THE BEDFORD SERIES IN HISTORY AND CULTURE

Postwar Immigrant America

A Social History

Reed Ueda

Tufts University

BEDFORD BOOKS *of* ST. MARTIN'S PRESS

Boston • New York

For my grandparents

For Bedford Books
Publisher: Charles H. Christensen
Associate Publisher/General Manager: Joan E. Feinberg
History Editor: Niels Aaboe
Developmental Editor: Jane Betz
Managing Editor: Elizabeth M. Schaaf
Copyeditor: Barbara G. Flanagan
Text Design: Claire Seng-Niemoeller
Cover Design: Richard Emery Design

Library of Congress Catalog Card Number: 92-75894
Copyright © 1994 by Bedford Books *of* St. Martin's Press

Manufactured in the United States of America.

8   7   6   5   4

f   e   d   c   b   a

For information, write: St. Martin's Press, Inc., 175 Fifth Avenue, New York, NY 10010
Editorial Offices: Bedford Books *of* St. Martin's Press, 29 Winchester Street, Boston, MA 02116

ISBN: 0-312-07526-X (paperback)
ISBN: 0-312-10279-8 (hardcover)

Acknowledgments

Janet Bode, *New Kids on the Block.* Copyright © 1989 by Janet Bode. Used with permission of Franklin Watts, Inc., New York.

Imogene Hayes, "Immigrant from Jamaica." Copyright © 1980 Joan Morrison and Charlotte Fox Zabusky. The current edition of *American Mosaic* is available from the University of Pittsburgh Press.

Miguel Torres, "Immigrant from Mexico, 1977." Copyright © 1980 Joan Morrison and Charlotte Fox Zabusky. The current edition of *American Mosaic* is available from the University of Pittsburgh Press.

Reed Ueda, "American National Identity and Race." Copyright © 1992 by the Massachusetts Institute of Technology and the editors of *The Journal of Interdisciplinary History.* "The Permanently Unfinished Country." This article appears in the October 1992 issue and is reprinted with permission from *The World & I,* a publication of *The Washington Times Corporation,* copyright © 1992.

Foreword

The Bedford Series in History and Culture is designed so that readers can study the past as historians do.

The historian's first task is finding the evidence. Documents, letters, memoirs, interviews, pictures, movies, novels, or poems can provide facts and clues. Then the historian questions and compares the sources. There is more to do than in a courtroom, for hearsay evidence is welcome, and the historian is usually looking for answers beyond act and motive. Different views of an event may be as important as a single verdict. How a story is told may yield as much information as what it says.

Along the way the historian seeks help from other historians and perhaps from specialists in other disciplines. Finally, it is time to write, to decide on an interpretation and how to arrange the evidence for readers.

Each book in this series contains an important historical document or group of documents, each document a witness from the past and open to interpretation in different ways. The documents are combined with some element of historical narrative—an introduction or a biographical essay, for example—that provides students with an analysis of the primary source material and important background information about the world in which it was produced.

Each book in the series focuses on a specific topic within a specific historical period. Each provides a basis for lively thought and discussion about several aspects of the topic and the historian's role. Each is short enough (and inexpensive enough) to be a reasonable one-week assignment in a college course. Whether as classroom or personal reading, each book in the series provides firsthand experience of the challenge—and fun—of discovering, recreating, and interpreting the past.

Natalie Zemon Davis
Ernest R. May

Preface

The uprooting and transplanting of people—the accelerating movements creating "worlds in motion," in the words of historian Bernard Bailyn—have been defining features of global transformation since the sixteenth century. Immigration to the United States in the post–World War II era unfolded into the most highly evolved manifestation of these changes. This book analyzes the history of that immigration in light of the global and international forces that prompted it.

In charting the latest evolutionary stage of the world's most welcoming "immigration country," this volume explores connections between the cycles of immigration and assimilation that have occurred throughout the nation's history. Late twentieth-century immigration from India, Mexico, and Vietnam has replaced earlier migrations from Scotland, Italy, and Russia and has shown both similarities with and differences from earlier patterns.

This volume also probes the impact of the arriving ethnic groups on the historic foundations of the American nation. The new Asian and Hispanic immigrants revitalized political and civic institutions inherited from the colonial founders. They reshaped the debate over how democracy could encompass ethnic groups with greater inclusiveness and egalitarianism.

Analyzing these features of postwar worldwide immigration requires an interdisciplinary approach joining history with the concepts and methodologies of the various social sciences. Thus, demographic and quantitative analysis are applied to the rise of worldwide immigration; sociology and demography provide an understanding of the development of group life; and ideas from political science and law illuminate the relationship of immigrants to American government and its ethnic policies.

In its global perspective and analytic treatment, *Postwar Immigrant America* endeavors to go beyond a narrative account of twentieth-century American immigration.

ACKNOWLEDGMENTS

I could not have completed this book without the capable support of publishers, editors, and production experts. I am indebted to Chuck Christensen and Sabra Scribner, who supported my idea for this book, and to Ernest May, who was my editorial consultant. I also wish to express appreciation to Joan Feinberg and Louise Townsend. In the final stages of writing, Jane Betz was a dynamic project editor; Richard Keaveny was a whiz with graphics; Barbara Flanagan supplied her excellent copyediting; and Elizabeth Schaaf smoothly managed the production. I am grateful to my colleagues at Tufts University and my former teachers at UCLA, Chicago, and Harvard who have knowingly and unknowingly over the years shaped the ideas set forth in this volume. I got a good start in organizing my thoughts for this book through my discussions with Peter Coclanis. I benefited from the comments of all the reviewers, especially Lawrence H. Fuchs and Stephan Thernstrom. All these individuals guided my course and decidedly improved the final result.

Reed Ueda

Contents

INTRODUCTION

The Historical Context
of Immigration

The United States became history's first "worldwide" immigration country in the twentieth century. By the 1990s, the flow of newcomers swelled to include people from every region and culture of the globe. Forty million of the sixty million immigrants since the founding of the country—two out of three newcomers—arrived in the twentieth century, making it the greatest era of immigration in national and world history (see Figure I.1).

The United States had long been distinguished for the continuous and unique role that immigrants played in its population history. From the early nineteenth to the early twentieth century, the United States attracted three-fifths of all the world's immigrants—more than received by all other large immigration-receiving countries in the world combined (Figure I.2). Among all the world's immigration countries, the United States accepted by far the greatest variety of nationalities. From the early nineteenth century to World War II, 16 percent of American immigrants came from Germany, 12 percent from Italy, 12 percent from Ireland, 12 percent from the multifarious ethnic enclaves of Austria-Hungary, 11 percent from Great Britain, and 10 percent from Russia. Other English-speaking immigration countries such as Australia and Canada drew their settlers almost wholly from other Anglophone nations. Immigration to Latin American societies also showed a narrow spectrum of national diversity, limited chiefly to Iberian and Italian origins. Ethnic variety in American immigration increased even more in the late twentieth century, especially with the rise of immigration from Asia, the Caribbean, Latin America, the Middle East, and Africa, from which few immigrants had come in the early twentieth century. The U.S. Immigration and Naturalization Service reported admissions in 1990 from thirty Asian countries (including

Figure I.1.   Immigrants Admitted to the United States by Period, 1820–1900

Immigration to the United States from 1820 to 1990 can be divided into three relatively equal parts: 1820–1900 (81 years, 33.6%); 1901–1940 (40 years, 33.6%); and 1941–1990 (50 years, 32.8%).

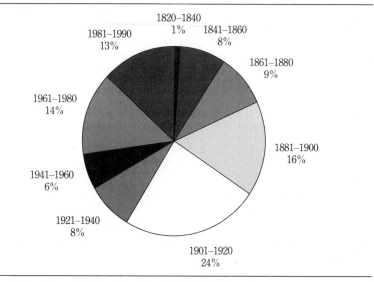

Source: Derived from *1990 Statistical Yearbook of the Immigration and Naturalization Service* (Washington, D.C.: U.S. Government Printing Office, 1991), p. 15.

the Middle East), seventeen Central and South American countries, thirteen Caribbean countries, and thirteen African countries.[1]

The United States is the great exception among world nations, most of which—including Germany, Japan, Norway, Scotland, Sweden, and Korea—have no tradition of immigration and little interest in developing one.[2] The German political leader Volker Ruhe expressed the viewpoint of such nations by announcing in 1991, "We [in Germany] are not an immigration country and we will not become one."

Despite the enormous numbers and variety of those who chose to come to America, immigrants were a minority among the peoples of the world. It is important to remember that the vast majority of Chinese, Mexicans, Swedes, and Italians chose to remain home. For every Irish immigrant who came to the United States during the potato famine of the 1840s, five people remained in Ireland. There were plenty of reasons to remain home. Leaving meant a painful separation from one's support system. When the immigrants left, they lost everything and everyone familiar. Historian Oscar Handlin has called this uprooting a trauma that left a permanent scar. Nearly all immigrants went

Figure I.2.   Destination of Immigration, 1820–1930

In the 110 years before the Great Depression, the United States attracted three-fifths of all immigrants—more than all other nations in the world combined. Countries in the British Empire attracted about one-fifth.

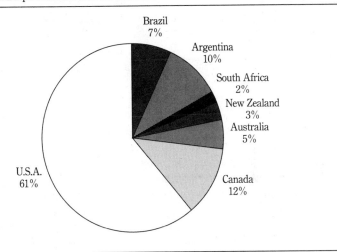

Source: Derived from William S. Bernard, ed., *American Immigration Policy* (New York: Harper and Brothers, 1950), p. 202.

through the pain of snapping the ties of extended family life. An immigrant woman arriving at Ellis Island recalled, "We hated to leave. I had a grandfather and grandmother living in Europe and my father was an only child. It was terrible to part with the two of them, but they wouldn't go along. They wanted to die in Europe." The loss of the old moorings filled the immigrants with self-doubt. In Abraham Cahan's early twentieth-century novel *The Rise of David Levinsky,* the protagonist David Levinsky recalls, "Who can depict the feeling of desolation, homesickness, uncertainty, and anxiety with which an emigrant makes his first voyage across the ocean? . . . And echoing through it all were the heart-lashing words: 'Are you crazy? You forget your place, young man!'"[3]

Most people chose to live with familiar oppression and poverty rather than throw everything away to uncertain, unfamiliar promises. The immigrant was a risk taker who had the courage or the recklessness to give up the known, with its limits, for the unknown, with its possibilities. Most immigrants—from Mexican farm laborers to Polish steelworkers—were bold adventurers on voyages of discovery who had to have the resiliency to cope with tremendous social change, pressures, and loss.

Despite the sacrifices and losses, many immigrants persevered to realize a new vision of the individual and society. They found that American conditions of tolerance toward diversity, compared with the rigid boundaries that existed in most other countries, made the forging of new identities and cultural ties inescapable. The immigrant absorbed new ways from neighboring people who were different. The children of Japanese immigrants in Hawaii learned new games, new words, new values, new tastes in food, new styles of dress, and new ways of forming relationships from neighbors, playmates, and class-mates who were Hawaiian, Filipino, German, Chinese, and Portuguese. The process of acculturating with unfamiliar surrounding elements had deep roots in the nation's social history. During the American Revolution, the French immigrant Hector St. John de Crèvecoeur described this mixing process in his community: *"He* is an American who, leaving behind him all his ancient prejudices and manners, receives new ones from the new mode of life he has embraced, the new government he obeys, and the new rank he holds."[4]

American immigrants created a new society differing fundamentally from old societies such as those they left in Sweden, Germany, or Japan. These societies took strength from homogeneity. Solidarity came from all people being the same. In the United States, the immigrants built a society whose strength came from the immense multiplicity of ethnic groups. Moreover, the society hinged on the existence of conditions that permitted dissimilar groups to act and live together without intrusive government. The resultant mutual-ism and interdependency helped integrate the nation.

Immigration created the American nation and defined its role in world history. Immigration to America adjusted the balance of human and material resources between nations, creating new international economic and cultural ties that affected the relations between countries. Otto von Bismarck, the "Iron Chancellor" who unified Germany in the 1870s, assessed American immigra-tion as the "decisive fact" of the modern world.[5]

At the heart of American history lay the cycle of national creation and re-creation through immigration. The new nation emerging from the Ameri-can Revolution grew out of the first immigration consisting of Protestant colonials from the British Isles and northern Europe. After the Civil War, with large numbers of Irish Catholics and newcomers from Germany and Scandi-navia, the immigrant nation continued to evolve. By the turn of the century, it received immigrants from southern and eastern Europe, East Asia, Mexico, and the Caribbean. These waves constituted the second immigration. After 1965, the American nation absorbed a great influx of immigrants from around the world in the third immigration.

As an ever-changing society formed out of three historical immigrations, the civic and social foundations of American nationhood shifted accordingly. The historian John Higham has called attention to the need to understand the differences immigration has made for national development. He has pointed out that the first immigration, by bringing diverse population elements before the founding of the country, prepared the way for an eclectic and universalistic form of citizenship. Higham found that the second immigration generated new communal and organizational modes for immigrant adaptation such as machine politics, organized labor, and ethnic associations, as well as cultural modes such as mass entertainment and media. The third immigration has reinforced the developments of the first and second immigrations but is contributing a unique shift: moving the nation toward a transnational, interracial world society and a multicultural politics.[6]

As a history of post–World War II immigrant America, this volume treats the third immigration, but it also touches on the multigenerational evolution of the second immigration and in a minor and oblique way the residual features of the first immigration. This work depicts a postwar immigrant America that was a cumulative fusion of these stages of ethnic incorporation, an expanding historical synthesis embodying a global international culture.

THE CHANGING WAVES OF IMMIGRATION

An immense tide of European immigration was the cardinal ethnic factor transforming the American nation from the birth of the industrial revolution to the Great Depression. Thirty-five million Europeans uprooted by economic and social distress moved to America in the century after 1830. During this period, the early American nation that grew out of colonization by Great Britain turned into a new immigrant nation of strikingly varied nationalities drawn from the metropolises and far-flung borderlands of the entire European continent.[7]

International migration spiraled toward the United States from wider and wider geographic circles. By the Civil War, the chief sources of immigration had spread outside of Great Britain to northern and western Europe. After 1890, the flow of American immigration was fed increasingly by streams originating from southern and eastern Europe, principally from the states of Italy, Austria-Hungary, and Russia (Figure I.3). The label "Old Immigrant" was affixed to groups arriving from northern and western Europe, the label "New Immigrant" to groups from southern and eastern Europe. In 1896, immigrants from the latter area for the first time in history composed a majority of newcomers, 57 percent of all immigrants in that year. Their numerical predominance continued into the 1920s.[8]

The largest groups among the New Immigrants from southern and eastern Europe were, in order of their numbers, the Italians, the Slavs, and the Jews.

Figure I.3.   Country of Origin of Immigrants to the United States, 1907 (Number of arrivals in thousands)

The rise of immigration from countries in southern and eastern Europe had become very pronounced in 1907, the peak year of annual immigration up to that time.

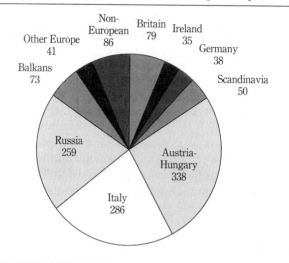

Source: Philip Taylor, *The Distant Magnet: European Emigration to the U.S.A.* (New York: Harper and Row, 1971), Diagram 1, p. 63.

Eighty percent of the Italians came from southern Italy. The Jews came chiefly from the multinational empires of Russia and Austria-Hungary. The Slavs comprised a huge variety of ethnic subgroups such as Poles, Czechs, Russians, Slovakians, Slovenians, Serbians, Bosnians, Montenegrins, Croatians, and Bulgarians, who had come from provincial areas in Germany, Austria-Hungary, and Russia. From 1899 to 1924, 3.8 million Italians, 3.4 million Slavs, and 1.8 million Jews entered the country.[9]

By comparison, in the early twentieth century, immigration from the non-European world was dwarfed in scale and impact. Asian immigration, flowing chiefly to the far western United States, was the first mass migration from outside Europe, coinciding approximately with the rise of southern and eastern European immigration. Chinese, Japanese, and Filipinos composed the bulk of Asian immigrants to America during this time; Koreans and Asian Indians constituted a much smaller influx. The major periods of immigration from the Asian countries ranged in a rough consecutive order. Between 1850 and 1924, 368,000 Chinese immigrants entered the United States. From 1890 to 1924, 270,000 immigrants came from Japan; from 1899 to 1924, 9,200 arrived from Korea and 8,200 from India; and between 1910 and 1930, at least 50,000 to 60,000 came from the Philippines. The American territory of Hawaii was a receiving area of a similarly timed and comparably sized immigration from China, Japan, Korea, and the Philippines.[10]

Although Asian immigration was relatively small, its pattern of short periodic bursts resembled the New Immigration from southern and eastern Europe. Ninety percent of all immigrants from Italy from the nineteenth century to World War II came in the thirty years from 1890 to 1920. Similarly, 92 percent of all immigrants from Austria-Hungary and Russia in that period arrived between 1890 and 1920. The brief yet intense intervals of immigration from Asia and southern and eastern Europe were circumscribed artificially by the passage of restrictionist laws that reduced the influx from these regions. Limits on admissions were first imposed on Asians at the end of the nineteenth century, but by the 1920s such restrictions affected the New Immigrants from Italy, Austria-Hungary, Russia, and the eastern Mediterranean.

As the supply of Asian laborers in the far west was cut off, agricultural and industrial capitalists began to look toward the reservoir of cheap workers across the border in Mexico. Because of the spread of "peonage," or debt servitude, northern regions of Mexico accumulated surplus labor that began to spill across the U.S. border. In the first decade of the twentieth century, only 31,000 Mexicans arrived, but in the second decade the influx swelled to 185,000. The drain on workers during World War I prodded the U.S. government in 1917 to issue passes to "temporary farmworkers" from Mexico. This was a preliminary experiment in a guest worker system of labor migration that would be expanded in the future.[11]

From 1900 to 1930, more than 100,000 blacks from the West Indies entered the United States. Increasing population and chronic seasonal unemployment in their home islands caused an inter-island migration of laborers. This circulating flow spilled over to Florida and the urban centers of the northeast as new economic, transportation, and communication links between the West Indies and the United States were forged by the spread of the commercial fruit industry.[12]

THE MATRIX OF PUSH AND PULL

Throughout the history of the United States, immigration was generated by an international force field of displacing "push" and attractive "pull" factors. These were by-products of economic reorganization and political centralization in the transatlantic and transpacific basins. The matrix of push and pull factors covered different regions and changed over time. It created a gigantic demographic watershed that drained off a growing flood of immigration to the United States.[13]

A key push factor was the unprecedented expansion of population in the modern era. In Europe, Asia, and the Western Hemisphere a "demographic transition"—a rise in the rate of population growth—resulted from improved nutrition and health support systems that lowered death rates. The resulting immense and rapid increase of population redefined economic prospects, eroding available resources for increasing numbers of people. The number of young workers seeking a livelihood grew faster than the number of slots the economy could generate anew or open by attrition. In this fashion, an economic surplus population expanded.[14]

Population increase coincided with regional economic stagnancy to determine the timing of exodus. The demographic transition moved across Europe roughly from west to east, encouraging the progressive "morselizing" or subdividing of land as it moved. Available land also shrank as large landowners accumulated small holdings to increase the output of commercial crops. In the late nineteenth century, the demographic and economic structure of southern and eastern Europe resembled that of western Europe a half-century earlier and became the source of the greatest exodus from Europe after 1890. In specific subregions of East Asia, economic decline and population pressure coincided to produce an impetus for migration that was roughly contemporaneous with that from southern and eastern Europe.[15]

The spread of capitalist manufacturing and marketing introduced new strains into the economic life of the populace. Early industrial capitalism in Europe displaced or marginalized artisans by creating the factory system of production. Peasants lost supplementary income from cottage manufactures when factory goods flooded the local markets. Cottage industries dwindled and eventually disappeared. Also, the emerging capitalist economy grew by boom and bust cycles. As the rural economies of Europe were drawn within an international market, peasants and laborers became more vulnerable to external vicissitudes. Intermittent economic setbacks came to farmers by fluctuating crop prices and to workers by slackening demand.[16]

The differential between the lower demand for labor in Europe, Asia, and Latin America and the higher demand in the United States created a pull factor that combined with push forces to exert pressure to immigrate to America. In contrast to provincial regions in the Eastern Hemisphere and Latin America, the United States was a leading sector of job growth. Commercial farms and plantations in the western states and Hawaii maintained a huge demand for Chinese, Japanese, Filipino, and Mexican laborers. Midwestern and Great Plains states promoted the development of family farms, attracting waves of

Scandinavians and Germans. The burgeoning factories of the industrial Midwest and Northeast attracted flocks of southern and eastern European laborers. Both agricultural and industrial labor were more valuable in the United States. Skilled as well as unskilled workers improved their chances for employment there.[17]

The forces of push and pull did not mechanistically determine departure because immigrants were not passive and homogeneous objects. The immigrants emerged with planning and deliberation at specific periods and from middling to lower sectors of homeland societies—not usually the most impoverished. The insecurity caused by the intersection of demographic change and economic transitions in agriculture and manufacturing was not in itself a sufficient cause of emigration. Insecurity prompted immigrants to rethink the shape of their lives and the odds for improvement by staying or moving. Those who were most venturesome and could espy timely opportunity in another country became immigrants. Furthermore, they developed an organized strategy, usually involving family members to help each other gain passage, obtain jobs, and find homes. As a result, most immigrants came to America in a cooperative process of chain migration.[18]

THE EBB AND FLOW OF IMMIGRATION

From 1820 to 1930, yearly arrivals climbed steadily, reaching several hundred thousand by the late nineteenth century. The movement of annual immigration, however, was not linear. It fluctuated in enormous oscillations of fifteen to twenty years, called "long swings" (Figure I.4). The peak surges in yearly arrivals occurred in three short upward swings from 1882 to 1893, 1903 to 1914, and 1921 to 1927.[19]

Annual immigration rose with economic expansion and declined during recession. A closer analysis of the "time-shape" of immigration, however, discloses a more subtle relationship between immigration and the American economy. It appears that during industrialization in the nineteenth century, immigration both stimulated a rise in economic activity and also responded to rises in economic activity. Before the Civil War, immigration preceded capital investment (particularly in railroads) and thus helped stimulate it. There is evidence that immigration also preceded and stimulated housing construction. From 1870, however, capital investment preceded changes in immigration. Moreover, throughout the industrializing era from the mid-nineteenth to the early twentieth century, immigration tended to respond to increases in economic productivity in the United States. Whether immigration preceded or responded to economic growth, it consistently had a positive and

Figure I.4.   Immigration to the United States, 1820–1944

Annual immigration has fluctuated in "long swings" of fifteen to twenty years. In general, immigration tended to rise in periods of economic expansion and fall during periods of recession.

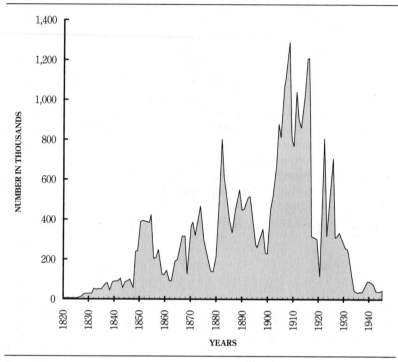

Source: Immigration and Naturalization Service, *Annual Report,* 1944.

galvanizing effect on it by increasing the pool of productive workers, savers, entrepreneurs, and consumers.[20]

Annual immigration totals alone do not tell the full story of how immigration affected American society. To gauge the impact of immigration it is necessary to compare the size of yearly admissions with the size of the host society. The resulting ratio is called the rate of immigration. When the rate is charted for the decades since the 1820s, it becomes clear that immigration had a greater impact in the nineteenth century than in the twentieth century (Figure I.5). Although the rate of immigration reached its apex in the first decade of the twentieth century, it dropped steeply to the 1920s. It bottomed out from the successive effects of restrictive admissions policies, the severe economic depression of the 1930s, and the disruptions of World War II.[21]

Figure I.5.   Rate of Immigration by Decade, 1821–1990

The rate of immigration, or the ratio of the number of immigrants to the number of people in the host society, measures the relative impact of immigration on society. Rates rose when the number of immigrants was relatively large.

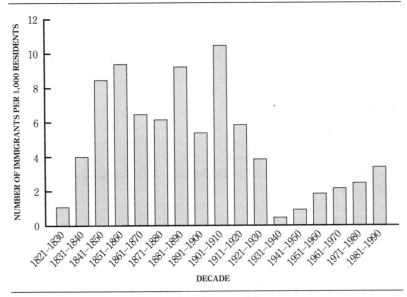

Source: Derived from *Statistical Abstract of the United States, 1992* (Washington, D.C.: U.S. Government Printing Office, 1992), Table 5, p. 10.

IMMIGRANTS IN THE EARLY TWENTIETH CENTURY

The social history of the twentieth century is impossible to understand without reference to the startling developments in immigration in its first decades. Immigrants flooded into the country with a magnitude and ethnic diversity never before seen. Half of all immigrants who came between the War of 1812 and the Great Depression arrived from 1900 to 1930 alone. The federal Bureau of Immigration classified thirty-nine "races or peoples" among immigrant arrivals in these three decades.[22]

Throughout the era of industrialization, laborers who could perform heavy physical work were in great demand. Thus, most immigrants were young males. In the late nineteenth century, more than two out of three immigrants were between fifteen and forty years old, and male immigrants constituted 60 percent of all arrivals (Tables A.1 and A.2, pp. 156, 157). At the turn of the century, the long-standing majorities of males and of prime-aged newcomers reached historical peaks while the share of females, minors, and the elderly dropped to all-time lows. Over the span of the industrial revolution, the share of industrial and service workers grew progressively larger while the share of agricultural workers fell (Figure I.6). Many of the former, however, had engaged in farm labor earlier in their working lives.[23]

The attractive power of the American economy, though exceedingly great, was not absolutely decisive. Many uprooted peasants and laborers decided to resettle in nearby provincial cities or national metropolises where new jobs were available. Such workers circulating within their homelands or neighboring countries outnumbered those who moved to America. Moreover, two out of five international migrants from the nineteenth to the early twentieth century chose to settle elsewhere, often in Argentina, Brazil, Canada, South Africa, or Australia. Emigration to America was, first, an alternative to local migrations, and, second, a preference among various possible destination countries.[24]

Figure I.6. Immigrants Admitted to the United States by Occupational Group, 1820–1900

As the industrial revolution took hold in the mid-1800s, immigrants in industrial labor and service jobs outnumbered those in agriculture.

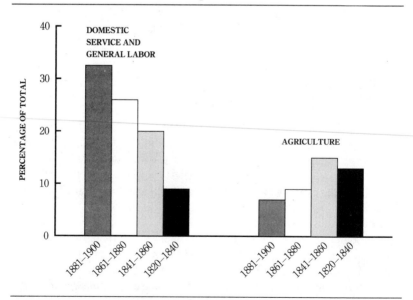

Source: 1990 Statistical Yearbook of the Immigration and Naturalization Service (Washington, D.C.: U.S. Government Printing Office, 1991), p. 20.

Capital-intensive manufacturing and labor-intensive agriculture and construction recruited a new form of immigrant labor characterized by transiency and low skill level. The number of immigrants returning to their country of origin rose sharply at the turn of the century. Transient labor migrants were quickly pooled into a work force or let go to leave the country. Their availability grew as increased modernization of international transportation and communications systems allowed them to change residency more easily and at lower cost.[25]

One of the notable changes in immigration patterns in the early twentieth century was the rising number of return immigrants. From 1908 to 1930, four million people departed from the United States permanently. In that period, one left for every three entering. Departures increased both absolutely and in proportion to arrivals in the decade of World War I. From 1911 to 1915, thirty-two people departed for every one hundred who arrived; from 1916 to 1920, fifty-five departed for every one hundred arriving.[26]

Immigrants from a variegated array of ethnic groups returned home. Return migration was an overseas extension of historic patterns of local circular migration. Many southern and eastern Europeans displayed an unusual propensity for temporary migration. From 1911 to 1915, among the Bulgarian-Serbian-Montenegrins, Magyars, and Slovaks, fifty or more immigrants journeyed home for every one hundred arriving in the United States; among the Greeks, Russians, southern Italians, and Croatian-Slovenians forty or more immigrants returned home for every one hundred arrivals. In the next five years surrounding World War I, the return migration rates for these groups multiplied several times. Many who went back were laborers who had come temporarily to the United States to earn income to send home or to take back later. The transient labor migrants from Europe were often called "birds of passage." Immigrants from Asia, such as the Chinese, Koreans, and Asian Indians, who also engaged in heavy return migration, were called "sojourners." Even Old Immigrant groups such as the English, Germans, and Scandinavians showed substantial return rates. Not all groups, however, conformed to the rising pattern of return migration. Most notably, the Welsh, the Jews, and the Armenians showed a strong reluctance to return home. Of course, Russian Jews and Turkish Armenians had little incentive to return to the repressive rule of tsars and pashas. From the 1880s on, the Russian imperial government intensified the ostracism of Jews and supported popular riots against their settlements. In the Ottoman Empire, Turkish potentates subjected the Armenians to similar injustices and brutalities.[27]

The social characteristics of immigrants varied enormously according to geographic and ethnic origin. Although a distinct differential in industrial and technological development separated northern and western Europe from southern and eastern Europe and other parts of the world, group differences did not follow a simple geographic correlation. Many of the groups with the highest proportions of skilled workers came from outside northern and western Europe. Jews, Bohemians, Moravians, Armenians, Spaniards, Cubans, Pacific Islanders, West Indians, and Africans ranked among those with the highest shares of skilled workers. Also, the groups with the highest proportions of male arrivals were a mix of Old Immigrant and New Immigrant groups. However, in illiteracy a clearer geographic pattern emerged: Old Immigrants were not represented among the groups with the highest percentages of illiteracy. Moreover, the differentials in illiteracy between Old Immigrants and New Immigrants were extremely large. In the first decade of the century, less than 2 percent of the Scandinavians and ethnic groups from Great Britain were illiterate; but more than 50 percent of southern Italians, Portuguese, Ruthenians, Mexicans, Syrians, and Turks and more than 40 percent of several southern Slavic groups were illiterate.[28]

The early twentieth century, however, marked the culmination of the industrial phase of immigration and the beginning of a new stage. New demographic trends started that would continue and grow more pronounced in the middle decades of the century. The proportions of laborers began to shrink, while the share of skilled craftworkers began to grow before 1920 (Table A.3, p. 158). Illiteracy rates began to decline significantly (Figure I.7). These changes were decisively consolidated by the creation of restrictive immigration quotas in the early 1920s that favored immigrants from the more industrialized societies of northern and western Europe. In the late 1920s,

Figure I.7.   Immigrants Illiterate by Period, 1900–1929

After the turn of the century, the percentage of illiterate immigrants began to decrease. Immigration quotas of the 1920s favored skilled immigrants from northern and western Europe, and illiteracy in Europe declined.

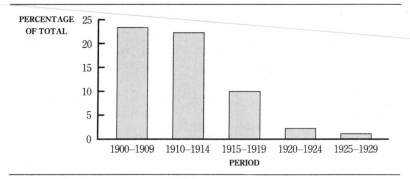

Source: Statistical Abstract of the United States, 1930 (Washington, D.C.: U.S. Government Printing Office, 1930), Table 104, p. 94.

northern and western European immigrants once more outnumbered immigrants from southern and eastern Europe and Asia. The globalizing immigration trends of the late industrial era that recruited mounting waves of low-skilled labor drew to a close because of revolutionary changes in American immigration policy.

NOTES

[1] For cumulative immigration from various countries, see William S. Bernard, ed., *American Immigration Policy* (New York: Harper and Brothers, 1950), Table XIII, p. 311. Bernard reports that 80 percent of immigrants to Australia came from Great Britain, while in Canada 37 percent arrived from Great Britain and another 37 percent from the United States; also he shows that in Argentina, 47 percent of the immigrants came from Italy and 32 percent from Spain; in Brazil, 34 percent came from Italy, 29 percent from Portugal, and 14 percent from Spain. For these breakdowns, see *American Immigration Policy,* Chart 13, p. 204. For historical immigration totals in the United States, see *1990 Statistical Yearbook of the Immigration and Naturalization Service* (Washington, D.C.: U.S. Government Printing Office, 1992), Table 1, p. 47. For countries of origin of immigrants in the late twentieth century, see *1990 Statistical Yearbook,* Table 3, pp. 52–53.

[2] Bernard, *American Immigration Policy,* ch. 10 and Table XVII, p. 314.

[3] Oscar Handlin, *The Uprooted,* 2nd ed. (Boston: Little, Brown, 1973), ch. 10; Dale R. Steiner, *Of Thee We Sing: Immigrants and American History* (San Diego: Harcourt Brace Jovanovich, 1987), p. 6. David M. Brownstone, Irene M. Franck, and Douglass L. Brownstone, *Island of Hope, Island of Tears* (New York: Viking Penguin, 1979), p. 24; Abraham Cahan, *The Rise of David Levinsky* (New York: Harper and Brothers, 1917), p. 85.

[4] J. Hector St. John de Crèvecoeur, *Letters from an American Farmer* (1782; New York: Viking Penguin, 1981), p. 70.

[5] Nathan Glazer, ed., *Clamor at the Gates: The New American Immigration* (San Francisco: Institute for Contemporary Studies, 1985), p. 3; Bernard Bailyn, *The Peopling of British North America* (New York: Alfred A. Knopf, 1977), p. i.

[6] John Higham, *Send These to Me: Jews and Other Immigrants in Urban America* (New York: Atheneum, 1975), pp. 17–28.

[7] The main outlines of the second immigration are conveyed in Marcus Lee Hansen, *The Atlantic Migration, 1607–1860* (Cambridge: Harvard University Press, 1940); Handlin, *The Uprooted;* Oscar Handlin, *The American People in the Twentieth Century* (Cambridge: Harvard University Press, 1954); Maldwyn Allen Jones, *American Immigration* (Chicago: University of Chicago Press, 1960); Philip Taylor, *The Distant Magnet: European Immigration to the U.S.A.* (New York: Harper and Row, 1971); Thomas Archdeacon, *Becoming American: An Ethnic History* (New York: Free Press, 1983); John Bodnar, *The Transplanted: A History of Immigrants in Urban America* (Bloomington: Indiana University Press, 1985); Roger Daniels, *Coming to America: A History of Immigration and Ethnicity in American Life* (New York: HarperPerennial, 1991).

[8] Oscar Handlin, *Race and Nationality in American Life* (Cambridge: Harvard University Press, 1957), pp. 74–77; U.S. Immigration Commission, *Statistical Review of Immigration* (Washington, D.C.: U.S. Government Printing Office, 1911), Table 6, p. 10.

[9] Archdeacon, *Becoming American,* pp. 121–27; Stephan Thernstrom, ed., *Harvard Encyclopedia of American Ethnic Groups* (Cambridge: Harvard University Press, 1980), Appendix I, Table 2, pp. 1036–37.

[10] These figures compiled from U.S. Commissioner-General of Immigration, *Annual Reports;* U.S. Commission on Immigration, *Reports,* vol. 3 (Washington, D.C.: U.S. Government Printing Office, 1911); Bruno Lasker, *Filipino Immigration to Continental United States and to Hawaii*

(Chicago: University of Chicago Press, 1931), Appendix A, pp. 348–49. For Asian immigration to Hawaii, see Eleanor C. Nordyke, *The Peopling of Hawai'i*, 2nd ed. (Honolulu: University of Hawaii Press, 1989), ch. 3. For an overview of the successive waves of specific Asian ethnic groups, see Sucheng Chan, *Asian Americans: An Interpretive History* (Boston: Twayne, 1991); Ronald T. Takaki, *Strangers from a Different Shore: A History of Asian Americans* (Boston: Little, Brown, 1989).

[11] Joan W. Moore, *Mexican Americans*, 2nd ed. (Englewood Cliffs: Prentice-Hall, 1976), pp. 38–40; Carlos Cortes, "Mexicans," in Thernstrom, *Harvard Encyclopedia*, p. 699.

[12] Ira deA. Reid, *The Negro Immigrant* (New York: AMS Press, 1939), pp. 61–74, 239–40; Thomas Sowell, *Ethnic America: A History* (New York: Basic Books, 1981), pp. 216–18; Philip Kasinitz, *Caribbean New York: Black Immigrants and the Politics of Race* (Ithaca: Cornell University Press, 1992), pp. 19–25.

[13] Brinley Thomas, *Migration and Economic Growth: A Study of Great Britain and the Atlantic Economy*, 2nd ed. (Cambridge: Cambridge University Press, 1973), chs. 7, 14; Daniels, *Coming to America*, pp. 16–22; Conrad Taeuber and Irene B. Taeuber, *The Changing Population of the United States* (New York: John Wiley and Sons, 1958), pp. 55–58; Richard A. Easterlin, *Population, Labor Force, and Long Swings in Economic Growth: The American Experience* (New York: National Bureau of Economic Research, 1968), p. 30.

[14] H. J. Habakkuk and M. Postan, *The Cambridge Economic History of Europe, The Industrial Revolutions and After: Incomes, Population, and Technological Change*, vol. 6 (Cambridge: Cambridge University Press, 1965), ch. 2; Taylor, *The Distant Magnet*, pp. 27–54; Archdeacon, *Becoming American*, pp. 31–32, 120.

[15] Habakkuk and Postan, *Cambridge Economic History*, pp. 60–69; Archdeacon, *Becoming American*, pp. 37–55, 117, 120–27; Bodnar, *The Transplanted*, pp. 23–32, 34–38; Sucheng Chan, "European and Asian Immigration into the United States in Comparative Perspective, 1820s to 1920s," in Virginia Yans-McLaughlin, ed., *Immigration Reconsidered: History, Sociology, and Politics* (New York: Oxford University Press, 1990), pp. 40–47; Lucie Cheng and Edna Bonacich, eds., *Labor Immigration under Capitalism: Asian Workers in the United States before World War II* (Berkeley: University of California Press, 1984), chs. 6–10; Jon Gjerde, *From Peasants to Farmers: The Migration from Balestrand, Norway, to the Upper Middle West* (Cambridge: Cambridge University Press, 1985), chs. 2–5; Walter D. Kamphoefner, *The Westfalians: From Germany to Missouri* (Princeton: Princeton University Press, 1987), ch. 1.

[16] Bodnar, *The Transplanted*, pp. 30–34; Taylor, *The Distant Magnet*, pp. 38–39.

[17] Taylor, *The Distant Magnet*, pp. 182–209; Taeuber and Taeuber, *The Changing Population*, pp. 202–6.

[18] Taylor, *The Distant Magnet*, chs. 2–3; Bodnar, *The Transplanted*, p. 56; Dino Cinel, *From Italy to San Francisco: The Immigrant Experience* (Stanford: Stanford University Press, 1982), pp. 38–70; John S. MacDonald and Leatrice D. MacDonald, "Chain Migration, Ethnic Neighborhood Formation, and Social Networks," in Charles Tilly, ed., *An Urban World* (Boston: Little, Brown, 1974).

[19] The changing annual numbers of immigrants found in historical graphs of immigration have the appearance of mathematical consistency and precision. Yet they are based on varying ways of counting immigrants and thus are not exactly comparable over time. In the nineteenth century, official annual totals included in different periods aliens who arrived but were not admitted, resident aliens returning from a trip abroad, temporary visitors, and travelers passing through the country. From 1894 to 1902, annual immigration totals excluded immigrant aliens traveling as cabin passengers. After 1906, official data for the first time were precise because they were based on a count of admitted aliens seeking permanent residency in the United States whose last permanent residence was a foreign country. Despite the changing rules for counting immigrants, the enumerations were sufficiently comparable to reveal the pattern of annual rise and fall. For a detailed history of the changing enumeration basis for immigration statistics, see U.S. Bureau of the Census, *Historical Statistics of the United States: Colonial Times to 1957* (Washington, D.C.: U.S. Government Printing Office, 1960), ch. C, p. 49. Also see U.S. Commission on Immigration, *Reports*, vol. 3 , Table 6, pp. 9–11. Also see Richard A. Easterlin, "Economic and Social Characteristics of Immigration," in Thernstrom, *Harvard Encyclopedia*.

[20] Harry Jerome, *Migration and Business Cycles* (New York: National Bureau of Economic Research, 1926), p. 208; Thomas, *Migration and Economic Growth,* ch. 7; Simon Kuznets and Ernest Rubin, *Immigration and the Foreign Born,* Occasional Paper 46 (New York: National Bureau of Economic Research, 1954), pp. 4–5; Easterlin, *Population, Labor Force,* pp. 30–32; Thomas Muller, *Immigrants and the American City* (New York: New York University Press, 1992), pp. 69–77.

[21] Archdeacon, *Becoming American,* p. 113.

[22] U.S. Commissioner-General of Immigration, *Annual Reports, 1899–1930* (Washington, D.C.: U.S. Government Printing Office, 1900–31).

[23] Oscar Handlin, *The American People in the Twentieth Century* (Cambridge: Harvard University Press, 1954), p. 8.

[24] Bodnar, *The Transplanted,* pp. 43–45; Taylor, *The Distant Magnet,* pp. 55–56; Cinel, *From Italy to San Francisco,* p. 69.

[25] Michael J. Piore, *Birds of Passage: Migration Labor and Industrial Societies* (Cambridge: Cambridge University Press, 1979), chs. 2, 6; Taeuber and Taeuber, *The Changing Population,* pp. 53–55; Taylor, *The Distant Magnet,* ch. 8; Cheng and Bonacich, *Labor Immigration under Capitalism,* pp. 27–28.

[26] Commissioner-General of Immigration, *Annual Reports, 1926,* Table 78; *Annual Reports, 1930,* Tables 76, 86, 87.

[27] Cinel, *From Italy to San Francisco,* pp. 43–70. An analysis that places return migration from the United States in an international and interregional context is J. D. Gould, "European Inter-Continental Emigration. The Road Home: Return Migration from the U.S.A.," *Journal of European Economic History* 9 (Spring 1980): 41–112.

[28] U.S. Commission on Immigration, *Reports,* vol. 3, Tables 15 and 21, pp. 84–85; Handlin, *Race and Nationality,* pp. 89, 96–99.

1

The Legacy of Restriction

THE RETREAT TO RESTRICTIONISM

The Origins of Immigration Policy

The principles guiding U.S. immigration policy until the eve of the twentieth century sprang from the universalism and republican ideology of the American Revolution. They embodied a cosmopolitan faith in the capacity of individuals, whether native- or foreign-born, for rational self-rule. By constitutional principles, immigrants could become American citizens; they, as much as natives, were Americans. George Washington extended the universal welcome to immigrants. "The bosom of America," he declared, "is open to receive not only the opulent and respectable stranger, but the oppressed and persecuted of all nations and religions; whom we shall welcome to a participation of all our rights and privileges, if by decency and propriety of conduct they appear to merit the enjoyment."[1]

The American Revolution had popularized a new conception of national identity. In their struggle to separate themselves from the English, Americans avowed that they were a new people bred from the frontier and from the mingling of many nationalities. The official motto "E Pluribus Unum" expressed the new government's faith in the unity that would arise from the diversity of the American people. The basis of government would be its relationship to individual citizens, not to special social orders. The founders assumed that persons of European ancestry would constitute the community of citizens. Thus they did not seek equal citizenship for blacks or naturalization rights for those who were not "free white persons."[2]

As a logical corollary to the idea of individual citizenship, rights to admission and to settlement were not apportioned according to group origin. Lawmakers consistently refused to support projects to build immigrant communities that would retain a separate and distinct identity. Congress refused a petition from the Irish Emigrant Society of New York in 1818 to reserve public lands in Illinois for exclusive settlement by Irish newcomers. In 1874, Congress turned down a petition from German Mennonite immigrants for special and exclusive settlement rights. Opponents of group incorporation invoked the republican axiom that no group had "a separate right to compact themselves as an exclusive community."[3]

Restrictions on Asian Admissions

A movement for new centralized control of immigration based on ethnic factors sprang from a xenophobic reaction against Chinese immigrants after the Civil War. From the 1850s, several thousand Chinese annually arrived on the Pacific coast. They were resented for their role as workers in mining, agriculture, transportation, and construction and for their success in business. Moreover, native whites ostracized the Chinese as an unassimilable race possessing a menacing, alien way of life.[4]

Workers who feared Chinese labor competition and middle-class reformers who were alarmed by their "heathen" culture applied pressure to stop the influx of Chinese immigrants. In 1882 Congress passed the Chinese Exclusion Act denying admission to Chinese laborers. In 1892, 1902, and 1904 Congress enacted successive laws that extended the Chinese Exclusion Act indefinitely.[5]

Policymakers then turned their attention toward the rising numbers of Japanese immigrants. A diplomatic arrangement between Tokyo and Washington in 1907–08, called the Gentlemen's Agreement, obtained the Japanese government's cooperation in preventing Japanese laborers from leaving for the United States in exchange for the integration of Japanese Americans in the San Francisco public school system. This policy had the additional effect of excluding laborers from Korea, a colony of Japan.[6]

Because of what most Americans regarded as ineradicable racial and cultural differences between Asians and whites, immigration from China and Japan could not be allowed to grow freely. It was treated as a special and separate case apart from European immigration and as perhaps a unique problem of far western communities. As historian John Higham points out, "At no time in the nineteenth century did immigration restrictionists argue that Chinese exclusion set a logical precedent for their own proposals."[7]

But within the evolving system of American immigration policy, the Chinese Exclusion Act and the Gentlemen's Agreement established new precedents of active regulation. They introduced the principle that federal authorities could set limits on the numbers of immigrants. They instituted the use of national origins to restrict immigration. In policies toward China and Japan, group characteristics superseded individual characteristics as a conditional standard for admission, a pivotal departure from the republican tradition of individual qualification for admissions.

The Creation of an Omnibus Restrictive Policy

The move from anti-Asian restriction toward a comprehensive policy received impetus from the U.S. Immigration Commission (1907–1910), which evaluated the role of mass immigration in the life of the nation. The commission announced in its forty-two-volume report of 1911 that the New Immigrants from southern and eastern Europe were highly unassimilable, that their presence caused a variety of social problems, and that they constituted a degenerate racial stock. The commission manipulated estimates of mental illness, crime, family breakup, transiency, prostitution, and labor problems among Italians, Jews, Slavs, Greeks, and other recent arrivals. The report cited the New Immigrants' supposed antisocial behavior and "pathological" racial characteristics—substantially the same objections raised against Asian immigrants to call for their exclusion. Many Americans found the commission's assertions plausible because they had come to feel that the nation's institutions could not adequately absorb so many aliens who appeared racially, socially, and culturally distant. The spreading slums and labor unrest seemed to signify that the immigrant masses would form a permanent and destructive underclass.[8]

In 1917 Congress passed a new law that was a stepping-stone toward an omnibus policy of discriminatory restriction. The Immigration Act of 1917 expanded the principle of exclusion based on national origins begun by Congress in the Chinese Exclusion Act of 1882. It established an Asiatic Barred Zone from which no laborers could come, covering all of India, Afghanistan, and Arabia as well as parts of East Asia and the Pacific.[9]

The 1917 act also introduced a literacy test administered to immigrants in their mother tongue upon arrival. Those who failed would not be admitted. The literacy test, sought by restrictionists since the 1890s, was expected to sharply reduce immigration from southern and eastern Europe.[10]

Despite these measures, a resurgence of immigration from southern and eastern Europe after World War I forced restrictionists to introduce radical new policies. Congress began to devise a ranked order of nationalities seeking admission that legally institutionalized pseudoscientific notions of the supposedly superior northern and western European capacity for assimilation. In 1921 Congress passed the First Quota Act, which ranked immigrant nationalities according to a discriminatory hierarchy of quotas. The act ruled that the number of aliens admitted annually from any country could not exceed 3 percent of the foreign-born of that nationality in the United States in 1910. The resultant quotas were distributed to countries in Europe, Africa, and the Middle East and to Australia, New Zealand, and Siberia. Quotas were not needed for nationalities already excluded by the Asiatic Barred Zone, the

Nativists seeking to restrict immigration before World War I depicted immigrants as barbaric invaders. They warned that the American republic, like ancient Rome, would be destroyed by primitive and inferior races unless the nation closed its gates to immigration.

THOMAS BAILEY ALDRICH'S NATIVIST POEM
"The Unguarded Gates"

Wide open and unguarded stand our gates,
And through them press a wild, a motley throng—
Men from the Volga and the Tartar steppes,
Featureless figures of the Hoang-Ho,
Malayan, Scythian, Teuton, Kelt, and Slav,
Flying the Old World's poverty and scorn;
These bringing with them unknown gods and rites,
Those tiger passions, here to stretch their claws.
In street and alley what strange tongues are these,
Accents of menace alien to our air,
Voices that once the tower of Babel knew!
O, Liberty, white goddess, is it well
To leave the gate unguarded? On thy breast
Fold sorrow's children, soothe the hurts of fate,
Lift the downtrodden, but with the hand of steel
Stay those who to thy sacred portals come
To waste the fight of freedom. Have a care
Lest from thy brow the clustered stars be torn
And trampled in the dust. For so of old
The thronging Goth and Vandal trampled Rome,
And where the temples of the Caesars stood
The lean wolf unmolested made her lair.

Source: From U.S. Immigration Commission, *Reports,* vol. 23 (Washington, D.C.: U.S. Government Printing Office, 1911).

Chinese Exclusion Act, and the Gentlemen's Agreement. Congress decided to place no restrictions on immigration from the Western Hemisphere, so quotas were not needed for that region either. The quota system limited annual admissions to 355,000 and made 200,000 visas (55 percent) available to immigrants from northern and western Europe and reserved 155,000 visas (45 percent) for immigrants from southern and eastern Europe. The rest of the world received less than one-fifth of 1 percent of the quota slots.[11]

In 1924, Congress passed a Second Quota Act that both further lowered the annual ceiling on total admissions and slashed the size of quotas. The quotas were recalibrated to 2 percent of the foreign-born of each nationality in the United States in 1890, when immigrants from southern and eastern Europe were much less numerous in the American population than in 1910, the former baseline year. Total immigration under quotas in any year could not exceed 165,000. Annual admissions from northern and western Europe was limited to 141,000 (86 percent) and from the rest of the world to 24,000 (14 percent). The visas allotted to countries in southern and eastern Europe fell to only 21,000 (12 percent).[12]

Restrictionism against Asian immigrants culminated with the Second Quota Act. It announced that henceforward "no alien ineligible to citizenship" could be admitted to the United States, an alien status reserved only for Asian immigrants. This status had been implied vaguely since the first naturalization law of 1790 permitted "free white persons" to naturalize, but it was made explicit for the Chinese by the Chinese Exclusion Act of 1882. It was extended by a series of judicial decisions to apply to all other immigrants from Asia. The exclusion of Asians from admission in the 1924 Quota Act was the logical endpoint of the exclusion of Asians from American citizenship. Interestingly, all Asian nations received small token quotas to ensure that whites born there would have the chance to immigrate.[13]

The Second Quota Act was intended to be a transitional measure until a permanent National Origins Quota system began to operate in 1929. The system continued to distribute visas in quotas sized according to the gradations of assimilability assumed to characterize different nationality groups. It lowered the annual ceiling for immigration once more to 154,000. Quotas were allocated to immigrants of an eligible nationality in proportion to their share in the American population of 1920. Their share was computed through a complicated extrapolation of national origins based on the 1790 federal census and casual samplings of surnames in directories and other listings. Through these questionable techniques, the desired favoritism toward immigrants from northern and western Europe was achieved. Those areas received 127,000 quota visas (83 percent of those available), southern and eastern Europe 23,000 (15 percent), and the rest of the world 4,000 (2 percent).[14]

In the early twentieth century, American lawmakers redefined the role of immigration in national life. They limited the future size of the foreign stock by adopting ceilings on yearly admissions. They built an ethnic hierarchy of admissible groups. They marginalized Asian immigrants as an immutably foreign social element and barred them from citizenship. Old Immigrant groups seen as historic members of the nation were given preferential access. New Immigrants were to be restricted out of a belief that they could be accepted only gradually into society. Moreover, as a consequence, the New Immigrants' representation would always be submerged by the demographic mass of immigrants from northern and western Europe to preserve the historic ethnic character of the nation. The restrictive devices used against southern and eastern Europeans and Asians were different, but they were based on the common assumption that these groups were difficult to assimilate. However, policymakers placed Asians at the far end of the spectrum of assimilability, viewed them as a separate problem, and enacted the harshest measures against them.[15]

Nevertheless, immigration restriction was neither inevitable nor irresistible. Industrial capitalists used their enormous power to lobby for open admissions to keep a steady supply of cheap immigrant labor. Missionaries and liberal assimilationists added their support. Immigrants and their adult children elected officials who fought to preserve an open admissions policy. Presidential vetoes stymied restrictive congressional proposals several times. Grover Cleveland vetoed a bill to enact the literacy test in 1896, William Howard Taft vetoed a similar proposal in 1913, and Woodrow Wilson vetoed restrictive laws in 1916 and 1921. A number of representatives and senators also adamantly opposed restrictive laws and fought against restriction out of a belief that it was undemocratic and at odds with the universal ideal of American citizenship. The movement in favor of restrictionism, supported by a xenophobic public who feared foreignization, however, gradually overwhelmed opposing influences.[16]

Political responses to immigration divided into socioeconomic issues and politico-cultural issues, engendering "odd couple" coalitions supporting and resisting restriction. One "odd couple" of liberal social reformers and conservative racist xenophobes supported both Asian exclusion and restrictive quotas against the New Immigrants from southern and eastern Europe. An opposite "odd couple" of conservative capitalists and liberal assimilationists and internationalists lobbied against exclusions and restrictions. In the 1920s, the former partnership triumphed over the latter. The pro-restriction odd couple in the 1920s focused less on the economic threat of New Immigrant competition but rather more on their alleged racial inferiority, which rendered them unadaptable to the social, cultural, and political order.[17]

Transition to an Omnibus Selective Policy

The series of restrictive laws beginning in 1917 reduced but did not eliminate mass immigration from Europe. After a slowdown in arrivals, caused mainly by the international disruption of World War I, annual immigration rebounded. Although the 1920s has been pictured as the era when mass immigration stopped, the numbers of immigrants actually remained quite high to the end of the decade. From 1921 to 1930, nearly 1.4 million newcomers arrived from southern and eastern Europe alone. Of these, 960,000 immigrated from 1921 to 1924 and 430,000 from 1925 to 1930. The volume of immigration for the 1920s was certainly smaller than for the decades surrounding the turn of the century, but it equaled the robust levels of the mid-nineteenth century (Figure I.4, p. 10). Given the expansionary economy of the 1920s, however, immigration would probably have been much larger had quotas and ceilings not been in place.[18]

Mass immigration continued during the 1920s partly because the restrictionist system allowed certain exemptions and exceptions. For example, the Immigration Act of 1917 mandating the literacy test for admission actually permitted thousands of immigrants who tested as illiterates to enter the country. According to this statute, any admissible alien could bring in or send for "his father or grandfather over fifty-five years of age, his wife, his mother, his grandmother, or his unmarried or widowed daughter, if otherwise admissible, whether such relative can read or not." This provision ensured that illiteracy would not be an obstruction to family reunification.[19]

As a result, 82,500 illiterates over the age of sixteen were admitted from 1918 to 1925; 20,800 more were admitted from 1926 to 1930. The exemption under the literacy test was especially important for female immigrants, who often received less education than males in their homelands. Females composed a large majority of exempted illiterates: 71,700 female illiterates were admitted from 1918 to 1925, while only 10,800 males were admitted; from 1926 to 1930, the number of female illiterates admitted was 17,500, compared with 3,300 males. New Immigrant groups in particular capitalized on the illiteracy exemption. For example, from 1926 to 1930, one out of seven southern Italians admitted were exempt illiterates as were one out of twenty Jews.[20]

The immigration acts of 1921 and 1924, often portrayed as purely restrictive devices, actually created a new category of unlimited immigration, the "nonquota" class. Among a host of admitted nationalities, the arriving aliens in this category greatly exceeded the allotted numbers in the quota class. The nonquota category expressed the value of selecting immigrants by occupational skills in demand and thus included professors, professionals, and domestic servants from 1921 to 1924. (After 1924, only professors, students, and ministers were in this class.) The nonquota class also expressed the principle of encouraging family reunion. After 1924, it included wives of American citizens and their unmarried children under twenty-one; it also included immigrants from other countries in the Western Hemisphere. This last category constituted a loophole for immigrants from countries with small quotas who could first migrate to a Western Hemisphere nation and subsequently gain entry to the United States as a nonquota immigrant from that nation.[21]

In addition, the 1924 law introduced a system of special preferences within quotas for skilled agriculturalists and their families, and for spouses, children, and parents of American citizens (Table A.4, p. 159). Special preferences conferred priority in gaining a visa. They became an elastic part of the immigration law, manipulated and expanded immensely in subsequent immigration acts.

To compensate for the small quotas allotted to them, southern and eastern European immigrants used the nonquota category much more frequently than northern and western European immigrants (Table A.5, p. 161). Well over 70 percent of all immigrants from southern and eastern Europe from 1925 to 1929 came as nonquota immigrants, a large number being wives and children of American citizens, many of whom were naturalized immigrants. Thus, selective policies reshaped the demography of immigration from this area to promote the reunification of families and the establishment of permanent residency.

Because of the exemptions and preferences, the reduction in immigration under restrictive policy was modulated, and it had a specific demographic direction. The exceptions inherent in the restrictive policy of the 1920s brought a change in admissions as momentous as discriminatory quotas based on national origins. They constituted a selective control system over immigration that would make it serve more efficiently the nation's economic needs and prerequisites for social order.

As with restrictionist measures, selective measures were first enacted on Chinese and Japanese immigration. The Chinese Exclusion Act of 1882, with its amendments, and the Gentlemen's Agreement of 1907–08 pioneered the basic principles for selective admissions. First, they considered occupational status as a standard for admitting immigrants. While Chinese and Japanese laborers were denied admission, those in nonmanual occupations were admissible. Second, they recognized family relationship as conferring the right of admission to particular classes of immigrants. The nonresident spouses and children of "domiciled," or permanently resident, Chinese merchants were admissible, as were the spouses and prospective spouses of Japanese adult male immigrants. Third, they allowed permanent residents to reenter the

United States after visits to their country of origin. Under Chinese exclusion, "domiciled" laborers and merchants could reenter after visits home of up to two years. The Gentlemen's Agreement permitted the Japanese government to issue passports to "laborers who, in coming to the [American] continent, seek to resume a formerly acquired domicile, to join a parent, wife, or children residing there, or to assume active control of an already possessed interest in a farming enterprise in this country."[22]

The nonquota and preference system of the Quota Acts of 1921 and 1924 were built on selective principles similar to those first applied to Asian immigrants. They recognized occupational status and family relationship as factors bringing the right to admission. They regarded established permanent residency as securing the right of readmission for aliens after visits home.

The Decline of Return Migration

Return migration—immigrants returning to their country of origin—peaked after 1910 and then slackened in the quota decade of the 1920s. From 1911 to 1920, the return migration rate was 37 immigrants returning home per 100 arriving in the United States (Table A.6, p. 162). In the following quota decade, return migration fell to 25 per 100. The return migration rate of male aliens and low-skilled workers declined, while for female aliens it also fell and remained only half that of males. All age brackets dropped in return rates.

Return migration dwindled sharply among immigrants from southern and eastern Europe, partly because the flow of transient labor migrants from that region had been cut by the quota system. In addition, the New Immigrants' use of nonquota admissions for immediate relatives reinforced family settlement. The combination of the quota system and nonquota system increased the geographic stability of the southern and eastern European population. Under restrictionist and selective policy, immigrant America became a more settled society.

TOWARD UNIFIED AND
RESTRICTED NATURALIZATION

Naturalization policy, which specified how immigrants would become citizens, shared its ideological parentage with immigration policy. The two policies were twin children of the American Revolution and the political charters it generated—the Declaration of Independence and the Constitution. They reflected the revolutionary era's vision of the popular and eclectic sources of the American nation. The Constitution as finally drafted repudiated the European notion of legally differentiated social status as well as the idea that native-born citizens and naturalized citizens possessed different sets of rights. A naturalized citizen had all the rights, without exception, of a native-born citizen. Most important, the origins of naturalized citizenship were presumed to lie in the idea of "volitional allegiance" that characterized citizenship generally. The adoption of American citizenship by aliens, the transference of allegiance to the United States, emanated from individual choice and self-interest. Naturalization was based on the autonomy and liberty of the individual. This theoretical character of naturalization meant practically that an alien had to initiate and control the pursuit of citizenship and nationality. Government would only set basic rules of procedure. The applicant would decide how and when naturalization would fit into his or her life. Naturalization would be a reflection of the republican values of personal liberty and consent.[23]

For most of the nineteenth century, naturalization policy reflected fully these inclusive and voluntary principles. Like immigration policy, naturalization policy was administered in a loose and decentralized form. With the coming of the twentieth century, however, policymakers succumbed to doubts about the continuation of these principles and practices.[24]

The System of Discriminatory Naturalization

Congressional lawmakers in the late nineteenth century perceived a growing crisis in the naturalization law and its administration. This crisis was connected with changes in the pattern of immigration and debate over how undesirable changes could be controlled through both immigration and naturalization laws.

Policymakers and social scientists tried to specify exactly which national groups could or could not receive American citizenship. As new peoples immigrated from East Asia and the Near East, questions abounded as to which of the newcomers should be designated eligible for naturalization. Under the Chinese Exclusion Act of 1882, which barred Chinese laborers, Congress declared the Chinese the first national group to be "aliens ineligible for citizenship." The ineligibility of the Chinese had a short time earlier been indirectly indicated by an act passed in 1870 granting naturalization rights to African immigrants but to no other racial groups.[25]

Although xenophobia and the fear of labor competition aroused hostility toward the Chinese, a major reason for denying citizenship to the Chinese was a general conviction that they could not acquire the civic habits—the egalitarian attitudes and democratic individualism—required to participate in a modernizing, industrial society. Those who opposed citizenship for the Chinese perceived these immigrants as absolutely and permanently foreign elements from a remote civilization. They were criticized for lacking the capacity for absorption into American life, for maintaining allegiance to their kin, village, chief, and emperor. An eminent jurist complained that the Chinese

> have never adapted themselves to our habits, modes of dress, or our educational system, have never learned the sanctity of an oath, never desired to become citizens, or to perform the duties of citizenship. . . . They remain the same stolid Asiatics that have floated on the rivers and slaved in the fields of China for thirty centuries of time. . . . Our institutions have made no impression on them during the more than thirty years they have been in the country. . . . They do not and will not assimilate with our people.

Historian Charles Price has concluded that Chinese exclusion was rationalized on the grounds that "the continued presence of the Chinese was a serious obstacle to the orderly process of nation-building and that continued Chinese immigration transformed this obstacle into a grave immediate danger."[26]

But what about other immigrants from Asia? What standard would policymakers use to determine the fitness for citizenship of Japanese, Koreans, Filipinos, Asian Indians, and other Asians entering the country in growing numbers? The original naturalization law of 1790 provided a crude rule of thumb: only "free whites" could apply for citizenship. The precise meaning of the term "white," however, caused serious problems. Until the 1870s, lawmakers and judges had given scant attention to which races would be included under the category of white persons. In fact, a number of Chinese had been naturalized before the Chinese Exclusion Act of 1882 declared them to be ineligible for citizenship.[27]

Another problematic facet of awarding citizenship according to racial criteria was the status of children whose parents were aliens ineligible for citizenship. Although they were obviously of the same excluded race as their parents, they were born within the United States and qualified for citizenship by the *jus soli* principle of the Fourteenth Amendment. The U.S. Supreme Court affirmed this point in the case of *United States v. Wong Kim Ark* in 1898. By ratifying the citizenship of second-generation Chinese Americans, the court brought the Constitution squarely into conflict with the federal naturalization law making race, not place of birth, the touchstone of naturalization.[28]

Newcomers from other Asian countries were considered by popular opinion not to be white, yet numerous courts found them to be white persons qualified for naturalization and granted them citizenship papers. The federal census of 1910 reported that 1,368 Chinese and 420 Japanese were naturalized citizens. Misuji Miyakawa, the chief counsel of the Japanese American plaintiffs in the

1906 San Francisco school desegregation case that led to the Gentlemen's Agreement, was born in Japan, but he had been admitted to American citizenship and the California bar, which required its members to be citizens. Another Japanese alien, Takuji Yamashita, was naturalized in 1902 although he had no competence in English. The judge found him to have the character requirements for citizenship and did not consider his race a disqualification.[29]

Slowly, however, policymakers and judges established a rule for drawing a line between eligible and ineligible aliens. Where any doubt existed, whether scientific or popular, that an applicant was not a member of the white or African race, that applicant was deemed an alien ineligible for citizenship. The federal Bureau of Naturalization issued an administrative order in 1910 that court clerks should deny all aliens whose racial qualification was in doubt. As early as 1893, a Japanese had been rejected for naturalization on the grounds of racial disqualification, but after 1910 the denials served to Japanese applicants became more regular and consistent. At last, in 1922 the U.S. Supreme Court in *Ozawa v. United States* declared once and for all that Japanese aliens were not white and hence were ineligible for American citizenship.[30]

After 1910 most applicants from other parts of Asia were denied naturalization. Burmese, Malaysian, Filipino, Thai, Indian, and Korean applicants were rejected by the courts as ineligible nonwhite aliens. Even persons of mixed Asian backgrounds were excluded. In *In re Young* (1912) a federal court rejected a "half-breed German and Japanese"; and in *In re Alverto* (1912) another federal court excluded an applicant who was one-fourth Spanish and three-fourths Filipino.[31]

The judges who denied applicants from Asia often used contradictory and divergent criteria to reach their decisions. In the *Ozawa* case, the Supreme Court held that scientific tests had to be applied to the applicant because misleading characteristics could be found "even among Anglo-Saxons, ranging by imperceptible gradations from the fair blond to the swarthy brunette; the latter being darker than many of the lighter hued persons of the brown or yellow races." In the case of *United States v. Thind* (1923), in which the Supreme Court found a high-caste Hindu ineligible for citizenship, the justices reasoned that although according to science the plaintiff had descended from the same stock as Europeans, he was not white "in accordance with the understanding of the common man." In sharp contrast to the reasoning used to dispose of the *Ozawa* case just the year before, the court concluded, "What ethnologists, anthropologists, and other so-called scientists speculate and conjecture in respect to races and origins may interest the curious and convince the credulous, but is of no moment in arriving at the intent of Congress in the statute aforesaid."[32]

By the 1920s, the United States had a naturalization policy that reflected both legal and scientific confusion. The policy of barring Asians on the basis of race stood in stark contradiction to the Fourteenth Amendment, which conferred citizenship on second-generation children of Asian ancestry. The welter of court decisions mixed scientific criteria and popular racial sensibilities to deny citizenship to ethnologically diverse Asians, from Hindus to Japanese. In the restrictionists' worldview such inconsistencies could be tolerated because of the overriding need to limit American nationality.[33]

The Centralized Administration of Naturalization

While closing off naturalization to Asian aliens, policymakers worried that the population of New Immigrants from southern and eastern Europe were not disposed toward acquiring American citizenship. The United States Immigration Commission in 1911, under the chairmanship of Senator William P. Dillingham from Vermont, discerned a significant difference between the New Immigrants and the Old Immigrants from northern and western Europe. The former had come to America primarily for material self-betterment and, unlike the latter, they had little experience with democratic institutions or republican government. The public and policymakers feared that the new alien population had little enthusiasm or capacity for becoming American citizens. They might remain a dangerous undigested mass; even if naturalized, they might be unsuited for the rights and duties of citizenship. Poorly qualified aliens might fail to vote or might turn their vote over to corrupt politicians. Even worse, they might be traitors or spies who would aid the cause of foreign subversion.[34]

To ensure that aliens were naturalized according to proper qualifications and procedures, Congress passed the Naturalization Act of 1906. This law centralized procedures and raised the standards for admission to citizenship. It was the first major revision of naturalization policy since the Naturalization Act of 1802 and set the stage for the federal government to manage immigration and the status of aliens in a coordinated fashion.

The law was enforced and interpreted by the Bureau of Immigration and Naturalization in the Department of Commerce and Labor. Later, in 1913, a separate Bureau of Naturalization was formed under the authority of a commissioner of naturalization to administer the 1906 law. The hodgepodge of procedures and tests used by state and federal courts to determine fitness for admission to citizenship were to be ironed into uniformity and interpreted with consistency under the guidance of the federal bureaucracy.

The passage of the Naturalization Act of 1906 reaffirmed the tradition of voluntary republican citizenship inherited from the late eighteenth century. It confirmed that the New Immigrants could qualify for naturalization on the same grounds as those had who preceded them from northern and western Europe. Following historical precedent, naturalized citizenship would be contingent on residency and race and, in contrast to the practice in European countries, would not reflect a person's occupation or social class. A knowledge of civics, decent character verified by witnesses, and English-speaking ability were specified as additional requirements. The criterion of naturalization remained the adoption of allegiance and loyalty to the United States by individual decision. The new citizens were allowed to enter electoral politics on the same terms enjoyed by the native-born. They acquired the complete array of civil rights that guaranteed all citizens opportunities for economic and social participation.[35]

THE CONTINUING INFLUX
AFTER RESTRICTION

Senator Albert Johnson of Washington, a principal sponsor of the Second Quota Act, in 1924 summed up the role of immigration in American life:

> [The American people] have seen, patent and plain, the encroachments of the foreign-born flood upon their own lives. They have come to realize that such a flood, affecting as it does every individual of whatever race or origin, cannot fail likewise to affect the institutions which have made and preserved American liberties. It is no wonder, therefore, that the myth of the melting pot has been discredited. It is no wonder that Americans everywhere are insisting that their land no longer shall offer free and unrestricted asylum to the rest of the world. . . . The United States is our land. If it was not the land of our fathers, at least it may be, and it should be, the land of our children. We intend to maintain it so. The day of unalloyed welcome to all peoples, the day of indiscriminate acceptance of all races, has definitely ended.[36]

The flow of immigration was indeed curbed. But this would turn out to be a temporary interruption. Mass immigration would rebound through the workings of selective policy and the abandonment of a restrictionism that became obsolescent and irrelevant.

A quarter-century after the Second Quota Act of 1924, the United States was one of only three countries in the world with restrictive immigration quotas. Nevertheless, in the years from 1924 to 1965 mass immigration continued. The numbers arriving were considerably smaller than in the early years of the century, but they were still quite substantial. More than 7 million immigrants and 4.7 million guest workers entered the United States during the forty years after the passage of the most restrictive immigration law in history, a period that included a decade of depression and five years of world war.[37]

It is true that immigration to the United States dwindled sharply in the 1930s. Worldwide depression and international conflict proved more potent in curtailing immigration than the restrictionist quota system. Large portions of annual quotas for many nations went unfilled. From 1930 to 1947, only 23 percent of all available quota spots were used. From 1930 to the end of World War II, less than 700,000 immigrants entered the country as compared with 5.4 million who entered in the decade and a half before 1930. Furthermore, because of the lack of opportunities in the Great Depression, more people left the United States than entered in the 1930s.[38]

With the exception of the Depression years, however, the Western Hemisphere sent large waves of newcomers throughout the restrictionist era because it was exempted from quotas and ceilings. Responding to the labor needs of industry and agriculture, lawmakers had left a gateway open for labor migration from the Western Hemisphere.[39] Canadian and Mexican immigration was especially high, supplying new reserves of labor to fill the shortages caused by restrictions on immigrants from Europe and Asia. Another important influx of replacement labor came from the U.S. territory of Puerto Rico.

Circular migration was a constant phenomenon shaping the lives of Canadians, Mexicans, and Puerto Ricans. The proximity of their homelands made the cost of migration low. Movement both going to and returning from the United States remained heavy. Canadians, Mexicans, and Puerto Ricans experienced a high degree of transiency, the continual presence of newcomers, and regular contact with their homeland culture. The Canadians and Mexicans were "transborder peoples" *par excellence:* they formed communities that were divided by an international border. Canadian, Mexican, and Puerto Rican immigrants developed an ambivalent identity. Circular migration encouraged them to divide their political and cultural identification between the United States and their homelands. Perhaps a key index of this ambiguity was that Canadians and Mexicans historically were slow to adopt U.S. citizenship.[40]

Exodus from Canada and Mexico

In the restrictionist era, Canadian and Mexican immigration grew into the two largest population movements to the United States. From the 1920s to the 1950s, more than 1.4 million Canadians arrived in the United States; three-quarters came from British Canada and one-quarter from French Canada.

More than 840,000 Mexicans came as permanent settlers and 4.7 million more arrived as temporary guest workers.

In the first half of the twentieth century, neither Canadian nor Mexican immigrants ever became a target of restrictionists as the southern and eastern Europeans and Asians did. In fact, industrial and agricultural capitalists saw Canadians and Mexicans as necessary replacements in the labor pool for the restricted Europeans and Asians.[41]

Mexicans in particular served as a reserve supply of labor that was recruited and sent away as necessary. During the Great Depression when many Mexican aliens were thrown onto the public relief rolls, federal, state, and local officials put pressure on them to return to Mexico, and the Mexican government cooperated because they wanted laborers back in their country. Some American officials threatened to cut off welfare payments to Mexican aliens if they did not accept a one-way railway ticket to Mexico. It is estimated that about half a million Mexicans were repatriated. Ten percent of these were persuaded to leave the midwestern states of Illinois, Michigan, Indiana, and Minnesota.[42]

Immigrants from both Canada and Mexico usually settled within short distances of the U.S. borders. Mexican migrants flocked particularly to the agricultural areas of southern California and the lower Rio Grande River valley of Texas. Since most of the Canadian immigrants arrived from Ontario, Quebec, and the maritime provinces of Nova Scotia, New Brunswick, and Prince Edward Island, they concentrated chiefly in New England and the Great Lakes region.

A sizable number of Mexicans, however, settled farther north from their homeland. Some traveled directly to Chicago, Detroit, Cleveland, and Milwaukee to take factory jobs, while others peeled off from the army of seasonal farm laborers and joined the enclaves in the big midwestern cities. Mexicans in the urban colonies in the Midwest assimilated in ways somewhat like their European immigrant neighbors and were unlike their counterparts in castelike communities isolated in the barrios of the Southwest.[43]

After the Great Depression, Mexican immigration surged under the stimulus of World War II. Wartime industrial activity, the drain of conscription on native labor, and the movement of rural whites to factory work in the cities renewed the demand for Mexican workers in agriculture and transportation. The U.S. and Mexican governments revived the guest worker program of World War I, which would be known as the *bracero* ("farmhand") program. Started in 1942, it admitted farmworkers on short-term contracts that guaranteed work and living arrangements. The *braceros* were classified as foreign laborers, not as immigrants. By 1947, an estimated 200,000 *braceros* worked in twenty-one states, 100,000 of them in California. Most were migrant farmworkers who fanned out all over the country (Figure 1.1). Congress renewed the program regularly from 1951 to 1964. The influx of *braceros* peaked in 1959 when 450,000 entered the country. In 1960, they made up 26 percent of the nation's migrant farm labor force. By the end of the *bracero* program in 1967, 4.7 million Mexican laborers had entered the United States under its terms.[44]

After the Second World War, illegal immigration from Mexico mounted. Thousands of *braceros* overstayed their work permits, thus becoming illegal residents. *Mojados* ("wetbacks") crossed the border surreptitiously to get temporary employment because they did not wish to immigrate permanently, to become involved in the complications of visa applications, or be tied to the arranged terms of work in the *bracero* system. The federal government used mass detention and deportation to control illegal immigration. From 1950 to 1955, Operation Wetback rounded up and expelled 3.8 million Mexicans. Officials of the Immigration and Naturalization Service raided factories, restaurants, bars, and even private residences in search of illegal immigrants. To avoid federal agents, these immigrants accepted without protest the poorest working conditions and lowest wages. Still, they continued to flood into the country because they were able to earn much more in the United States than in Mexico.[45]

By the end of the restrictionist era, Mexican immigration grew into a more dynamic force than Canadian immigration. Increasing population and diminishing resources in Mexico stimulated the potential for mass exodus. In 1960, with a population rising by 3.5 percent each year, Mexico was one of the fastest-growing nations in Latin America. High rates of natural increase and the transfer of impoverished masses from rural to urban areas swelled the towns and cities in the northern Mexican states adjoining the U.S. border. Four out of five people changing residence moved from the state of their birth to an urban *municipio* in 1960. From 1950 to 1960 the nine largest border cities doubled their population. Ciudad Juarez grew by 136 percent, Mexicali by 123 percent, Tijuana by 115 percent, and Ensenada by 113 percent. These overcrowded urban centers were the launching places for the mounting waves of Mexican immigrants. The mass movement of Mexicans to the United States was a spillover of the migratory currents of a surplus population that would grow ever larger in the 1970s and 1980s.[46]

Figure 1.1. Patterns of Migration (right)
The army of migrant farmworkers followed these routes into different agricultural regions according to the cycle of planting and harvesting.

Source: The Immigration and Naturalization Systems of the United States (Washington, D.C.: U.S. Government Printing Office, 1950), App. VIII, p. 855.

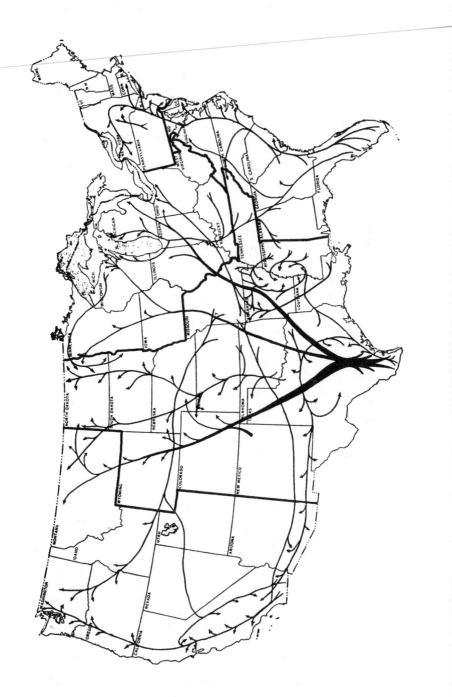

The Airplane Migration from Puerto Rico

Puerto Rican migration to the United States was, like Canadian and Mexican immigration, part of the pattern of replacement migration from the Western Hemisphere. Like Canadians and Mexicans, Puerto Ricans filled the labor demand caused by the restriction of immigrants from Asia and Europe. As in Mexico, the decline of the rural economy—which in Puerto Rico was based on plantation commercial agriculture—created a growing pool of underemployed workers. Puerto Rico, like Mexico, also lacked an urban industrial economy that could absorb a mushrooming population.[47]

The Puerto Ricans represented a special case of immigration for they originated in a U.S. territory and as such were American citizens who could enter the mainland without restriction. Because of Puerto Rico's proximity to the United States, Puerto Rican settlements displayed a high degree of transiency and return migration, much like Mexican and Canadian communities. The Puerto Rican influx was America's first airplane immigration. In the 1940s, cheap mass air travel was established between Puerto Rico and the mainland, and it became possible to fly from the island to New York City in six hours for less than fifty dollars. The air links quickened and expanded the movement from Puerto Rico and thus the Puerto Rican–born population in the United States jumped from 53,000 in 1930 to approach a quarter of a million by 1950. Some of the postwar newcomers came first as contract farmworkers who eventually gravitated to nearby cities in the Southeast, much like Mexicans did in the Midwest, but the majority headed directly to New York City and its surrounding communities. As the size of the New York Puerto Rican community grew, it became the chief magnet for new arrivals.[48]

The Rise of the Refugee Class

Refugees and displaced persons constituted the second important stream of immigrants after the influx of newcomers from the Western Hemisphere. Most came from Europe in the 1940s and 1950s, but by the end of the 1950s refugees from Asian nations augmented the flow of uprooted European masses. Congress passed an unprecedented series of refugee and displaced persons laws that creatively combined the traditional notion of the United States as a humanitarian sanctuary with the realpolitik of cold war internationalism. The United States sought to assist the millions uprooted by World War II and by the spread of Communist power in order to bolster its relations with allies who supported this country as the leader of the free world.[49]

The plight of persecuted people fleeing from nazism and fascism raised public concern that the United States should make room for refugees in spite of restrictive admissions policies. The federal government, however, turned its back on these refugees—most of whom were Jews—and refused to make special provisions for their admission from 1938 to 1941. President Harry S. Truman broke new ground when he issued an executive order in 1945 admitting 40,000 refugees and displaced persons, starting a train of new initiatives by the United States to relocate the millions uprooted by war and the spread of Communism. To keep intact the families of military personnel who married overseas, Congress passed the War Brides Act in 1945, enabling 120,000 alien wives, husbands, and children of armed services members to enter the United States, irrespective of racial criteria. In 1948, Congress passed a Displaced Persons Act, which provided 202,000 visas to refugees to settle permanently in the United States over a two-year period. This measure gave priorities to refugees from the Baltic states while discriminating against Jewish applicants through technicalities such as the requirement that 30 percent of those admitted be farmers by occupation. Displaced persons had to have sponsors who would guarantee their housing and employment, and strict security screening of all refugees was required to prevent spies and saboteurs from entering. The new law prescribed that visas issued to displaced persons be "mortgaged"—that is, the numbers of such visas were counted against respective nationality quotas for each subsequent year, up to a maximum of one-half a given quota per year. This stipulation revealed the intention of Congress to preserve discriminatory admissions based on nationality and provoked charges that lawmakers lacked the vision to create a fair immigration policy. Congress passed an amended Displaced Persons Act in 1950 to continue the program begun in 1948. It liberalized the terms of admission and increased annual admissions for displaced persons to 341,000. The provisions that tended to discriminate against Jewish refugees were removed. The 1950 law retained the requirement of sponsor guarantees for housing and employment and the principle of quota mortgaging. In 1953, however, Congress passed the Refugee Relief Act, which provided for 205,000 nonquota visas, a major breakthrough because it abandoned the much-criticized practice of quota mortgaging. In the late 1950s, new provisions were established to facilitate the transition of refugees to permanent resident status. Under the unprecedented refugee policy of the postwar era, southern and eastern Europeans as well as Asians who had been the chief targets of restrictionism were admitted in numbers far exceeding their annual quotas.[50]

The series of congressional refugee laws started the process of reevaluating and changing the historic principle of restriction. Progressively, refugee policy became more open, responsive, and generous. It was in the area of refugee legislation that quota effects were first weakened significantly by the rejection of quota mortgaging.

Continuation of the Demographic Shift

The swing away from the nineteenth-century industrial pattern of immigration began between 1900 and 1930 and accelerated from 1930 to 1960 (Tables A.1, A.2, and A.3, pp. 156–58). For the first time in history, female immigrants outnumbered males. The share of white-collar and skilled workers grew rapidly, and the share of laborers shrank correspondingly. In fact, the proportion of low-skilled workers fell to its lowest historic levels. The age distribution shifted from adolescents and young adults toward children and the elderly. Return migration also remained low.

The four decades after the installation of full restriction in 1924 constituted a pivotal era of change in the origins and characteristics of immigrants. These shifts in demography resulted from the open gate to immigration from the Western Hemisphere and the introduction of refugee policies. They helped to maintain a mass immigration that produced both economic and political dividends to the nation as it gradually forged new international ties. The legacy of restriction was to control immigration in new and limited channels where it would help stabilize a postindustrial society.

NOTES

[1] Henry Steele Commager, ed., *Living Ideas in America* (New York: Harper, 1951), p. 145.

[2] Gordon S. Wood, *The Creation of the American Republic, 1776–1787* (Chapel Hill: University of North Carolina Press, 1969), pp. 609–15.

[3] Marcus Lee Hansen, *The Immigrant in American History* (Cambridge: Harvard University Press, 1940), pp. 131–32; Maldwyn Allen Jones, *American Immigration* (Chicago: University of Chicago Press, 1960), p. 123; John Higham, *Strangers in the Land: Patterns of American Nativism, 1860–1925* (New Brunswick: Rutgers University Press, 1955), p. 17.

[4] Stuart Creighton Miller, *The Unwelcome Immigrant: The American Image of the Chinese, 1785–1882* (Berkeley: University of California Press, 1969), provides a unified account of the various features of anti-Chinese xenophobia. Also see Gunther Barth, *Bitter Strength: A History of the Chinese in the United States, 1850–1870* (Cambridge: Harvard University Press, 1964), ch. 6; Alexander Saxton, *The Indispensable Enemy: Labor and the Anti-Chinese Movement in California* (Berkeley: University of California Press, 1971).

[5] E. P. Hutchinson, *Legislative History of American Immigration Policy, 1798–1965* (Philadelphia: University of Pennsylvania Press, 1981), pp. 64–84, 430–31.

[6] Thomas A. Bailey, *Theodore Roosevelt and the Japanese-American Crises* (Stanford: Stanford University Press, 1934), ch. 7, 8; Roger Daniels, *The Politics of Prejudice: The Anti-Japanese Movement in California and the Struggle for Exclusion* (Berkeley: University of California Press, 1962), ch. 3.

[7] Higham, *Strangers in the Land,* p. 167.

[8] U.S. Immigration Commission, *Reports,* 42 vols. (Washington, D.C.: U.S. Government Printing Office, 1911); William S. Bernard, ed., *American Immigration Policy* (New York: Harper and Sons, 1950), p. 11; Oscar Handlin, *Race and Nationality in American Life* (Cambridge: Harvard University Press, 1957), pp. 77–82; Robert A. Divine, *American Immigration Policy, 1924–1952* (New Haven: Yale University Press, 1957), p. 4; Higham, *Strangers in the Land,* ch. 10.

[9] Hutchinson, *Legislative History,* pp. 431–32.

[10] Higham, *Strangers in the Land,* p. 203; Barbara Miller Solomon, *Ancestors and Immigrants: A Changing New England Tradition* (Cambridge: Harvard University Press, 1956), pp. 115–17; Divine, *American Immigration Policy,* pp. 4–5.

[11] Hutchinson, *Legislative History,* ch. 14; Higham, *Strangers in the Land,* pp. 308–11; Divine, *American Immigration Policy,* pp. 5–9. A tabulation of quota distribution that is particularly helpful is in Bernard, *American Immigration Policy,* Table 2, p. 27.

[12] Divine, *American Immigration Policy,* p. 17; Higham, *Strangers in the Land,* pp. 319–24; Hutchinson, *Legislative History,* pp. 484–85; Bernard, *American Immigration Policy,* pp. 25–26.

[13] Luella Gettys, *The Law of Citizenship in the United States* (Chicago: University of Chicago Press, 1934), pp. 36–37, 62–66; Sidney Kansas, *Citizenship of the United States of America* (New York: Washington Publishing Co., 1936), pp. 28–32; Hutchinson, *Legislative History,* p. 479.

[14] Divine, *American Immigration Policy,* pp. 28–33; Bernard, *American Immigration Policy,* pp. 26–31; Thomas Archdeacon, *Becoming American: An Ethnic History* (New York: Free Press, 1983), p. 175.

[15] Report of House Committee (H. Rept. 350 [68-I], pp. 13–14), quoted in Hutchinson, *Legislative History,* p. 484; Roy L. Garis, *Immigration Restriction: A Study of the Opposition to and Regulation of Immigration into the United States* (New York: Macmillan, 1927), pp. 352–54.

[16] Divine, *American Immigration Policy,* p. 16; Solomon, *Ancestors and Immigrants,* ch. 9; Higham, *Strangers in the Land,* pp. 104–5, 191–93, 311.

[17] Aristide R. Zolberg, "Reforming the Back Door: The Immigration Reform and Control Act of 1986 in Historical Perspective," in Virginia Yans-McLaughlin, ed., *Immigration Reconsidered: History, Sociology, and Politics* (New York: Oxford University Press, 1990), p. 316; Aristide R. Zolberg, "International Migrations in Political Perspective," in Mary M. Kritz, Charles B. Keely, and Silvano M. Tomasi, eds., *Global Trends in Migration: Theory and Research on International Population Movements* (New York: Center for Migration Studies, 1981); Thomas Muller, *Immigrants and the American City* (New York: New York University Press, 1993), pp. 36–47.

[18] Commissioner-General of Immigration, *Annual Report, 1930,* Table 82, p. 201; Table 84, pp. 204–07.

[19] First proviso, section 3 of the 1917 Immigration Act; continued by section 212b of the 1952 McCarran-Walter Act.

[20] Computed from tabular data in Commissioner-General of Immigration, *Annual Reports, 1918–1925,* Tables VII and VIIB; *Annual Reports, 1926–1927,* Table 11; *Annual Reports, 1928–1930,* Table 13.

[21] Hutchinson, *Legislative History,* pp. 185, 194; Bernard, *American Immigration Policy,* pp. 34–35; Roger Daniels, *Coming to America: A History of Immigration and Ethnicity in American Life* (New York: HarperPerennial, 1991), p. 292.

[22] U.S. Commissioner-General of Immigration, *Annual Report, 1906* (Washington, D.C.: U.S. Government Printing Office, 1907), pp. 83–87; *Annual Report, 1908,* pp. 125–26.

[23] The early legal foundations of citizenship and naturalization are explained in Frederick Van Dyne, *Citizenship of the United States* (Rochester, N.Y.: Lawyers' Co-operative Publishing Co., 1904), and Frederick Van Dyne, *A Treatise on the Law of Naturalization of the United States* (Washington, D.C.: Frederick Van Dyne, 1907), pp. 43–48; Frank George Franklin, *The Legislative History of Naturalization in the United States from the Revolutionary War to 1861* (Chicago: University of Chicago Press, 1906); John S. Wise, *A Treatise on Citizenship* (Northport, N.Y.: E. Thompson, 1906); Gettys, *The Law of Citizenship;* and John P. Roche, *The Early Development of United States Citizenship* (Ithaca: Cornell University Press, 1949). The contractual character of American citizenship is explored in James H. Kettner, *The Development of American Citizenship, 1608–1870* (Chapel Hill: University of North Carolina Press, 1978), ch. 7; and I-Mien Tsiang, *The Question of Expatriation in America Prior to 1907* (Baltimore: Johns Hopkins University Press, 1942).

[24] Arthur Mann, *The One and the Many: Reflections on the American Identity* (Chicago: University of Chicago Press, 1979), pp. 79–92.

[25] Ibid., pp. 86–94; Charles A. Price, *The Great White Walls Are Built: Restrictive Immigration to North America and Australasia, 1836–1888* (Canberra, Australia: Australian National University Press, 1974), pp. 128–29; Alexander Saxton, *The Indispensable Enemy: Labor and the Anti-Chinese Movement in California* (Berkeley: University of California Press, 1971), pp. 36–37.

[26] Price, *The Great White Walls,* pp. 257, 269–70.

[27] Sydney L. Gulick, *American Democracy and Asiatic Citizenship* (New York: Charles Scribner's Sons, 1918), p. 59.

[28] Norman Alexander, *Rights of Aliens under the Federal Constitution* (Montpelier, Vt.: Capital City Press, 1931), p. 46.

[29] U.S. Bureau of the Census, *Population, 1910* (Washington, D.C.: U.S. Government Printing Office, 1913), Table 21, p. 1067; Gulick, *American Democracy and Asiatic Citizenship,* p. 71; Ray Malcolm, "American Citizenship and the Japanese," *Annals of the American Academy* 93 (1921): 79.

[30] *Toyota v. United States,* 268 U.S. 408 (1925); *Ozawa v. United States,* 260 U.S. 178 (1922); *Yamashita v. Hinkle,* 260 U.S. 198 (1922). Also see D. O. McGovney, "Race Discrimination in Naturalization," *Iowa Law Bulletin* 8 (1923): 129–61, 211–44; Malcolm, "American Citizenship and the Japanese," pp. 77–81; Kansas, *Citizenship of the United States,* pp. 28–33.

[31] *In re San C. Po,* 7 Misc. 471, 28 N.Y. Supp. 383 (1894); Petition of Easurk Emsen Charr (D.C. Mo. 1921), 273 F. 207 (1921); *Wadia v. U.S.C.C.A.,* N.Y. 1939, 101 F. 2d. 7 (1939); *In re Young,* 198 Fed. 715 (1912); *In re Alverto,* 198 Fed. 688 (1912).

[32] *Ozawa v. United States,* 260 U.S. 178 (1922); *United States v. Bhagat Singh Thind,* 261 U.S. 204 (1922).

[33] Paul S. Rundquist, "A Uniform Rule: The Congress and the Courts in American Naturalization, 1865–1952," Ph.D. thesis (University of Chicago, 1975), chs. 2–4.

[34] Solomon, *Ancestors and Immigrants,* pp. 198–99; *United States v. Schwimmer,* 279 U.S. 644; Harry H. Hull, Commissioner-General of Immigration, "Statement," in Commissioner-General of Immigration, *Annual Report, 1927,* p. 21.

[35] Ira Katznelson, *City Trenches: Urban Politics and the Patterning of Class in the United States* (New York: Pantheon, 1981), pp. 65–72; T. H. Marshall, *Citizenship and Social Class* (Cambridge: Cambridge University Press, 1950), p. 35.

[36] Cited in William S. Bernard, "Immigration: A History of U. S. Policy," in Stephan Thernstrom, ed., *Harvard Encyclopedia of American Ethnic Groups* (Cambridge: Harvard University Press, 1980), p. 493.

[37] The other countries with admissions quotas were the Philippines and Brazil. See U.S. Congress, Senate, Committee on the Judiciary, *The Immigration and Naturalization Systems of the United States* (Washington, D.C.: U.S. Government Printing Office, 1950), p. 27.

[38] U.S. Congress, *Immigration and Naturalization Systems,* Table 4, p. 889; Muller, *Immigrants and the American City,* p. 46; Conrad Taeuber and Irene B. Taeuber, *The Changing Population of the United States* (New York: John Wiley, 1958), Table 91, p. 294.

[39] *1984 Statistical Yearbook of the Immigration and Naturalization Service* (Washington, D.C.: U.S. Government Printing Office, 1985), Table IMM1.1, p. 1; Jones, *American Immigration,* p. 279; Oscar Handlin, *The Uprooted,* 2d ed. (Boston: Little, Brown, 1973), p. 260; Zolberg, "Reforming the Back Door," pp. 316–17.

[40] Nathan Glazer and Daniel Patrick Moynihan, *Beyond the Melting Pot: The Negroes, Puerto Ricans, Jews, Italians, and Irish of New York City,* 2nd ed. (Cambridge: MIT Press, 1970), pp. 99–110; Peter Skerry, "The Ambiguity of Mexican American Politics," in Nathan Glazer, ed., *Clamor at the Gates: The New American Immigration* (San Francisco: Institute for Contemporary Studies, 1985), pp. 241–44; Raymond H. Carr, *Puerto Rico: A Colonial Experiment* (New York: Vintage, 1984), pp. 298–304; Reed Ueda, "Naturalization and Citizenship," in Thernstrom, *Harvard Encyclopedia,* Table 4; Handlin, *Race and Nationality,* p. 163; F. J. Brown and J. S. Roucek, *One America* (New York: Prentice-Hall, 1945), p. 657; Myron Weiner, "Transborder Peoples," in Walker Connor, ed., *Mexican-Americans in Comparative Perspective* (Washington, D.C.: Urban Institute Press, 1985), pp. 130–33. A useful description of circular migration is provided in Peter Clark and David Souden, *Migration and Society in Early Modern England* (Totowa, N.J.: Barnes and Noble, 1988), pp. 16–17.

[41] Oscar Handlin, *The American People in the Twentieth Century* (Cambridge: Harvard University Press, 1954), pp. 48–55, 156–59.

[42] Carlos Cortes, "Mexicans," in Thernstrom, *Harvard Encyclopedia,* p. 703. See repatriation figures in Joan Moore, *Mexican Americans,* 2d ed. (Englewood Cliffs: Prentice-Hall, 1976), p. 42, based on estimates of Abraham Hoffman, *Unwanted Mexicans in the Great Depression* (Tucson:

University of Arizona Press, 1974). Also see Vernon M. Briggs, Jr., *Immigration Policy and the American Labor Force* (Baltimore: Johns Hopkins University Press, 1984), pp. 54–56.

[43] Paul S. Taylor, *Mexican Labor in the United States: Chicago and the Calumet Region* (Berkeley: University of California Press, 1932), pp. 48–49; Julian Samora and Richard A. Lamanna, *Mexican Americans in a Midwest Metropolis: A Study of East Chicago* (Los Angeles: UCLA Graduate School of Business Administration, 1967); Dennis Nodian Valdes, *Al Norte: Agricultural Workers in the Great Lakes Region, 1917–1970* (Austin: University of Texas Press, 1991), pp. 26–27, 72–73, 111–12; Leo Grebler, Joan W. Moore, and Ralph C. Guzman, *The Mexican American People: The Nation's Second Largest Minority* (New York: Free Press, 1970), p. 112; Arnaldo De Leon, *They Called Them Greasers: Anglo Attitudes toward Mexicans in Texas, 1821–1900* (Austin: University of Texas Press, 1983), ch. 2.

[44] Grebler, Moore, and Guzman, *The Mexican American People,* pp. 66–69; John Stone, "Ethnicity and Stratification: Mexican-Americans and European *Gastarbeiter,*" in Connor, *Mexican Americans in Comparative Perspective,* pp. 106–11; Lawrence H. Fuchs, *The American Kaleidoscope: Race, Ethnicity, and the Civic Culture* (Hanover, N.H.: University Press of New England, 1990), pp. 120–27.

[45] Moore, *Mexican Americans,* pp. 42–44.

[46] Walter Fogel, "Mexican Migration to the United States," in Barry Chiswick, ed., *The Gateway: Immigration Issues and Policy* (Washington, D.C.: American Enterprise Institute, 1982); Ellwyn R. Stoddard, *Mexican Americans* (New York: Random House, 1973), pp. 27–28; Grebler, Moore, and Guzman, *The Mexican American People,* p. 41.

[47] Virginia E. Sanchez Korrol, *From Colonia to Community: The History of Puerto Ricans in New York City, 1917–1948* (Westport, Conn.: Greenwood Press, 1983), pp. 17–39; Oscar Handlin, *The Newcomers: Negroes and Puerto Ricans in a Changing Metropolis* (Cambridge: Harvard University Press, 1959), pp. 49–50.

[48] Joseph Fitzpatrick, *Puerto Rican Americans: The Meaning of Migration to the Mainland* (Englewood Cliffs: Prentice-Hall, 1971), pp. 10–15.

[49] David M. Reimers, *Still the Golden Door: The Third World Comes to America* (New York: Columbia University Press, 1985), pp. 21–23.

[50] David S. Wyman, *Paper Walls: America and the Refugee Crisis, 1938–1941* (New York: Pantheon, 1985); Marion T. Bennett, *American Immigration Policies: A History* (Washington, D.C.: Public Affairs Press, 1963), pp. 86–87; Hutchinson, *Legislative History,* pp. 280–81, 291–92, 317–19; Reimers, *Still the Golden Door,* p. 23.

2

The Transformation
of Policy

THE PATH TO A WORLDWIDE
IMMIGRATION POLICY

From World War II to the Vietnam War, the United States recast the parameters of immigration and naturalization policy, as lawmakers pried open the ethnic and racial closures on admissions and citizenship. Congress completely replaced the system of "ethnic screening" in force from 1924 to 1965 with an expanded selective system of "family and skill screening." The pace of activity in immigration legislation accelerated steadily in an effort to keep the massive and complicated system updated.[1]

World War II marked the end of American isolationism and the beginning of a new international leadership role for the nation. Henceforth, lawmakers saw immigration and naturalization policy as a tool for shaping foreign relations to further American self-interest. To cement the alliance between China and the United States during World War II, Congress in 1943 repealed the Chinese Exclusion Act of 1882. Furthermore, in 1946, Congress established naturalization rights for Filipinos and admitted aliens from India who had been excluded since the act of 1917 created the Asiatic Barred Zone.[2]

Conflict with international rivals such as the Axis powers and Soviet Russia forged a closer linkage between immigration restriction and national security. Seeking to meet new security and defense needs, Congress passed the Smith Act in 1940, authorizing American consuls to refuse visa applicants who might endanger the "public safety." It also empowered the president to deport any alien if such deportation was "in the interest of the United States." Continuing in the vein of the Smith Act, Congress passed the Internal Security Act of 1950, requiring that all aliens who had been Communist party members or had belonged to front organizations be barred from entry or deported if necessary. The new emphasis on security added urgency to the need to revise and recodify the welter of immigration laws passed in the years since the onset of restrictionism.[3]

The McCarran-Walter Act

Finally, in 1952, Congress passed the voluminous McCarran-Walter Act, which assembled all previous legislation into one uniform code reaffirming restrictionist policy. First and foremost, it retained the precedent of national origins in fixing discriminatory quotas. Northern and western European nations received 85 percent of annual admissions. Moreover, inhabitants of colonies and dominions of quota-receiving countries could no longer qualify for admission under the quotas of the mother countries. Each colony received a subquota of one hundred visas a year. This provision cut sharply into immigration from the West Indies. Offended by the preservation of national origins discrimination, President Truman vetoed the bill, but his veto was overridden.[4]

The McCarran-Walter Act was a counterpoint to the expansion of refugee legislation. It "represented the triumph of nationalism over international considerations," observes historian Robert A. Divine, because it perpetuated the legacy of restriction out of fear that immigration would undermine national strength. The act expressed an isolationist nationalism. McCarran-Walter stood in contrast to the growth of refugee legislation aimed at forming international linkages "to have the respect of people all around the world," in the words of Senator Hubert H. Humphrey.[5]

Despite its basic conservatism, the McCarran-Walter Act did loosen some cornerstones of restrictionist policy. It declared the denial of admission based on racial factors invalid. Culminating the trend begun by the acts ending Chinese exclusion in 1943 and Asian Indian exclusion in 1946, it abolished the principle of the closed door toward immigrants from Asian nations. Japan received a quota of 185, China a quota of 105, and countries within a zone called the Asia-Pacific Triangle a quota of 100. While these were token quotas, the 1952 law demolished the long-standing principle of Asian exclusion. As a whole, the 1952 omnibus law reaffirmed the validity of discriminatory admissions, but it made the national origins system apply without racial exclusion to the entire world for the first time.[6]

The 1952 immigration act also reaffirmed the value of selective and unlimited admissions categories by retaining and revising the preference system for visa assignment (Table A.4, p. 159). Each preference class received a designated share of the quota visas annually available, and those applicants with the highest preference standing received the first available visa until the number allotted to their preference class was exhausted. The 1952 law awarded the highest preference to immigrants who had desirable technical or professional job expertise and their immediate family members. The parents and adult children of U.S. citizens received secondary preference. The immediate relatives of permanent resident aliens were given the next preference, followed by siblings (with their immediate relatives) of American citizens. The 1952 law also retained the nonquota class, which still included spouses and minor children of American citizens, who could also enter as quota immigrants through the preference system. All Western Hemisphere immigration remained in the nonquota category, maintaining the conditions for the rapid growth of Latin American immigration that occurred subsequently.[7]

With the limited breakthroughs of the 1952 immigration act and the introduction of displaced persons legislation, Congress moved away gingerly from old restrictive principles. Refugees gained yearly admissions that exceeded annual quotas for their home countries. Discrimination according to national origin seemed less likely to serve the interests of the United States as it sought to establish itself as the leader of free and democratic nations in the Cold War.

Presidents from Harry Truman to Lyndon Johnson tried to nudge Congress away from restrictionism. In his veto of the McCarran-Walter Act, Truman denounced the "basis" of the restrictionist quota system as "false and unworthy." A presidential commission convened by Truman recommended in its 1953 report *Whom We Shall Welcome* the complete abrogation of the national origins system. In 1960, President Dwight Eisenhower declared to Congress, "I again urge the liberalization of some of our restrictions upon immigration." President John F. Kennedy in 1963 assailed the quota system as having "no basis in either logic or reason." He complained, "It neither satisfies a national need nor accomplishes an international purpose. In an age of interdependence among nations, such a system is an anachronism for it discriminates among applicants for admission into the United States on the basis of the accident of birth." President Lyndon B. Johnson urged Congress to heed his predecessor's appeal for reform of the entire immigration and naturalization system.[8]

The Hart-Celler Act

Finally, in 1965 Congress amended the McCarran-Walter Act by passing a revolutionary new law, the Hart-Celler Act, which abolished the discriminatory national origins quotas and the Asia-Pacific Triangle, the last vestige of the exclusionary Asiatic Barred Zone. This act can be understood as a part of the evolutionary trend in federal policy after World War II to end legal discrimination based on race and ethnicity. The liberalization of immigration policy was a concomitant of the Civil Rights Act of 1964 and the Voting Rights Act of 1965, the federal pacemaking laws designed to abolish racial discrimination, particularly against black Americans. The 1965 immigration act, with its amendments in 1976 and 1978, produced, according to labor policy analyst

Vernon M. Briggs, Jr., a "worldwide immigration system . . . a single policy that applies uniformly to the people of all nations."[9]

The architects of the 1965 law, however, did not see it as a means of increasing the flow of immigration in a major way. Moreover, they had no inkling that the law would become an avenue for globalizing immigration. Many senators and congressional representatives believed that the new equal quotas would be underutilized by European, Asian, and Middle Eastern nations. In addition, they did not foresee the expansion of nonquota admissions under the act's strengthened provisions for family reunification.[10]

The 1965 law in fact had new restrictionist content. It created stricter control over labor migration and limited the power of the president to provide special refugee admissions. Most important, it put admissions from the Western Hemisphere under numerical limitations for the first time. Admissions openings were apportioned in two blocs: 170,000 visas were allocated to countries in the Eastern Hemisphere and 120,000 were reserved for countries in the Western Hemisphere. Thus the law moderately raised the annual ceiling on admissions from 150,000 to 290,000. Each country in the Eastern Hemisphere was permitted no more than 20,000 visas in a year; the equal per country ceilings were conceived as the antidote to the discriminatory quotas under the old national origins system. Congress later amended these provisions to provide greater uniformity. In 1976, it passed an amendment applying the per country ceiling of 20,000 visas yearly to the Western Hemisphere as well as the Eastern; in 1978 it abolished hemispheric annual ceilings by creating a single worldwide ceiling of 290,000 annual admissions.[11]

The 1965 law ensured the continuation of selective admissions by revising the visa preference system. For the first time in history, immediate relatives of American citizens and permanent resident aliens enjoyed a higher preference standing than applicants with special job skills (Table A.4, p. 159). Preferences for those with special job skills were extended only to nations in the Eastern Hemisphere, while a small block of refugee visas was set aside annually.[12]

The 1965 law also maintained selective admissions by continuing the old nonquota class started in 1921. It was relabeled as "exempt from worldwide limitation" and included "immediate relatives" of U.S. citizens, now expanded to include parents as well as spouses and children of U.S. citizens. The exempt class now applied to Western Hemisphere nations that had been given per country annual ceilings of 20,000 visas.

The 1965 law departed from the labels *quota* and *nonquota* immigrants in use since the First Quota Act of 1921. The term *immigrant* replaced the term *quota immigrant; immediate relative* replaced *nonquota immigrant;* and *special immigrant* replaced *nonquota immigrant from the Western*

Hemisphere. Nevertheless, the law still operated by allotting functional visa quotas and providing a nonquota visa class not subject to numerical limitations. In essence, the 1965 law converted the old system of quota and nonquota classes into an equivalent two-pronged system consisting of a visa class subject to worldwide limitation and a visa class exempt from worldwide limitation.[13]

The 1965 law established conditions under which the problem of illegal immigration from Western Hemisphere countries, particularly from Mexico, would worsen. Because the 1965 immigration law and its 1976 amendment imposed annual ceilings and national quotas on Western Hemisphere countries, many applicants who desired temporary work were tempted to enter the United States surreptitiously rather than go through the time-consuming and uncertain application process for limited visa slots. The abrupt ending of the *bracero* program, coinciding with the passage of Hart-Celler, diverted those who would normally have come as guest workers into illegal entry channels. Seasonal migration continued after 1965, for the most part illegally. Through a recruitment and communications network operating over two decades, the *bracero* program had built an enormous social infrastructure for migration that could not be suddenly eliminated. The Immigration and Naturalization Service arrested and deported 500,000 illegal aliens each year in the decade following the Hart-Celler Act. Most were low-skilled, low-paid Mexican workers, but others came from Central America, the Caribbean, and Europe.[14]

The rise in illegal immigration became the chief stimulus for new departures in policies dealing with immigrants. In charting a legislative course of action, Congress studied the recommendations of the Select Commission on Immigration and Refugee Policy (1978–1981). The thrust of the select commission's views were in diametric opposition to the findings of the U.S. Immigration Commission of 1907–1910, which compiled the federal case for closing the nation's gates. Despite opinion surveys showing that many Americans felt that immigration levels were too high, the commission found much evidence to affirm the positive role of immigration in American life. It advised that the United States continue to accept large numbers of immigrants and even consider an amnesty program for undocumented aliens that would include a mechanism for legalizing their status. The commission found that evidence on the impact of illegal immigration was inconclusive, but it sought ways to close the "back door" of influx, recommending legislation that would make knowing employment of illegal aliens unlawful and punishable. Specific elements of these proposals for immigration policy were packaged in the Simpson-Mazzoli bill, which Congress put through protracted and discouraging deliberations in the early 1980s.[15]

The Human Element in Immigration

Recruiting agents operated a network of communication and transportation to facilitate illegal immigration from Mexico.

I was born in a small town in the state of Michoacán in Mexico. When I was fifteen, I went to Mexico City with my grandmother and my mother. I worked in a parking lot, a big car lot. People would come in and they'd say, "Well, park my car." And I'd give them a ticket and I'd park the car and I'd be there, you know, watching the cars. I got paid in tips.

But I wanted to come to the United States to work and to earn more money. My uncle was here, and I thought if I could come to him, I could live with him and work and he would help me.

It's not possible to get papers to come over now. So when I decided to come, I went to Tijuana in Mexico. There's a person there that will get in contact with you. They call him the Coyote. He walks around town, and if he sees someone wandering around alone, he says, "Hello, do you have relatives in the United States?" And if you say yes, he says, "Do you want to visit them?" And if you say yes, he says he can arrange it through a friend. It costs $250 or $300.

The Coyote rounded up me and five other guys, and then he got in contact with a guide to take us across the border. We had to go through the hills and the desert, and we had to swim through a river. I was a little scared. Then we come to a highway and a man was there with a van, pretending to fix his motor. Our guide said hello, and the man jumped into the car and we ran and jumped in, too. He began to drive down the highway fast and we knew we were safe in the United States. He took us to San Isidro that night, and the next day he took us all the way here to Watsonville. I had to pay him $250 and then, after I'd been here a month, he came back and I had to give him $50 more. He said I owed him that.

—Miguel Torres, immigrated from Mexico, 1977

Source: Joan Morrison and Charlotte Fox Zabusky, *American Mosaic: The Immigrant Experience in the Words of Those Who Lived It* (New York: New American Library, 1980), p. 347.

The Immigration Reform and Control Act

In 1986, Congress finally passed the Immigration Reform and Control Act (IRCA), a modification of the Simpson-Mazzoli Act that dealt centrally with the issue of illegal immigration. The rising population of illegal aliens was estimated by 1986 to be as high as three to five million. Instead of launching massive deportations, a measure often employed in the past to deal with Mexican aliens, the law created a radically new program aimed at legalizing the status of undocumented aliens. Aliens who had been unlawfully resident in the country since January 1, 1982, had up to a year from May 1987 to apply for legal status. Temporary-resident agricultural workers who had overstayed their permits were permitted to apply for legal status from June 1987 to November 1988.[16]

The 1986 law broadened admissions opportunities in other ways as well. It normalized the status of 100,000 special entrants from Haiti and Cuba and increased annual quotas for former colonies and dependencies from 500 to 6,000. It also created a small quota for aliens from countries underrepresented in annual immigration allotments.

While opening the "front door" of admissions wider, the 1986 law tried to close the "back door" of illegal immigration by placing sanctions against employers who knowingly hired undocumented aliens. This was a hotly debated feature of the law, vehemently opposed by Mexican American advocacy groups who feared that it would lead to discrimination against Mexicans in general. Congress tried to defuse the potential for discrimination by passing a law that made discrimination based on immigrant status illegal.[17]

To many observers, the Immigration Reform and Control Act was the most generous immigration law passed in United States history. IRCA was "pro-immigration," based on the view that immigration was an asset to the nation. It established novel and generous provisions for the legalization of illegal aliens and enlarged a host of quota allotments based on special needs and status. Even its controversial program to impose sanctions on employers to discourage employment of illegal aliens was conceived as ending the exploitation of powerless and voiceless workers and expanding civil rights protections for Hispanics.

Amnesty for illegals was not a political prize won by a powerful "odd couple" lobby of civil libertarians and capitalist employers. The former did not assert themselves in the immigration policy arena and the latter tended to favor guest worker programs or permitting the government to do little about the situation for illegals. Even Mexican American advocacy groups were hesitant over amnesty because they felt it was a bargaining chip to obtain their support of employer sanctions. The amnesty provision passed in the

House by only seven votes. Despite weak support, amnesty for illegals became part of IRCA through the persistence and leadership of an influential cadre of congressional representatives who served on the Select Commission for Immigration and Refugee Policy and decided that legalization best combined social pragmatism and democratic values. As a consequence of the admission of legalized aliens, all-time highs of 1.5 million and 1.8 million immigrants were officially admitted in 1990 and 1991, respectively. The 1990 annual total included 880,000 former undocumented aliens who had been legalized, the 1991 total 1.1 million.[18]

The "pro-immigration" ethos persisted into 1990 when Congress enacted a new law that revised numerical ceilings and the system of preferences. Its provisions, effective in 1992, created a new "overall flexible cap" of 700,000 visas for all categories of admissions; the cap would be reduced to 675,000 in 1995. The per country ceiling of yearly available visas was retained, but the basis for its computation was changed. The law divided preference classes into three broad groups (Table A.4, p. 159): a "family-based" class for immigrants reuniting with family members; an "employment-based" class for immigrants with desirable occupational skills and training; and a miscellaneous class including applicants from countries deemed to be underrepresented in immigration. The share of immigrants selected to meet occupational and economic needs was enlarged, but those reuniting with family members still were granted the highest percentage of visas. Lawmakers anticipated that about 700,000 immigrants would be admitted each year through the mid-1990s, with about 100,000 refugees added to that number. Finally, the 1990 law empaneled a new Commission on Immigration Reform to report recommendations in 1994 and 1997 on questions such as how to control illegal immigration, but it was not clear whether it would entertain a major change in the immigration system.[19]

The Expansion of Refugee Legislation

From the end of World War II to 1990, 2.5 million out of 18.6 million immigrants—almost one out of seven—arrived as refugees. Europe and Asia each sent nearly a million refugees, while Latin America sent half a million refugees, nearly all from Cuba. Refugees from each region arrived in a series of waves. Most of the refugees arriving from 1946 to 1950 fled from the spread of Communist regimes in central and eastern Europe. In the 1960s, the largest wave of refugees came from Cuba to escape the revolutionary government of Fidel Castro; in the 1970s and 1980s, an exodus of Southeast Asian refugees arrived in the wake of the regional chaos following the Vietnam War; in the late 1980s and 1990s refugees from central and eastern Europe resurged anew as the Soviet bloc governments disintegrated. The 1970s and 1980s became the two greatest decades of refugee admissions in American history because of the confluence of refugee streams from Cuba, Southeast Asia, and eastern Europe (Figure 2.1).[20]

As the tide of refugee admissions rose well above the quota apportioned to it by the 1965 immigration law, Congress moved to revise the entire program for admitting refugees. Lawmakers passed the 1980 Refugee Act, which broke new ground by creating a separate admissions system for refugees. Henceforward, refugee admissions did not compete for visas with the class of regular admissions.[21]

The strengthening of refugee policy demonstrated the continuing vitality of humanitarian idealism, but it was also an opportunity for the United States to cultivate political power on the world stage. Each year the president reviewed worldwide refugee problems and consulted with Congress on appropriate measures to resettle refugees in the United States. Like the general immigration policy of which it was a part, refugee policy was a device to manage diplomatic ties and promote goodwill toward the United States. In the Refugee Act of 1980, Congress defined a refugee as a person

Figure 2.1.   Number of Refugees from Different Regions, 1946–1990
From the end of the Second World War to 1990, 2.5 million refugees were admitted to the United States. In the 1940s and 1950s, the majority of refugees came from Europe; from the 1960s to the 1980s, the flow from Cuba and Southeast Asia grew fastest; recently the flow from the former Soviet bloc countries of Europe has raised the European total from low points in the 1960s and 1970s.

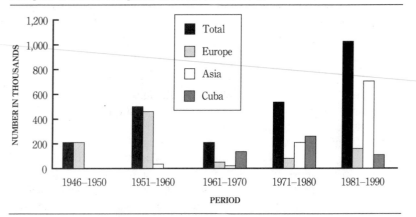

Source: Tabulated from the *1990 Statistical Yearbook of the Immigration and Naturalization Service* (Washington, D.C.: U.S. Government Printing Office, 1991), p. 109.

who is outside his or her country of nationality and is unable or unwilling to return because of persecution or a well-founded fear of persecution. Lawmakers conferred refugee status based on homeland conditions of political persecution. Critics of this admissions criterion argued that the federal government eagerly admitted persons such as Cubans or Vietnamese fleeing political persecution by states opposed to American interests—especially those with left-wing governments—but refused persons such as Salvadorans or Haitians fleeing from economic distress or undemocratic regimes supporting American interests. Despite acrimonious controversy over the partisan and diplomatic realpolitik of the cold war that underlay the framing of refugee policy, all lawmakers agreed that accepting refugees was a vital responsibility of the United States as a leader of democracy and a historic world sanctuary.[22]

The Human Element in Immigration

Because they were caught in the complications of international politics, refugees faced difficult legal procedures in their effort to resettle and reunite family members.

My father and I have been here for a long time now, eight, nine years. For five years we have had all the papers in order to have my mother and my brothers and my sisters come here. We have sent a letter to the United States ambassador to Thailand. We have written to the United States representative at the United Nations. We contacted our congressman and he wrote a letter. The congressman said, "Your family is qualified to come to the United States. They are at the top of the list." Still we wait and we wait and we wait. The Communist government doesn't want to give them visas.

—A Vietnamese refugee boy

Source: Janet Bode, *New Kids in Town: Oral Histories of Immigrant Teens* (New York: Scholastic, 1989), p. 121.

The Liberalization
of Naturalization Policy

World War II engendered new concerns over national security and international alliances that raised questions about naturalization policy. Congress passed the Nationality Act of 1940, which unified and tightened laws controlling naturalization. It reaffirmed the exclusion of Asians from naturalization but offered naturalized citizenship to American Indians native to foreign countries and to Eskimos.[23]

The quest for Allied unity during the war initiated a gradual reversal of restrictive naturalization policy. Congressional repeal of Chinese exclusion in 1943 permitted foreign-born Chinese to naturalize. In 1946, Congress gave rights of admission and naturalization to aliens from India who had been excluded since the Immigration Act of 1917 created the Asiatic Barred Zone. In the same year, Congress decided to allow Filipinos the right to naturalized citizenship.

The abolition of racial or marital qualifications for citizenship by the 1952 McCarran-Walter Act consummated the trend toward an egalitarian naturalization policy. The standard that henceforth would be utilized to afford the right to naturalize would not discriminate on the basis of race, nationality, or sex. The status of "aliens ineligible for citizenship" was banished from the statute books. Individual qualifications became the sole standard for achieving American citizenship.[24]

The 1952 McCarran-Walter Act installed a new requirement for naturalized citizenship. Afterwards, applicants not only had to be able to speak and understand English, but they had to be able to read and write "simple words and phrases." Despite this tightening of qualifications, the number of unsuccesful petitioners rejected in subsequent years was two-thirds lower than in the decade before the act.[25]

THE GLOBALIZATION OF IMMIGRATION

After World War II, immigration flowed increasingly from Latin America, Asia, and Africa to Western metropolitan centers. This "backward" flow from developing to developed nations reversed the nineteenth-century pattern of "forward" immigration that took white settlers from Western core areas to colonial dominions on the periphery. The worldwide immigration to the United States after 1965 continued this shift in the direction of international population movements.[26]

Push and Pull Factors in the Postindustrial Era

The push forces that had uprooted more than thirty-five million people from Europe in the century before World War II began to expand in the developing world of the twentieth century. A new population crisis beset societies in Latin America, Asia, and the Middle East, which experienced the same demographic transition Europe had undergone a century earlier. The introduction of modern sanitation and public health care in the third world turned the tide against the effects of contagious disease. In many of these areas, gradually rising standards of nutrition and living conditions improved the survival chances of children until adulthood. Population spiraled upward. The Caribbean and Mexico doubled in population from World War II to the 1970s. The countries of the Middle East, India, Pakistan, Bangladesh, and the Philippines also experienced comparable acceleration in population growth. Two factors combined to intensify the pressures of population on resources. First, arable land in these regions suffered from severe and long-standing overuse and overcrowding, thus sharply restricting the capacity of the agricultural economy to absorb the rising numbers. Second, the local metropolitan economies had barely developed new industries and new technologies that afforded jobs.[27]

Immigration from the third world was not a mechanical response to the push force of intensifying population pressure on resources. As in the European industrializing era, immigrants did not spring from the lowest economic class. For example, many immigrants from Mexico had better-than-average education and were established in the urban working class. These people, however, had been in a shifting and unpredictable situation. Furthermore, many immigrants were highly educated elites who made sophisticated judgments about opportunities offered by immigration, deciding to take advantage of the economic and social conditions in the United States. Their departure was characterized by economists as the "brain drain," the flight of valuable human capital to locations where their training and skills could be applied with greater rewards.[28]

Everywhere uncertainty over the future determined how people reacted to the push and pull forces. Often it was the prospect of economic decline—the perception of a future gap between possibility and capability—that precipitated a decision to move. Unstable governments, regional armed conflicts, and political transitions arising in the third world induced people to rebuild their lives elsewhere. In general, push forces acted to put people into a transitional and insecure status, thus making them more sensitive to pull forces, which appeared to be on the rise worldwide after World War II.[29]

The American economy after World War II exerted a powerful magnetic pull on people in transition in the third world. The economy received its greatest productive boost in history, particularly from the 1950s to the 1970s. American workers doubled their family incomes. The labor force multiplied in the white-collar, professional, and technical fields on one hand and in service industries on the other. During the 1980s, the economy was not growing as healthily, but the relative advantages of the American economy were still tangible and desirable.

The technological revolution in international transportation and communications quickened the movement of newcomers to the United States. Jet air travel made time-consuming ocean and land journeys unnecessary and obsolete. Travel from distant and even remote regions experiencing population crisis and economic stagnation was now easier and less expensive than ever. The international airports of Los Angeles, Miami, New York, San Francisco, and Chicago became the Ellis Islands of the jet age. Equally important in generating immigration was the creation of a global, high-technology communications system. Alluring television images of daily life in the United States were transmitted to the villages of places as distant as Pakistan and the Philippines. News about economic and political conditions in the United States was regularly communicated in much more systematic and accurate form than available in the nineteenth century. The spread of communications and transportation networks to immigration sources worldwide was associated with "globalization," the intensification of functional interconnections among societies across national boundaries.[30]

The immigrants arriving after the 1965 Hart-Celler Act were more likely than the New Immigrants of the early twentieth century to settle permanently. Their rates of transient and return migration remained far smaller than the rates in the early twentieth century (Figure 2.2). The movement of many post-1965 immigrants was opportunistic and rationally planned for the long-term project of rebuilding their lives into American lives.

NOTES

[1] Rosemarie Rogers, "Migration Theory and Practice," in Walker Connor, ed., *Mexican-Americans in Comparative Perspective* (Washington, D.C.: Urban Institute Press, 1985), pp. 171–73; Vernon M. Briggs, Jr., *Immigration Policy and the American Labor Force* (Baltimore: Johns Hopkins University Press, 1984), pp. 42–45.

[2] Fred W. Riggs, *Pressures on Congress: A Study of the Repeal of Chinese Exclusion* (New York: Columbia University Press, 1950), pp. 195–96; David M. Reimers, *Still the Golden Door: The Third World Comes to America* (New York: Columbia University Press, 1985), pp. 11–16; Edward P. Hutchinson, *Legislative History of American Immigration Policy, 1798–1965* (Philadelphia: University of Pennsylvania Press, 1981), pp. 264–65.

Figure 2.2. Annual Average Number of U.S. Immigrants Admitted and Departing, by Period, 1900–1979

In the early years of the twentieth century, many immigrants to the United States returned home after earning money to bring back to their families. After World War II, a greater proportion of immigrants remained permanently, but since the 1960s the rate of return migration has been rising again.

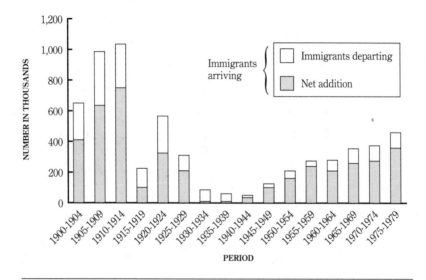

Source: Robert Warren and Ellen Percy Kraly, *The Elusive Exodus: Emigration from the United States* (Washington, D.C.: Population Reference Bureau, 1985), p. 4.

[3] Robert A. Divine, *American Immigration Policy, 1924–1952* (New Haven: Yale University Press, 1957), pp. 105–7, 162–63.

[4] Ibid., ch. 9; President Harry S. Truman, "Message on Veto of McCarran-Walter Bill," June 25, 1952, reproduced in Milton R. Konvitz, *Civil Rights in Immigration* (Ithaca: Cornell University Press, 1953), Appendix I, pp. 159–72.

[5] Divine, *American Immigration Policy,* pp. 190–91.

[6] Roger Daniels, *Coming to America: A History of Immigration and Ethnicity in American Life* (New York: HarperPerennial, 1991), pp. 328–29; Hutchinson, *Legislative History,* pp. 311–13.

[7] Daniels, *Coming to America,* p. 342; Hutchinson, *Legislative History,* pp. 308–10.

[8] Reimers, *Still the Golden Door,* pp. 63–66; Hutchinson, *Legislative History,* pp. 314–15, 344, 359, 363; President's Commission on Immigration and Naturalization, *Whom We Shall Welcome* (Washington, D.C.: U.S. Government Printing Office, 1953), p. 13.

[9] Nathan Glazer, ed., *Clamor at the Gates: The New American Immigration* (San Francisco: Institute for Contemporary Studies, 1985), pp. 6–8; Briggs, *Immigration Policy,* p. 68.

[10] David M. Reimers, "An Unintended Reform: The 1965 Immigration Act and Third World Immigration to the United States," *Journal of American Ethnic History* 3 (1983): 9–28; Glazer, *Clamor at the Gates,* pp. 7–8; Daniels, *Coming to America,* p. 341.

[11] Briggs, *Immigration Policy,* pp. 67–68.

[12] Hutchinson, *Legislative History,* pp. 366–79, 580–81.

[13] Briggs, *Immigration Policy*, p. 64; Guillermina Jasso and Mark R. Rosenzweig, *The New Chosen People: Immigrants in the United States* (New York: Russell Sage Foundation, 1990), pp. 38–40.

[14] Briggs, *Immigration Policy*, pp. 68, 128–31, 155–56; Glazer, *Clamor at the Gates*, p. 10; Douglas S. Massey, Rafael Alarcon, Jorge Durand, and Humberto Gonzalez, *Return to Aztlan: The Social Process of International Migration from Western Mexico* (Berkeley: University of California Press, 1987), pp. 285–97; *1984 Statistical Yearbook of the Immigration and Naturalization Service* (Washington, D.C.: U.S. Government Printing Office, 1985), Table ENF 1.1, p. 188.

[15] Lawrence H. Fuchs, "Immigration Reform in 1911 and 1981: The Role of Select Commissions," *Journal of American Ethnic History* 3 (1983): 58–89; Lawrence H. Fuchs, "The Search for a Sound Immigration Policy: A Personal View," in Glazer, *Clamor at the Gates;* Lawrence H. Fuchs, *The American Kaleidoscope: Race, Ethnicity, and the Civic Culture* (Hanover, N.H.: University Press of New England, 1990), pp. 249–50, 251–52; Briggs, *Immigration Policy*, pp. 88, 171; Aristide R. Zolberg, "Reforming the Back Door: The Immigration Reform and Control Act of 1986 in Historical Perspective," in Virginia Yans-McLaughlin, ed., *Immigration Reconsidered: History, Sociology, and Politics* (New York: Oxford University Press, 1990), pp. 322–23.

[16] Fuchs, *The American Kaleidoscope*, pp. 250–55.

[17] Ibid., p. 252.

[18] This account of the politics behind IRCA is indebted to a memo from Professor Lawrence H. Fuchs, Chair of the Select Commission on Immigration and Refugee Policy. Also see his "The Corpse That Would Not Die: The Immigration Reform and Control Act of 1986," *Revue Européenne de Migrations Internationales* 6 (1990): 111–27. For another view of the process, see Zolberg, "Reforming the Back Door," pp. 336–37. For immigration totals, see *1990 Statistical Yearbook of the Immigration and Naturalization Service* (Washington, D.C.: U.S. Government Printing Office, 1991), p. 11; and *1991 Statistical Yearbook*, p. 15.

[19] *1991 Statistical Yearbook*, pp. A.1-20 to A.1-21, and pp. A.2-2 to A.2-3. Also see Peter H. Schuck, "The Emerging Political Consensus on Immigration Law," *Georgetown Immigration Law Journal* 5 (1991): 1–33; Peter H. Schuck, "The Politics of Rapid Legal Change: Immigration Policy in the 1980s," *Studies in American Political Development* 6 (1992): 37–92.

[20] *1990 Statistical Yearbook*, p. 97.

[21] Briggs, *Immigration Policy*, pp. 72–73.

[22] Daniels, *Coming to America*, pp. 348–49; *1990 Statistical Yearbook*, p. 96; Reimers, *Still the Golden Door*, ch. 6.

[23] Paul S. Rundquist, "A Uniform Rule: The Congress and the Courts in American Naturalization, 1865–1952," Ph.D. thesis (University of Chicago, 1975), ch. 10.

[24] Hutchinson, *Legislative History*, pp. 308 (and n. 105), 312; Daniels, *Coming to America*, p. 329.

[25] Reed Ueda, "Naturalization and Citizenship," in Stephan Thernstrom, ed., *Harvard Encyclopedia of American Ethnic Groups* (Cambridge: Harvard University Press, 1980), p. 746.

[26] Elsa M. Chaney, "National Boundaries and Moral Boundaries: A Cosmopolitan View," in Peter G. Brown and Henry Shue, eds., *Boundaries: National Autonomy and Its Limits* (Totowa, N.J.: Rowman and Littlefield, 1981), pp. 44–45; Thomas Muller and Thomas J. Espenshade, *The Fourth Wave: California's Newest Immigrants* (Washington, D.C.: Urban Institute Press, 1985), pp. 25–28.

[27] Francisco Alba, "The Mexican Demographic Situation," and Sergio Diaz-Briquets, "The Central American Demographic Situation: Trends and Implications," in Frank D. Bean, Jurgen Schmandt, and Sidney Weintraub, eds., *Mexican and Central American Population and U.S. Immigration Policy* (Austin, Tex.: Center for Mexican American Studies, 1989); Thomas Kessner and Betty Boyd Caroli, eds., *Today's Immigrants: Their Stories* (New York: Oxford University Press, 1982), Introduction; Reimers, *Still the Golden Door*, pp. 126–28.

[28] Alejandro Portes and Ruben Rumbaut, *Immigrant America: A Portrait* (Berkeley: University of California Press, 1990), pp. 9–12; Alejandro Portes, "Illegal Immigration and the International System," *Social Problems* 26 (1979): 425–38; Alejandro Portes, "Determinants of the Brain Drain," *International Migration Review* 10 (Winter 1976): 489–508; Massey et al., *Return to Aztlan*, pp.

131–33; William A. Glaser and Christopher Habers, "The Migration and Return of Professionals," *International Migration Review* 8 (Summer 1974): Maxine Greer Seller, *To Seek America: A History of Ethnic Life in the United States,* rev. ed. (Englewood, N.J.: Jerome S. Ozer, 1989), pp. 294–96.

[29] Muller and Espenshade, *The Fourth Wave,* p. 17.

[30] Elliott R. Barkan, *Asian and Pacific Islander Migration to the United States: A Model of New Global Patterns* (Westport, Conn.: Greenwood Press, 1992), Pt. I.

3

The Changing Face of
Post-1965 Immigration

AN IMBALANCED WORLDWIDE IMMIGRATION

The liberalization of immigration policy following the 1965 Hart-Celler Act did not produce geographic balance in immigration sources; instead it reversed the former imbalance in which Europe predominated over other regions (Figure 3.1). In the 1960s the traditional dominance of immigration from Europe began to decline. By the 1980s only 11 percent of the total immigration came from Europe, as compared with 90 percent in 1900.

Latin Americans and Asians made up a large majority of immigrants arriving after 1970. The Mexican influx remained the largest factor in Latin American immigration, even without undocumented aliens (Table A.7, p. 163). But immigration grew faster from other Hispanic nations such as the Dominican Republic, El Salvador, Peru, and Ecuador. Immigration from Asia grew fastest of all. Immigration rose spectacularly from the Philippines, Korea, China, Vietnam, and India—the principal sources of Asian immigration after the Hart-Celler Act. By the early 1980s, nearly half of all immigrants came from Asian points of origin. The number of nations producing immigrants also grew, making the variety of arriving nationalities the largest in history.[1]

The reassignment of highest preference to family reunification after the 1965 Hart-Celler Act had important repercussions for the patterns of immigration. Because most immigrants would qualify for admission through family

Figure 3.1. Immigration to the United States by Worldwide Geography (Fiscal Year 1991) (right)
The dotted patterns indicate the spread of the sources of U. S. immigration to virtually all regions of the world in the 1990s. Moreover, they show that the distribution of immigration sources was worldwide but not balanced: areas in Latin America and Asia served as the greatest suppliers of immigrants, eclipsing countries in Europe and Africa.

Source: 1991 Statistical Yearbook of the Immigration and Naturalization Service (Washington, D.C.: U.S. Government Printing Office, 1992), p. 12.

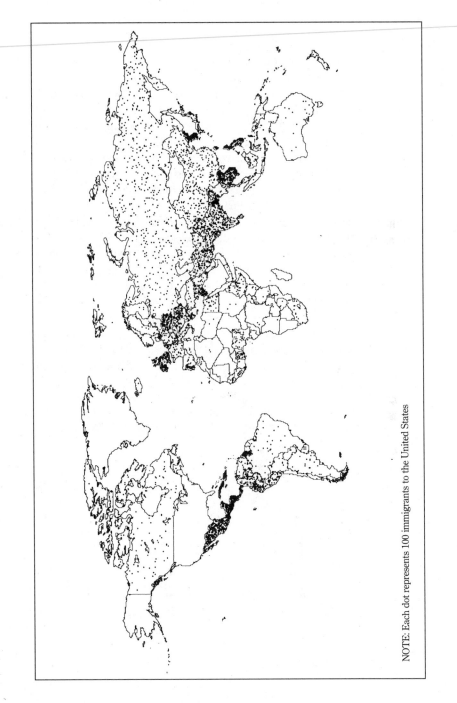

NOTE: Each dot represents 100 immigrants to the United States

relationship, the family preference had an unprecedented potential to multiply admissions from the major immigrant-sending countries. Thus it tended to heighten the numerical dominance of immigration from particular Latin American and Asian nations.[2]

Annual immigration rebounded after 1965 (Figure 3.2), rising gradually from an average of 450,000 immigrants in the 1970s to 730,000 in the 1980s. International diversity coupled with economic and demographic complexity in the wave of immigration from 1965 to the 1990s. Although annual immigration rose after 1970 to very high levels, it was far more heterogeneous and balanced in its demographic aspects than at the turn of the century. In part, this was because post-1965 immigration was a continuation of immigration patterns established from 1924 to 1965.

The increased proportions of white-collar personnel, females, and children that began after 1924 persisted after 1965. Because in the 1970s and 1980s employment opportunities for females improved, while heavy manual labor jobs historically attracting male immigrants dwindled, female immigrants continued to outnumber males. The unlimited class of visas for immediate relatives of citizens and preferences for immediate relatives of resident aliens paved the way for the admission of spouses, parents, and children to rise steadily (Figure 3.3). Indeed, experts on immigration demography found that marriage became the principal route to obtaining visas by the 1980s. Family migration and reunification contributed to continuing low levels of return

Figure 3.2. Immigrants Admitted, 1900–1990
Annual immigration formed peaks in the early and late twentieth century.

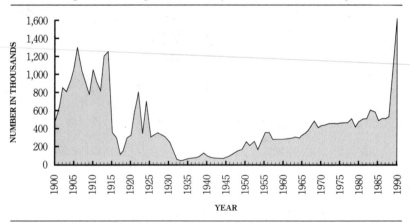

Source: 1990 Statistical Yearbook of the Immigration and Naturalization Service (Washington, D.C.: U.S. Government Printing Office, 1991), Chart C, p. 38.

The Human Element in Immigration

Overcrowding and underemployment motivated people to search for new opportunities in the United States. After 1965, women made up a growing number of immigrant "pioneers." They worked in the United States to help family members back home or to bring immediate relatives into the country.

I had a job in the post office in the town I was from and I wanted to leave Jamaica because my mother had nine of us at home, and it was a customary thing for the bigger ones to start working and help with the smaller kids. Coming here was being in a position to help my smaller brothers and sisters. Coming here was much more a challenge to me than going to England, although it's much easier going to England.

When I came here I heard about an employment agency in New York that were getting sponsors for foreigners. So I went to the agency and they got me a sponsor. It was a small family in Westchester County. It was a sleep-in job. You know, it's easier for a woman, because she gets a live-in job; she has a place to sleep and she gets food and it's easier.

—Imogene Hayes, immigrated from Jamaica, 1962[1]

If you come here alone first, it's more complicated. When I know the place and everything, I bring my brothers and my mother and my sister. She marry a good man, they got a big house. My brother's got a new car. I was the first one to do farm work in this country. Second, my sisters; next, my brother. Because if you here first you don't know nothing. When they come here, my husband have a good job and he help my brothers. It's more good to come like that than alone.

—Graciela Valencia, farmworker
from Mexico, 1976[2]

[1]*Source:* Joan Morrison and Charlotte Fox Zabusky, *American Mosaic: The Immigrant Experience in the Words of Those Who Lived It* (New York: New American Library, 1980), p. 399.

[2]*Source:* June Namias, *First Generation: In the Words of Twentieth-Century American Immigrants* (Boston: Beacon Press, 1978), p. 179.

Figure 3.3.   Immigrants Admitted as Immediate Relatives of U.S. Citizens, 1970–1990

With the 1965 Hart-Celler Act, which expanded opportunities for family reunification, admissions of immediate relatives rose steadily.

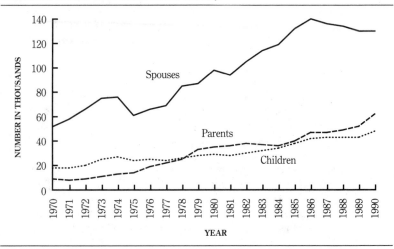

YEAR

Source: 1990 Statistical Yearbook of the Immigration and Naturalization Service (Washington, D.C.: U.S. Government Printing Office, 1991), Chart D, p. 43.

migration. Low levels of return combined with high levels of immigration in the 1980s to make net immigration in that decade the highest in history.[3]

The global immigrants of the 1970s and 1980s could be divided into two economic classes, whereas the immigrants before the Great Depression were almost uniformly working class. The post-1965 influx possessed the largest contingents of human capital—highly educated and trained workers—in history, reflecting the development of admission preferences that favored newcomers in fields requiring a high level of training. In the 1970s, 25 percent of immigrants were professionals and more than 40 percent were white-collar workers (Table A.3, p. 158). These rates of human capital migration continued into the early 1980s. From 1976 to 1990, more than 35 percent of employed immigrants were in professional and other white-collar jobs, and 12 percent were in skilled crafts (Figure 3.4). Many who worked in these areas brought capital, entrepreneurial skills, and ethnic and familial networks to support new business ventures.[4]

The human capital migration was counterbalanced by a large contingent of low-skilled workers. Service workers, laborers, and semiskilled operatives composed about 46 percent of employed immigrants arriving from 1976 to 1990 (Figure 3.4). Poor and transient illegals, estimated at somewhere between

Figure 3.4. Immigrants Admitted to the United States by Occupational Group, 1976–1990

While the immigrants before the Great Depression were almost uniformly working class, a large fraction of recent immigrants have been professional and white-collar workers.

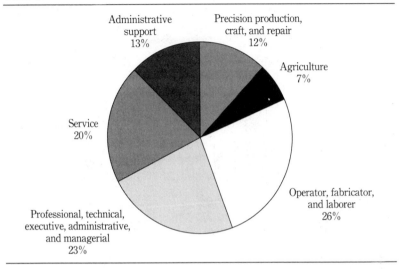

Source: 1990 Statistical Yearbook of the Immigration and Naturalization Service (Washington, D.C.: U.S. Government Printing Office, 1991), p. 32.

three and six million in the early 1980s, sought low-paid, labor-intensive jobs. The flow of the low-skilled and undereducated rose in numbers and in percentage of arrivals in the 1980s and 1990s. Hispanic, Asian, and West Indian workers moved into the service and semiskilled job markets in big cities like Los Angeles and New York City, causing increasing friction and conflict with native black workers.[5]

In the 1980s, the social class division in immigration corresponded to two different sets of nationality groups. The first consisted of groups possessing large numbers and shares of white-collar and highly educated workers. It included nationalities from India, the Philippines, Korea, Taiwan, and China, as well as from Great Britain and Canada (Figure 3.5). These groups often exhibited close to even sex ratios and had a median age near thirty (Tables A.8 and A.9, pp. 164, 165). The second group of nationalities had large totals and proportions of less-skilled and less-educated operatives, laborers, and service employees (Tables A.9 and A.10, pp. 165, 166). Some had a higher percentage of male immigrants or a lower median age than the first group. These were from Mexico, Central America, Southeast Asia, and the Caribbean:

Figure 3.5.   Immigrant Nationalities with the Largest Number of Professionals and Managers, 1987

In the 1980s, immigrants from Asian countries, Great Britain, and North America contributed large numbers of white-collar workers. This was partly due to admissions policies that favored highly trained immigrants.

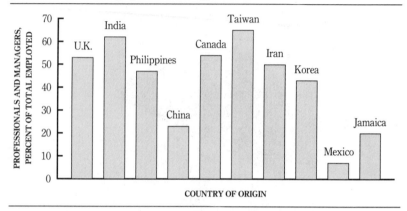

Source: Computed from *1987 Statistical Yearbook of the Immigration and Naturalization Service* (Washington, D.C.: U.S. Government Printing Office, 1988), Table 20, pp. 40–41.

Specifically, Haiti, the Dominican Republic, Cuba, the West Indies, and Puerto Rico.[6]

Mexican immigration in many ways was the bellwether of changes in immigration patterns after 1965, becoming the preeminent example of the rising influx of poor migrants from the third world. More immigrants came from Mexico than from any other country. The share of low-skilled workers was higher from Mexico than from the large majority of countries in the world. More than 70 percent of employed Mexican immigrants in the 1970s and 1980s were laborers, farmers, and service workers (Table A.10, p. 166). Finally, Mexicans constituted the largest share of illegal immigrants in the United States—as much as 60 percent in one estimate.[7]

The New Asian Immigrants

After World War II, the door to Asian immigration began to reopen slightly. The repeal of Chinese and Asian Indian exclusion had been the first wedge in the door, and the passage of the McCarran-Walter Act in 1952 opened it still wider by providing token quotas to all Asian nations, as did the enactment of displaced persons and "war brides" policies.[8]

Asian mass immigration returned fully with the liberalization of the quota system under the Hart-Celler Act of 1965. Old Asian communities were transformed, and a multitude of new Asian ethnic colonies sprouted in the backwash of an immense wave of Asian arrivals. The Asian America that had long been constituted chiefly by Chinese and Japanese communities derived from the turn of the century was infused with new diversity by groups from East and South Asia. The variety of national and ethnic Asian subpopulations rose to rival that found historically among immigrants from Europe. By the 1970s, Asians constituted the largest share of newcomers admitted yearly from a continental region: one and one-half million immigrants from Asia arrived in that decade, compared with 840,000 from Europe. After 1965, the fastest-growing ethnic groups were Asians who had virtually no significant previous representation in the American population. Immigrants arrived from South Korea, Cambodia, Vietnam, Laos, Thailand, Indonesia, Burma, Sri Lanka, Singapore, Malaysia, Pakistan, India, and Bangladesh, while others came from areas where immigrant Asian communities had been established earlier in the century, such as the West Indies and Latin America.[9]

The social complexity of Asian mass immigration after 1965 contrasted sharply with the laborer influx of the late nineteenth and early twentieth centuries. A human capital migration of professionals and highly educated technical workers from homeland elites grew into a large influx (Figures 3.5 and 3.6). Arrivals from the Philippines and India included an unusual number of health care professionals. In the late 1980s, immigrants from India, the Philippines, China, and Korea ranked in the ten nationalities with the largest representation of professional and managerial workers (Figure 3.5). In 1975, three-quarters of employed Indian immigrants were professional, technical, or managerial workers. Highly trained elites often came through a two-stage process in which they first entered the United States on temporary visas as students in American universities and later applied successfully for permanent residency.[10]

Large waves of low-skilled and impoverished immigrants also arrived from Asia, consisting of two distinct groups. The first were immigrants who moved to big cities such as New York, Boston, Chicago, and Los Angeles to take jobs in service industries and light manufacturing. The Chinatowns of the United States, particularly the burgeoning Chinese community of New York City, received a huge influx of newcomers from Hong Kong seeking jobs in the sweatshop garment industries, restaurants, and hotels. The second group of poor newcomers from Asia were the one million refugees who fled from war, persecution, and political upheaval in the troubled homelands of Northeast and Southeast Asia from the end of World War II to 1990. The Chinese became the first Asian refugee population in the aftermath of World War II. The ending of the Vietnam War brought new refugee populations from Cambodia,

Figure 3.6.   Immigrant Nationalities with the Highest Percentages of College Graduates, 1980

Many of the immigrant nationalities with the most professionals in the 1980s also included the most college-educated immigrants.

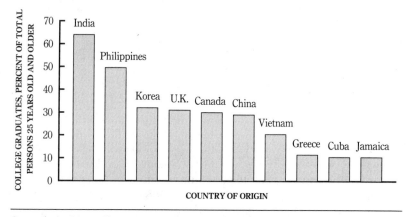

Source: Derived from U.S. Bureau of the Census, *1980 Census: Detailed Population Characteristics,* PL80-1-D1-A (Washington, D.C.: U.S. Department of Commerce, 1984), Table 255.

Laos, and Vietnam, including minority subgroups such as the ethnic Chinese from Vietnam and the ethnic Hmong from Laos. The tide of Asian refugees mounted higher from the 1970s to the 1980s; the pace of refugee arrivals stepped up from 20,000 admissions a year in the 1970s to nearly 100,000 admissions annually in the early 1980s. By 1990, 800,000 refugees from Indochina, constituting half of all refugees from that region, were resettled in the United States.[11]

The refugees suffered a traumatic uprooting and were equipped with the fewest resources to make the difficult transition to American life. Some groups had more advantages than others in the struggle to rebuild their lives. Many refugees from Vietnam came from urban centers where educational opportunities and better jobs had been available. They had historic ties with French and American culture and familiarity with English that in some cases aided adjustment. In comparison, the refugees from Cambodia and Laos were poorly suited to the conditions of American life and were by far the most disadvantaged of the new Asian refugees. With very little education and job skills, they encountered the most difficult entrance to American society, and by necessity they made their adjustment through the welfare system.[12]

The discipline of migrating in family units determined the movement of human capital elites, poor laborers, and refugees alike in the Asian immigration after 1965. In sharp distinction with transient Asian labor migrants early in the twentieth century, post-1965 Asian immigrants by and large were determined to settle permanently in the United States. Thus the transference of families* was a critical necessity, and many Asians immigrated in whole families and used the family preference. Other Asians capitalized heavily on the right of naturalized citizens to bring family members to the United States as "immediate relatives" above annual visa limitations. Asian immigrants were quick to take out citizenship papers and composed a disproportionate share of the newly naturalized in the 1970s and 1980s. They began a spiral of chain migration: the numerous spouses, children, and parents who entered in the unlimited class of "immediate relative" in turn sponsored their "immediate relatives," and so on. Consequently, annual admissions from each Asian country greatly exceeded the visa allotment of 20,000. These factors caused total immigration from Asia to skyrocket.[13]

Female immigrants from Asia achieved increasing representation as a result of policies that promoted family reunification. Wives planned their moves with the intention of obtaining gainful employment because of the new job opportunities of the 1970s and 1980s for female workers in light manufacturing, personal service, and industrial service in hotels, restaurants, and hospitals. After 1965, the numbers of female immigrants admitted annually from Asia equaled the numbers of male immigrants, altering the historic overrepresentation of males in Asian immigration.

The Asian ethnic populations of the United States grew rapidly from the swelling tide of immigration. The growth rate of the Chinese population, measured by decade, increased from the 1950s to the 1970s from 58 percent to 85 percent and for the Filipino population from 44 percent to 126 percent. Certain Asian populations increased with exceptional speed from the arrival of immigrants. The number of foreign-born in the Filipino population grew 171 percent from 1970 to 1980, in the Korean population 649 percent. In the 1980s, the Koreans, Indians, and Vietnamese surpassed other Asian nationalities in the rate of population growth (Figure 3.7). Despite the fact that Asian ethnic groups grew faster than all others, they still constituted less than 3 percent of the U.S. population in 1990 because of their small representation in the population before 1965.[14]

Population growth became a revolutionary force that started a new generational cycle in Asian ethnic communities. The small historic enclaves of Chinese, Koreans, and Filipinos evolved from earlier migrations were galvanized into new life by the injection of newcomers with families. Along with the families in the new communities from southern Asia, they formed the beginnings of a new progression of generations among Asian Americans.

Figure 3.7. Population Growth of Asian and Hispanic Ethnic Groups, 1980–1990

After passage of the Hart-Celler Act in 1965, Asian and Hispanic immigrants became the fastest-growing ethnic groups.

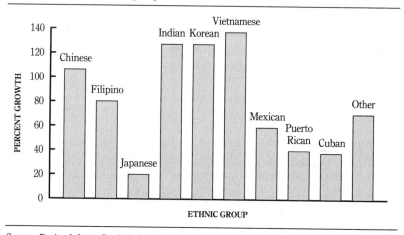

Source: Derived from *Statistical Abstract of the United States, 1992* (Washington, D.C.: U.S. Government Printing Office, 1992), Table 16, p. 17.

The New Latin American Immigrants

Central America and South America contributed a rapidly increasing portion of immigrants who arrived after 1965. Although labeled by nationality—as Hondurans or Colombians, for example—these groups were not homogeneous and included important subelements because they came from Latin American nations that were multiethnic in character. Italians, Spaniards, Germans, Chinese, Japanese, and Jewish immigrants came from various countries in Central and South America. *Mestizo* Hondurans, black Panamanians, and mulatto Colombians (*costeños*) arrived in rising numbers. A particularly large share of Panamanians and Hondurans were nonwhite: 28 percent of all foreign-born Hondurans and 59 percent of foreign-born Panamanians, according to the 1970 federal census.[15]

Notwithstanding the ethnic and racial diversity of immigrants from Latin America, the overwhelming majority of these immigrants reported themselves as white in the federal census. In 1970, more than 90 percent of all foreign stock from Costa Rica, Guatemala, El Salvador, and Nicaragua were white. But since all Central American nations, with the possible exception of Costa Rica, possessed a majority or a large proportion of *mestizos,* many who identified themselves as whites on the 1970 census probably were *mestizos.*

From the 1950s to the 1970s, an average of a few thousand immigrants each year arrived from Costa Rica, El Salvador, Guatemala, Honduras, Nicaragua, and Panama. In 1970, the Panamanians, numbering 48,000, and the Hondurans, numbering 31,000, constituted the largest Central American groups in the United States. By the 1980s, however, the populations from El Salvador and Guatemala grew faster as a result of an exodus from war and civil strife (Table A.7, p. 163).[16]

Many of the immigrants from Central America were women in service or low white-collar jobs who came on their own to earn income that they periodically sent back in remittances to their families. They responded to the growing demand for workers who could provide household help, child care, elder care, and maintenance service in office buildings, hotels, and hospitals. The percentage of employed newcomers who were domestic servants remained high, ranging between 15 and 28 percent annually from each country. The number of immigrant males per hundred females was quite low in the late 1960s, falling to sixty for Nicaragua and fifty-one for Panama.[17]

The social and demographic features of immigration from South America differed in important respects from those of the wave from Central America. Immigration from South America was larger, and it began to rise earlier, in the 1950s. The population of South Americans in the United States in 1970 was 389,000, well over twice as many as the total of Central Americans. During the 1970s and 1980s again, immigration from South America was nearly twice as large as immigration from Central America.

The various migrant streams from Central and South America were differentiated by key social and demographic characteristics from the 1960s to the mid-1970s. The sex ratios among migrants from many South American countries were significantly more balanced than those for Central American countries. An average of eighty to more than one hundred males per one hundred females came from Argentina, Ecuador, Colombia, Peru, and Venezuela at various intervals from the 1950s to the 1960s. In the 1970s, the ratio remained almost even for immigrants from most South American countries.

Differences in age patterns could be found between the waves from Central America and South America. Male immigrants from Central America were younger on the average than those from South America. Also, the age distribution among South Americans tended to remain the same from the 1960s to the 1970s, while among Central Americans it shifted more toward the young.

Immigrants from South America contrasted with those from Central America in occupational distribution, especially in the areas of professional work and domestic service. The percentages of professionals from South American nations in most cases were twice as great or more as among arrivals from Central American countries. Professionals constituted over 30 percent of the immigrants from South American nations such as Bolivia, Chile, and Venezuela; entrepreneurs and managers made up a comparatively small portion of the "brain drain" from South America. Also, every South American country sent an appreciably smaller percentage of domestic workers than did the Central American countries. For example, from 1968 to 1975, 27 percent of immigrants from Honduras and 22 percent from El Salvador were domestic workers, but only 4 percent and 5 percent were domestic workers from Argentina and Venezuela, respectively.[18]

South American migrations displayed unusual and individual features according to country of origin. The volume of immigration from South America varied enormously from country to country, with Colombia, Ecuador, and Argentina sending by far the greatest numbers of immigrants in the 1960s and 1970s. Brazil was several times more populous than these nations, yet it sent fewer immigrants to the United States. By the 1980s, however, immigration from Brazil was rising. Venezuelan immigrants were much younger than those from any other South American country, probably because they included large numbers of wives and children. An unusually high proportion—over one-third—of Bolivians were professionals. Bolivia and Venezuela sent the largest percentages of clerical workers from South American countries. Argentina, Colombia, Ecuador, and Uruguay sent the highest percentages of skilled and semiskilled workers.[19]

The effects of human capital migration were somewhat beneficial to some Latin American nations. Many of the immigrants returned to their home countries, bringing ideas and techniques acquired while working in the United States. Thus, Colombian medical facilities and services were upgraded by the return of physicians and technicians who had acquired knowledge and training abroad.

Despite significant variations among the immigrant nationalities from Central and South America, they exhibited common social patterns and characteristics. First, because they possessed the education, occupational orientations, and lifestyles suited to urban society, they flocked to the metropolitan regions of the Northeast, Pacific Coast, and Gulf Coast states. Very few rural laborers and farmers migrated, although the economies of most Central and South American countries were greatly dependent on agricultural production. Thus the immigrants represented a mobile, urban-oriented part of their homeland societies. Second, New York City assumed a unique role in attracting nonwhite immigrants from both Central and South America. Third, a trend developed beginning in the 1970s toward migration of the less-educated and poorer elements, as the proportion of blue-collar workers among immigrants from Central and South America rose (Table A.11, p. 166). The share of domestic and service workers, especially from Central America, increased, while the proportion of white-collar workers from a number of Central and South American nations declined. In the 1980s, low-skilled immigrants were a half or more of arrivals and continued to include many women and young adults. Undocumented immigration from Central and South America, especially from El Salvador and Nicaragua, was substantial, according to impressionistic accounts and journalistic reports. The flow of low-skilled and undocumented immigrants intensified in the 1980s as people fled to the United States from turmoil and revolution in this region.

Two important new Hispanic groups arrived from Caribbean islands a generation apart in time. The Cuban immigrants who fled from Castro's Communist regime beginning in 1959 constituted the first large wave of refugees from Latin America. Many migrated in well-established families and thus displayed a broad range of age levels and a balanced sex ratio; they also were drawn from the professional and business classes. After 1965, however, the composition of Cuban immigrants changed as more laborers and young couples began to arrive. By the 1980s, Cubans were the single largest nationality of refugees in American history, with about 500,000 arrivals, as compared with 470,000 arrivals from the nation of Vietnam. In the 1980s, immigrants from the Dominican Republic began to arrive in rapidly rising numbers. They challenged the Puerto Ricans as the largest Hispanic group in New York City by the 1990s. Many Dominicans originated from rural communities as the Puerto Ricans did, but they tended to come from moderately well-off farming families. The majority, however, were workers and middle-class migrants from cities, many of whom obtained employment in the service and mass-production industries of the urban Northeast. Many young male immigrants came to establish an economic foothold without wives, but eventually they married other female immigrants, who by the 1980s increased in numbers as a result of the flow toward jobs in personal and industrial service.[20]

The West Indian and Haitian Immigrants

With the growth of employment opportunities during and after World War II, black immigrants once more moved from the British West Indies to the United States. Twenty thousand immigrants arrived from Jamaica between 1948 and

1954. Many worked as contract laborers in Florida agriculture. This flow was halted by provisions of the McCarran-Walter Act that reduced the quotas for British territories in the Caribbean. From 1954 to 1965, British West Indian immigrants moved chiefly to the United Kingdom, where they found entry easier.[21]

Political changes in the Caribbean, the United Kingdom, and the United States, however, stimulated a new rise in immigration from the British West Indies and Haiti. Beginning in the 1960s, many West Indian islands moved toward independence from Britain, thus also gaining an independent standing with respect to the immigration policies of the United States. In Haiti, the abuses of the dictatorial François Duvalier regime precipitated an exodus to the United States. At roughly the same time, in 1962, the United Kingdom enacted new policies to curb the influx of West Indian immigrants. In 1965, the Hart-Celler Act abolished colonial quotas and created equal access for the micro-nations of the West Indies. These developments in combination established the political and legal conditions for the upsurge of black West Indian immigration to the United States. In the decade after the passage of the Hart-Celler Act, more immigrants from the British West Indies and Haiti arrived than in the previous seventy years. The newly independent countries of Jamaica, Trinidad and Tobago, Guyana, the Bahamas, and Barbados supplied the bulk of the West Indian newcomers to the United States.[22]

Like Latin America, the West Indies and Haiti had rapid population growth in impoverished rural regions after World War II. The underemployed in the labor force, like the migrants from Puerto Rico, secured cheap and fast access to the United States by jet airways linking the West Indies with American international airports in cities such as Miami, New York, and Boston.

The rate of immigration accelerated. The number of Jamaican immigrants arriving yearly grew more than ten times from 1962 to 1970, when a total of 150,000 immigrants from the British West Indies arrived. An average of 20,000 West Indians entered the United States each year from the 1960s to the 1970s, while thousands more came as illegal immigrants. In the 1960s and 1970s, more females than males immigrated. Females were especially likely to migrate from Jamaica, where twice as many females as males left in the 1960s. Many were young adults who came to the United States for service and manufacturing work.[23]

While the majority of West Indian immigrants in the 1960s were young, unmarried adults, the share of children and adolescents rose sharply in the 1970s and more immigrants arrived as family dependents. Fifty percent of all immigrants arriving from Jamaica were under the age of twenty; in the 1980s, the average age of Jamaicans remained among the lowest of all immigrant groups. These trends along with growing sex-ratio balance showed that immigration from Jamaica included many people who were arriving in families or were joining family members already established in the United States.

As in the immigration from Latin America, the occupational concentrations of immigrants from black Caribbean nations shifted from those employed in white-collar and skilled jobs toward those in low-skilled occupations. During the early 1960s, half of the employed immigrants arriving each year from Jamaica, Barbados, Trinidad and Tobago, and the other British West Indies were professional, white-collar, and skilled workers. In the same period, wealthy and middle-class Haitians dominated in the movement to the United States. Unskilled workers constituted only one out of five immigrants from Jamaica and less than one out of three immigrants from the other islands. Beginning in the late 1960s, however, white-collar and skilled workers from the West Indies declined relative to the influx of low-skilled and poorly educated workers. In the 1980s and recurring intermittently into the 1990s, rural laborers poured out of Haiti. Because they could not afford the cost of transportation to the United States, they tried to enter illegally by taking small boats on a dangerous ocean voyage to Florida. Poor female labor migrants made up a rising share of the influx from the British West Indies and Haiti.[24]

The Declining Factor
of European Immigration

Once an overwhelmingly dominant demographic force, European immigration dwindled rapidly after 1965 (Figure 3.8). Whereas in the late 1950s and early 1960s Europeans composed half of all immigrants admitted, they amounted to less than 10 percent of immigrants in the late 1980s. The average number of annual arrivals from Europe declined from 80,000 in the 1970s to 70,000 in the 1980s. Immigrants from northern and western Europe, who once formed a huge majority of immigrants, accounted for only 3 percent of arrivals in 1990. The European countries sending the largest numbers of immigrants from the 1970s to the 1980s were the United Kingdom, Italy, Germany, and Portugal. With political collapse, war, and ethnic conflict in eastern Europe, a new wave from the former Soviet Union and eastern bloc countries arrived in mounting numbers in the 1990s. European immigrants were no longer a significant labor factor, as more than half of employed European newcomers were professional and white-collar employees. A small number of European immigrants were undocumented and employed in industrial or personal service occupations.[25]

Figure 3.8.   Immigrants Admitted by Region of Birth, Selected Years, 1955–1990

While Europeans represented the bulk of immigrants until about 1960, more permissive admissions policies and economic forces in the developing world led to increased admissions from Asia and Latin America after 1965.

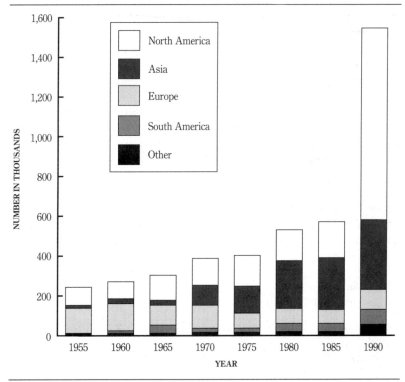

Source: *1990 Statistical Yearbook of the Immigration and Naturalization Service* (Washington, D.C.: U.S. Government Printing Office, 1991), p. 36.

SEEDING THE NEW FRONTIER
OF IMMIGRANT COLONIES

In the first half of the twentieth century, immigrants settled in distinctive regional constellations. Immigrants from Europe predominated in the urban Northeast and the Great Lakes region; immigrants from East Asia flocked to Hawaii and the Pacific Coast; Mexican immigrants settled heavily in the Southwest. Since the Great Depression, these regional concentrations began to spread out gradually as newcomers edged beyond the initial perimeter of settlement.[26]

Before 1920, Mexican migrants usually located in towns and farm districts near the Mexican border, specifically in the agricultural areas of southern California and the lower Rio Grande River of Texas. In the 1920s, however, the scope of movement widened as Mexicans traveled as far north as Chicago, Detroit, Cleveland, and Milwaukee to take factory jobs. Although Mexican colonies continued after World War II to flourish in the urban centers of the Midwest, the Mexican population still chiefly concentrated in the South and West, where about 90 percent of the Mexican American population lived. In 1970, one of every six persons in Arizona, California, Colorado, New Mexico, and Texas was of Mexican origin. In 1970, about 50 percent of all Mexicans in the Southwest lived in California, and 36 percent lived in Texas. Outside of Mexico City and Guadalajara, Los Angeles was the largest Mexican city in the world in 1970, home to more than one million Mexican Americans.[27]

Since World War II, urbanization has been the key to the forming of Mexican communities. In 1940 Mexicans were the most rural of the major ethnic groups in the United States, but by 1970 they were among the most urbanized. Sixty-six percent of all Mexican Americans lived in urban areas in 1950, while 85 percent did so in 1970.

The Puerto Ricans initially settled within a much smaller geographic space than the Mexicans, collecting mainly around the New York City metropolitan area. In fact, the regional concentration of Puerto Ricans was much higher than that of Mexicans. Although the Puerto Rican population fanned out to other cities in New Jersey and New England, 70 percent of all first- and second-generation Puerto Ricans lived in New York City in 1960. In 1970, most of the 820,000 Puerto Ricans on the mainland still resided in New York City,

Figure 3.9.   Immigrants Admitted by State of Intended Residence, 1986 (per 100,000 Population) (page 76)
The newest immigrants spread over all regions. Nevertheless, they concentrated most heavily in the states of the Northeast and the West. Illinois, Texas, and Florida also had substantial settlements.

Source: 1986 Statistical Yearbook of the Immigration and Naturalization Service (Washington, D.C.: U.S. Government Printing Office, 1987), p. x.

Figure 3.10.   Immigration to the United States by Consolidated Metropolitan Area of Residence, 1989 (page 77)
In recent years, large numbers of immigrants from Asia, Latin America, the Caribbean, and the Middle East have settled in cities across the United States. About 53 percent of all immigration to the United States in 1989 concentrated in the eight metropolitan areas in the figure.

Source: Derived from *1989 Statistical Yearbook of the Immigration and Naturalization Service* (Washington, D.C.: U.S. Government Printing Office, 1990), Table 18, pp. 36–38.

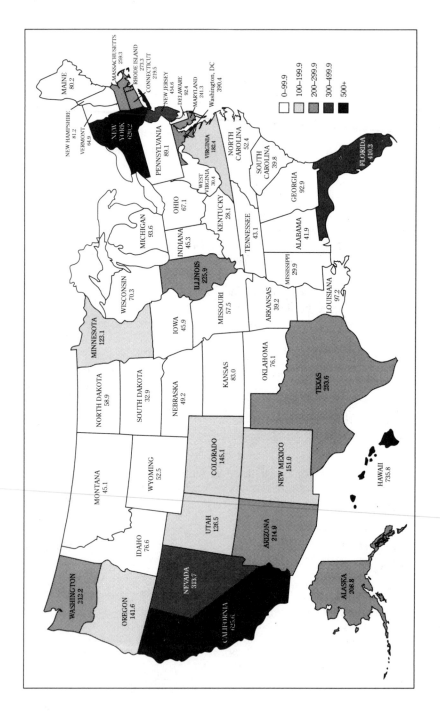

Legend:
- 0–99.9
- 100–199.9
- 200–299.9
- 300–499.9
- 500+

MAINE 80.2
NEW HAMPSHIRE 81.2
VERMONT 64.9
MASSACHUSETTS 259.3
RHODE ISLAND 273.3
CONNECTICUT 219.5
NEW JERSEY 454.6
DELAWARE 92.4
MARYLAND 241.3
Washington, DC 390.4
NEW YORK 620.2
PENNSYLVANIA 89.1
VIRGINIA 182.4
WEST VIRGINIA 30.4
NORTH CAROLINA 52.4
SOUTH CAROLINA 39.8
GEORGIA 92.9
FLORIDA 410.3
OHIO 67.1
KENTUCKY 28.1
TENNESSEE 43.1
ALABAMA 41.9
MICHIGAN 93.6
INDIANA 45.3
ILLINOIS 225.9
MISSISSIPPI 29.9
LOUISIANA 97.2
WISCONSIN 70.3
IOWA 45.9
MISSOURI 57.5
ARKANSAS 39.2
MINNESOTA 123.1
OKLAHOMA 76.1
TEXAS 253.6
NORTH DAKOTA 58.9
SOUTH DAKOTA 32.9
NEBRASKA 49.2
KANSAS 83.0
COLORADO 145.1
NEW MEXICO 151.0
HAWAII 735.8
MONTANA 45.1
WYOMING 52.5
UTAH 126.5
ARIZONA 214.9
ALASKA 208.8
IDAHO 76.6
NEVADA 313.7
CALIFORNIA 625.6
WASHINGTON 212.2
OREGON 141.6

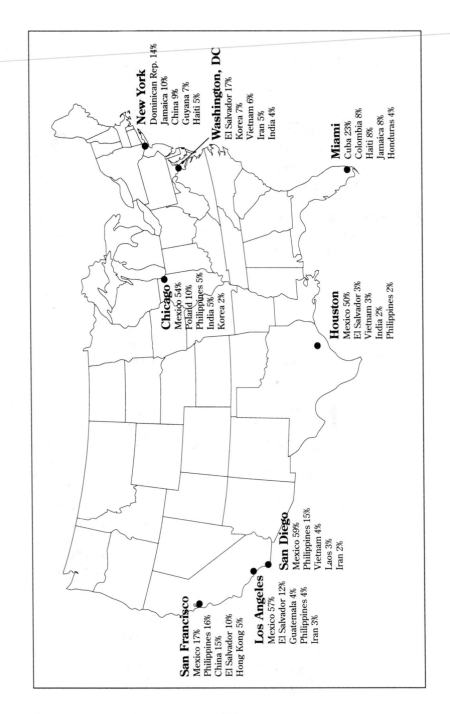

New York
Dominican Rep. 14%
Jamaica 10%
China 9%
Guyana 7%
Haiti 5%

Washington, DC
El Salvador 17%
Korea 7%
Vietnam 6%
Iran 5%
India 4%

Miami
Cuba 23%
Colombia 8%
Haiti 8%
Jamaica 8%
Honduras 4%

Chicago
Mexico 54%
Poland 10%
Philippines 5%
India 5%
Korea 2%

Houston
Mexico 50%
El Salvador 3%
Vietnam 3%
India 2%
Philippines 2%

San Diego
Mexico 59%
Philippines 15%
Vietnam 4%
Laos 3%
Iran 2%

Los Angeles
Mexico 57%
El Salvador 12%
Guatemala 4%
Philippines 4%
Iran 3%

San Francisco
Mexico 17%
Philippines 16%
China 15%
El Salvador 10%
Hong Kong 5%

which housed the most sizable and important of all Puerto Rican communities on the mainland. The first neighborhoods grew up after World War I around the Brooklyn Navy Yard and East Harlem, which turned into the hub of the Puerto Rican community. After World War II, Puerto Ricans moved from there into the South Bronx, the Lower East Side and the Upper West Side of Manhattan, and the Williamsburg section of Brooklyn. Despite the historic geographic focus of Puerto Ricans in the Northeast, they settled increasingly in the 1970s in the north central, southern, and western regions of the country.[28]

The historic geographic clusters created by immigrant groups of the early twentieth century endured into the late twentieth century, but with the advent of the mass immigration after 1965 the old ethnic configuration was overlaid by colonies of immigrants from Asia, Latin America, the Caribbean, and the Middle East that spread over the entire nation, particularly into regions where few of these nationalities had lived before (Figure 3.9). Multicultural geography was being nationalized.

The residential distribution of the newest immigrants was highly selective. Overwhelmingly, they gravitated to several gateway metropolitan areas: New York City, Los Angeles, San Francisco, Chicago, Miami, Houston, San Diego, and Washington, D.C. These major entry points also appealed as places of settlement because they possessed host colonies and the fastest expanding areas of the economy and residential construction (Figure 3.10).[29]

The complex array of Central American nationalities displayed a more variegated pattern of settlement than either the Mexican or Puerto Rican population. By the 1970s, these newcomers had settled in urban areas of the New England, Middle Atlantic, Great Lakes, Gulf Coast, and Pacific Coast states. The largest populations of Central Americans clustered in New York City, Los Angeles, San Francisco, Miami, and Chicago. Central American groups displayed varying rates of concentration in these areas and cities. Costa Ricans, El Salvadorans, and Nicaraguans were most numerous in the West in 1970. Within California, El Salvadorans and Nicaraguans flocked to San Francisco, while Guatemalans favored Los Angeles. By contrast, Hondurans flocked to the urban centers on the Gulf Coast and in the Northeast, where Panamanians also tended to congregate. New York City possessed the largest population of Hondurans and Panamanians. *Mestizo,* black, and Indian Central Americans of all nationalities were more numerous in New York City than in any other U.S. city.[30]

The Cubans and Dominicans, two of the largest groups of new Hispanic immigrants, diverged with respect to geographic settlement. Cubans preferred to locate in areas close to their homeland, especially in Florida, where Miami became a focal point of Cuban arrival and permanent settlement. Dominicans flocked to New York City, but in the 1970s and 1980s they spread northward to New England and southward to Washington, D.C. A substantial migration also flowed to Florida. By the 1990s they vied with the Puerto Ricans for numerical dominance of Hispanic districts in New York City.[31]

The colonies of West Indians, like those of Puerto Ricans, were located initially in New York City. Earlier in the century, New York State alone contained almost two-thirds of the Jamaican blacks in the United States; most resided in the Harlem section of New York City. But even then, West Indians were numerous in Massachusetts and Florida. After World War II, West Indian immigrants surged into the Midwest and the West Coast, settling in Michigan, Illinois, and California.[32]

Asian immigrants showed a new willingness to move outside of Hawaii and the West Coast, their historic zone of settlement from the late nineteenth century to World War II. Newcomers from China, Hong Kong, Taiwan, South Korea, and Vietnam migrated to the East Coast, the Midwest, and the South, settling in Washington, D.C., New Jersey, Massachusetts, Illinois, and Texas. The state of Virginia, which once had virtually no Asians, served as a significant indicator of this trend. Economist Thomas Muller noted that Virginia in the 1990s "rank[ed] eighth in the admission of immigrants" and was "a major center for Asian enterprises." Most Asians formed rapidly growing communities in metropolitan centers, but many Cambodian and Laotian immigrants could be found in rural areas and small cities. The geographic distribution of Asian ethnic groups shifted away from the Far West as a result of the creation of new enclaves. The percentage of population on the West Coast among the historic Asian groups shrank steadily from 1950 to 1980. So rapid was the nationwide spread of the Asian population that a major demographic study concluded in 1993 that the "spatial assimilation of Asian Americans may well happen at a greater speed than for either Hispanics or blacks."[33]

At the micro-level of community geography, clusters of third world immigrants formed out of the shift of population from central-city districts to suburbs. From metropolitan centers, the southern and eastern European stock moved increasingly into suburban areas, while the Hispanic, Asian, and Caribbean immigrants replaced them, rehabilitating commerce and housing in the declining urban neighborhoods abandoned by the Europeans. The third world immigrants assumed a central role in light manufacturing, service industries, and small shopkeeping. They became the new dynamic force in the metropolitan economy and society. But over time, they too appeared to be following the earlier waves of European immigrants along the "tenement trail" to the suburbs. An important clue to this movement was that the proportions of Mexicans, Central and South Americans, Cubans, and Puerto Ricans living in central cities tended to decline gradually in the 1980s and 1990s. In the long run, class and generation exerted growing control over geographic location. As the descendants of immigrants rose economically through better jobs and education, they moved into neighborhoods defined by higher income levels.[34]

The regional and community clusters of immigrant settlement formed distinctive patterns but did not become rigid. As a result of the fluidity of geographic movement, the United States possessed a lower degree of spatial isolation of immigrant groups than found in other societies. A changing ethnic geography reduced the potential for ethnic separatism and strengthened the forces of inclusion.[35]

NOTES

[1] Vernon M. Briggs, Jr., *Immigration Policy and the American Labor Force* (Baltimore: Johns Hopkins University Press, 1984), pp. 78–82; Frank D. Bean and Marta Tienda, *The Hispanic Population of the United States* (New York: Russell Sage Foundation, 1987), pp. 119–21; Thomas Muller and Thomas J. Espenshade, *The Fourth Wave: California's Newest Immigrants* (Washington, D.C.: Urban Institute Press, 1985), pp. 14–15; U.S. Department of Commerce, *Statistical Abstract of the United States, 1990* (Washington, D.C.: U.S. Government Printing Office, 1991), Table 7, p. 10.

[2] Guillermina Jasso and Mark R. Rosenzweig, *The New Chosen People: Immigrants in the United States* (New York: Russell Sage Foundation, 1990), p. 38.

[3] Ibid., pp. 185–86; Muller and Espenshade, *The Fourth Wave*, p. 14.

[4] Alejandro Portes and Ruben G. Rumbaut, *Immigrant America: A Portrait* (Berkeley: University of California Press, 1990), pp. 14–23.

[5] Briggs, *Immigration Policy*, ch. 5; Bean and Tienda, *The Hispanic Population*, p. 119; Jack Miles, "Blacks versus Browns: The Struggle for the Bottom Rung," *The Atlantic*, October 1992, pp. 41–68.

[6] Portes and Rumbaut, *Immigrant America*, pp. 58–72.

[7] Bean and Tienda, *The Hispanic Population*, p. 121.

[8] David M. Reimers, *Still the Golden Door: The Third World Comes to America* (New York: Columbia University Press, 1985), Table 1.1, pp. 24–25.

[9] Herbert R. Barringer, Robert W. Gardner, and Michael J. Levin, *Asians and Pacific Islanders in the United States* (New York: Russell Sage Foundation, 1993), p. 44; Reimers, *Still the Golden Door*, ch. 4; Laurence H. Fuchs, *The American Kaleidoscope: Race, Ethnicity, and the Civic Culture* (Hanover, N.H.: University Press of New England), pp. 291–92; Peter I. Rose, "Asian Americans: From Pariahs to Paragons," in Nathan Glazer, ed., *Clamor at the Gates: The New American Immigration* (San Francisco: Institute for Contemporary Studies, 1985), pp. 196–203; Peter Kwong, *The New Chinatown* (New York: Hill and Wang, 1987), pp. 38–41.

[10] Barringer, Gardner, and Levin, *Asians and Pacific Islanders*, p. 195; Reimers, *Still the Golden Door*, pp. 100–02, 107, 114; Portes and Rumbaut, *Immigrant America*, pp. 58–72.

[11] Roger Daniels, *Coming to America: A History of Immigration and Ethnicity in American Life* (New York: HarperPerennial, 1991), pp. 354–55, 368–70; Valerie O'Connor Sutter, *The Indochinese Refugee Dilemma* (Baton Rouge: Louisiana State University Press, 1990), p. 165.

[12] Barringer, Gardner, and Levin, *Asian and Pacific Islanders*, pp. 32–35; Nathan Caplan, John K. Whitmore, and Marcella H. Choy, *The Boat People and Achievement in America: A Study of Economic and Educational Success* (Ann Arbor: University of Michigan Press, 1989), and *Children of the Boat People: A Study of Educational Success* (Ann Arbor: University of Michigan Press, 1991); Reimers, *Still the Golden Door*, pp. 173–84.

[13] Elliott R. Barkan, *Asian and Pacific Islander Migration to the United States: A Model of New Global Patterns* (Westport, Conn.: Greenwood Press, 1992), pp. 74–76; Daniels, *Coming to America,* p. 343.

[14] Richard T. Gill, Nathan Glazer, and Stephan Thernstrom, *Our Changing Population* (Englewood Cliffs: Prentice-Hall, 1991), Table 19-6, pp. 339–40; U.S. Bureau of the Census, *1990 Census of Population and Housing,* Summary Tape File 1C, "Detailed Race."

[15] Ann Orlov and Reed Ueda, "Central and South Americans," in Stephan Thernstrom, ed., *Harvard Encyclopedia of American Ethnic Groups* (Cambridge: Harvard University Press, 1980), pp. 210, 212.

[16] Because their numbers were relatively small until after World War II, the United States Census Bureau did not record statistics for individual Central and South American nationalities until 1960. The bureau had hitherto aggregated all data concerning these groups under the rubric "Central and South Americans" and it continued this practice in publications such as its series of *Current Population Reports* on persons of Spanish origin. The Immigration and Naturalization Service began to report immigrants from specific Central and South American countries in the mid-1950s.

[17] These and following statistical data on Central and South American immigrants come from the author's tabulation of demographic characteristics published in the *Annual Reports* of the U.S. Immigration and Naturalization Service.

[18] Ian R. H. Rockett, "Immigration Legislation and the Flow of Specialized Human Capital from South America to the United States," *International Migration Review* 19 (1976): 47–61.

[19] Ines Cruz and Juanita Castano, "Colombian Migration to the United States," Part 1, and Elsa M. Chaney, "Colombian Migration to the United States," Part 2, in *The Dynamics of Migration* (Washington, D.C.: Smithsonian Institution, 1976).

[20] Reimers, *Still the Golden Door,* pp. 164–73; Nancy Foner, ed., *New Immigrants in New York* (New York: Columbia University Press, 1987), pp. 2, 4, 9, 18, 28, 55, 62, 65–67. Also see in Foner, Patricia R. Pessar, "The Dominicans: Women in the Household and the Garment Industry," pp. 104–7. Also see Lisandro Perez, "Cubans," and Glenn Hendricks, "Dominicans," in Thernstrom, *Harvard Encyclopedia.*

[21] Aspects of British West Indian immigration since World War II have been examined in the following articles in the journal *Social and Economic Studies:* W. F. Maunder, "The New Jamaican Immigration," 4 (1955): 39–63; G. E. Cumper, "Working Class Emigration from Barbados to the U.K., October 1955," 6 (1957): 77–83; R. W. Palmer, "A Decade of West Indian Migration to the United States, 1962–1972," 23 (1974): 571–87; and G. W. Roberts, "Emigration from the Island of Barbados," 4 (1955): 245–87. For a synopsis of West Indian group history see Reed Ueda, "West Indians," in Thernstrom, *Harvard Encyclopedia.* Thomas Sowell, *Essays and Data on American Ethnic Groups* (Washington, D.C.: Urban Institute Press, 1978), provides useful data on the socioeconomic features of the West Indian population.

[22] Philip Kasinitz, *Caribbean New York: Black Immigrants and the Politics of Race* (Ithaca: Cornell University Press, 1992), pp. 26–27.

[23] Reed Ueda, "West Indians." The demographic tabulations for this article, both published and unpublished, are used in this sketch of the characteristics of West Indian immigrants. Also see Nancy Foner, "The Jamaicans: Race and Ethnicity among Migrants in New York City," in Foner, *New Immigrants,* p. 199.

[24] Ueda, "West Indians"; Michel S. Laguerre, "Haitians," in Thernstrom, *Harvard Encyclopedia;* Reimers, *Still the Golden Door,* p. 148; Susan Buchanan Stafford, "The Haitians: The Cultural Meaning of Race and Ethnicity," in Foner, *New Immigrants,* pp. 104–7.

[25] These data are derived from *1990 Statistical Yearbook of the Immigration and Naturalization Service* (Washington, D.C.: U.S. Government Printing Office, 1991), Table B, p. 39; and *Statistical Abstract of the United States, 1992* (Washington, D.C.: U.S. Government Printing Office, 1992), Table 8, p. 11.

[26] David Ward, "Immigration: Settlement Patterns and Spatial Distribution," in Thernstrom, *Harvard Encyclopedia.*

[27] Bean and Tienda, *The Hispanic Population,* Table 5.1, p. 139; Joan W. Moore, *Mexican Americans,* 2d ed. (Englewood Cliffs, N.J.: Prentice-Hall, 1976), pp. 55, 112.

[28] Joseph Fitzpatrick, *Puerto Rican Americans: The Meaning of Migration to the Mainland* (Englewood Cliffs, N.J.: Prentice-Hall, 1971), pp. 10–11, 15–16, 53–57; Joseph Fitzpatrick, "Puerto Ricans," *Harvard Encyclopedia*, pp. 858–59; Bean and Tienda, *The Hispanic Population*, Table 5.1, p. 139.

[29] Thomas Muller, *The Immigrant and the American City* (New York: New York University Press, 1992), pp. 111–14.

[30] Bean and Tienda, *The Hispanic Population*, Table 5.1, p. 139.

[31] David Gonzalez, "Dominican Immigration Alters Hispanic New York," *New York Times*, 1 September 1992, p. 1.

[32] Ira deA. Reid, *The Negro Immigrant: His Background, Characteristics, and Social Adjustment, 1899–1937* (New York: AMS Press, 1939), pp. 85–89.

[33] Muller, *The Immigrant and the American City*, p. 65; Gill, Glazer, and Thernstrom, *Our Changing Population*, Table 19-6, pp. 339–40; Barringer, Gardner, and Levin, *Asians and Pacific Islanders*, p. 133.

[34] Bean and Tienda, *The Hispanic Population*, Table 5.6, p. 147.

[35] Stanley Lieberson and Mary C. Waters, *From Many Strands: Ethnic and Racial Groups in Contemporary America* (New York: Russell Sage Foundation, 1988), p. 83.

4

The Making
of a World Melting Pot

In the early years of the twentieth century, advocates of Anglo-Saxon supremacy and Americanization proposed the melting pot as an ideal type of assimilation. They hoped that American society would gradually "melt" different groups into homogeneous Anglo conformity. Today, in the era of multiculturalism, politicians, journalists, and educators compare ethnic groups to the discrete and static parts of a mosaic, a metaphor for ethnic relations that emphasizes differences and the preservation of distinct cultures. When the first black mayor of New York City, David Dinkins, delivered his inaugural address in 1989, he paid homage to his city as a "beautiful mosaic."[1]

Since the ethnic revival of the 1960s, critics have either repudiated the melting pot as a pernicious formula for ethnic self-annihilation or dismissed it as irrelevant, saying that the melting pot never happened: it never melted groups. Obviously, these polemics described mutually contradictory scenarios. Reality lay somewhere between the extremes of cultural change and static tradition. As historian Dino Cinel points out, "Explaining the dialectical relationship between change and continuity may be more rewarding than studying either by itself." Cultures and identities endured to an extent, but they metamorphosed in variable degrees and intermixed in complex ways. In other words, rejections of the concept of the melting pot notwithstanding, a real historical melting pot that was neither Anglo conformist nor homogeneous had formed through the gradual processes of social mobility and intergroup acculturation. It produced a shared national culture and a heterogeneous and constantly changing set of ethnic cultures. Even Anglo-Saxons were in the mix, and they were blending with others too. The changes in the melting pot occurred in a cumulative way, but not with linear simplicity, over a succession of generations. New cultural elements, once recognizably foreign, over time became quintessentially American. Thus the melting pot itself changed irresistibly and unpredictably.[2]

The history of food and nutrition styles illustrates the process by which the melting pot transformed itself as new elements were added. The hot dog was said to have been introduced as an ethnic food novelty in the 1880s by the German immigrant Antoine Feuchtwanger. A century later, in the 1980s, it was seen as the symbol of all-American food, in contrast with "real" ethnic food. At a 1989 Fourth of July celebration in the multiracial suburb of Monterey Park, California, a Chinese girl hawked hot dogs, shouting, "Get your hot dogs here, they're so American," while a rival male vendor replied, "No, hot dogs are an American cliché. Expand your cultural experiences. Eat an egg roll." The subtle reshaping of the melting pot over time could easily escape notice, as this anecdote illustrates.[3]

Ethnic groups reshaped the melting pot, as much as it reshaped them, in complex and fluid ways. Assimilation revolved around a multidirectional process of mutual acculturation among groups. Like the images in a kaleidoscope, group identities and cultures intermixed into novel and unpredictable patterns of diversity that cohered into a unity. Yet various features of group life were left unmelted and unfused. Acculturation was incomplete, not always direct, and proceeded at different paces for different groups. The melting pot was like a simmering stew of various ingredients in various states. Northern European groups who were two or more generations removed from the Old World had the weakest sense of ethnic identity. Some European groups who no longer stressed specific loyalties in the second half of the twentieth century were the Scotch-Irish, the Welsh, and the Dutch. Although they retained a stronger sense of identity, the Norwegians, Danes, Swedes, and Germans also grew distant from an ethnic identity centered on the homeland. Groups descended from forebears who came from southern and eastern Europe, Asia, the Caribbean, and Latin America exhibited a stronger tendency to retain distinctive ethnic features. But they, too, were altered by the transformative forces of the host society.

The descendants of even the most impoverished and powerless immigrants such as the Jews, Armenians, Italians, Poles, Irish, Japanese, Chinese, and Koreans who came before the Great Depression of the 1930s obtained better jobs, more education, and higher status than their immigrant ancestors. In the media culture and political culture of mass parties, they achieved more representation and greater influence. Any verdict on America's identity as a land of opportunity must take into account the broader view of the promise of American life as extended to the children and grandchildren of immigrants. Each succeeding generation from a variety of origins usually edged ahead in social and economic standing over its predecessor. Immigrants from Latin America, Asia, the Caribbean, and the Middle East arriving since the 1960s exhibited signs of following the path of economic betterment traveled by Europeans and other previous immigrant minorities.

To tap the full range of opportunities in American society, immigrants have had to overlook ethnic differences and loyalties. Ethnic groups in America lacked the size and power to isolate their members completely. An immigrant's options increased according to his or her ability to diversify social contacts. Ethnic group members were willing to ignore the religion or ancestry of outsiders with whom they developed instrumental and mutually beneficial relations. Self-interest inspired them to forge and dissolve social and economic ties with people from other groups. In politics, immigrants could gain power and office only by forming alliances with outsiders, for no ethnic group could be assured of a majority except at the most local level. To become a force, groups had to form coalitions that spanned their divisions.[4]

The dynamic conditions of American society that detached people from families and groups of origin and reabsorbed them into new families and new communities led to a leapfrogging of the boundaries of ethnic identity. The life of Fiorello La Guardia, mayor of New York City during the Great Depression, reflected the ineluctable workings of this process. Historian Arthur Mann provides an unforgettable glimpse of La Guardia:

> Tammany Hall may have been the first to exploit the vote-getting value of eating gefüllte fish with Jews, goulash with Hungarians, sauerbraten with Germans, spaghetti with Italians, and so on indefinitely, but Fiorello La Guardia not only dined every bit as shrewdly but also spoke, according to the occasion, in Yiddish, Hungarian, German, Italian, Serbian-Croatian, or plain New York English. Half Jewish and half Italian, born in Greenwich Village yet raised in Arizona, married first to a Catholic and then to a Lutheran but himself a Mason and an Episcopalian, Fiorello La Guardia was a Mr. Brotherhood Week all by himself."[5]

The multiethnic fusion of Fiorello La Guardia's life exemplified a general social experience. The children of immigrants forged lifestyles that could not avoid mixing the ingredients of ethnic customs and the wider pluralistic culture. As a son of Japanese immigrants, Aiji Tashiro, explained in 1934:

> I sat down to American breakfasts and Japanese lunches. My palate developed a fondness for rice along with corned beef and cabbage. I became equally adept with knife and fork and with chopsticks. I said grace at meal times in Japanese, and recited the Lord's Prayer at night in English. I hung my stocking over the fireplace at Christmas and toasted "mochi" at Japanese New Year. The stories of "Tongue-cut Sparrow" and "Momo-taro" were as well known to me as those of Red Riding Hood and Cinderella. . . . On some nights I was told bedtime stories of how Admiral Togo sent a great Russian fleet down to destruction. Other nights I heard of King Arthur or from *Gulliver's Travels* and *Tom Sawyer*. I was spoken to by both parents in Japanese and English. I answered in whatever was convenient or in a curious mixture of both.[6]

The diverse parts of ethnic identity were loosely related in overlap and tension. They were not always logically or self-consciously arranged in accordance with clear organized agendas. To be sure there were inherited qualities but others were adapted *ad hoc* from social surroundings to suit individual needs, tastes, and self-interest. The individualized activity of cultural improvisation and combination accelerated the pace of boundary crossing. The resulting dynamism of ethnic identity could be threatening to traditionalists wishing to preserve customary forms, but immigrants and their children usually anticipated change and growth in their lifestyles.

Members of ethnic minorities created overlapping bonds to other communities that expanded as one generation succeeded the next. The entry of grandchildren and great-grandchildren of immigrants into integrated workplaces, schools, residential communities, nonethnic voluntary associations, and even friendships and marriages outside the ethnic circle entailed the creation of multiple and layered identities. Various crossover experiences kept boundaries loose, changing, and blurry, creating a host of possibilities for cultural and intergroup integration.[7]

Although the complex ethnic pluralism of American society made the direction and forms of fusion highly variegated, Anglo-American official culture still exerted a unifying effect on all groups in cultural transition. As immigrants participated in mass party politics and as their children studied in school, ethnic groups absorbed the civic values and forms of Anglo-American culture. The descendants of immigrants who gained occupational and educational mobility encountered the codes of conduct, taste, and manners defined by the Anglo-American middle class, which they adopted to validate their social inclusion in the mainstream.

PATTERNS OF SOCIAL MOBILITY

The Structure of Economic Opportunity

The American economy from the industrial revolution to the twentieth century supplied the basic conditions for immigrants to rebuild their lives so as to broaden their access to occupations, property, and education. A gigantic spectrum of jobs in mass manufacturing and urban labor provided more regular and better-paying employment than was available in the immigrants' homelands. From the turn of the century, the differentiation of the occupational structure offset the compressing and degrading effects of mass production on industrial labor. As technology made traditional skilled manufacturing jobs obsolete, the need for other skilled trades (particularly in construction) expanded enormously. Since many of the craftworkers under pressure from technological change had generalized skills, they moved quickly into these new posts. A growing fraction of workers were also able to open shops and other small businesses. Furthermore, many artisans supplied their children the option of white-collar employment by sponsoring their high school education. Generalized clerical skills became more valuable with the steady expansion of white-collar occupations.[8]

Equally important for keeping fluidity in the social structure in the twentieth century were opportunities for accumulation of savings and property. The continuous increase in real wages and the disciplined saving habits of immigrants stimulated property mobility. The development of suburban tracts increased opportunities for homeownership. The growth of business ventures generated new forms of personal property increasingly within the purchasing power of the working populace. The spread of property in the form of investment securities gave a stake in entrepreneurial operations to a wider segment of the population. Corporate employers facilitated the distribution of financial properties by offering stock to their employees.[9]

The state was unable to limit entry into certain occupations as it had in Europe. The organized labor unions were more powerful in controlling access to the handicrafts. But neither regional nor municipal controls were strong enough to exclude any branch of commerce from ambitious entrepreneurs.

The educational system, in the long run, tended to facilitate social mobility. Schooling developed the disciplined habits and attitudes that were useful for job performance. Although the skills taught were more basic than vocational, the facility with words and numbers that they afforded could be translated into an acceptable white-collar alternative to intergenerational or family succession to manual occupations.[10]

Immigrants throughout the twentieth century found self-employment in small business to be an attractive route toward economic betterment. The most humble enterprise, street vending, attracted Jews and Chinese in the early twentieth century and Asian Indians and Koreans in the late twentieth century. Japanese in prewar Honolulu and Seattle and Koreans in Los Angeles and New York City of the 1980s established commercial domains of "mom and pop" grocery stores. Workers all over the country who amassed sufficient savings in the building trades started hardware and supply stores; auto mechanics opened gas stations and repair shops. Virtually all immigrant groups produced restaurant and foodstand entrepreneurs. In the 1980s and 1990s, Asian, Hispanic, and Caribbean immigrants revitalized the declining small-business sector of the urban economy in New York City, Chicago, Los Angeles, and Boston.[11]

Although the American economy and immigration historically formed a mutually rewarding match, it was not clear how well immigration corresponded to the workings of the economy after the 1970s. The post–World War II American economy was the most dynamic and prosperous in history as measured by its gross production, and it created a residual buoyancy that lasted into the 1970s and 1980s. But it contained structural weaknesses that eroded its strength over time. The postindustrial economy did not possess a deep, stable, and wide base of manufacturing jobs to accommodate the ranks of poor and uneducated newcomers expanding since the 1970s. Rising productivity rates from high-technology production reduced the demand for industrial labor. The growth of manufacturing jobs was inhibited by the move of many American companies to foreign countries for cheap labor. Furthermore, the labor market became increasingly crowded. Rising labor force participation rates among minorities and females and the maturation of the "baby boom" cohort steadily increased the civilian labor force. The widening array of service-sector jobs were low-paying and restricted in long-range opportunities.[12]

In spite of the limiting structural changes, it appeared that recent immigrants over time advanced themselves and strengthened the economy, thus helping to raise overall economic levels. Opportunities in the United States were still superior to those in the developing world. But increasingly it became evident that the growing pool of poor newcomers tended to increase unemployment and widen socioeconomic gaps in the short term. They thus depressed opportunities for natives or at least increased competition for them. Competition in the low-skilled urban labor market intensified between Hispanic and Caribbean immigrants on the one hand and poor blacks on the other, spilling over into acute political and social tensions. In the 1990s, the mutual relationship between economic development and immigrant labor was increasingly perceived as problematic.[13]

The Ethnic Dimensions of Economic Progress

Inequality has constantly shaped the social order in the United States, but the ethnic parameters of inequality have constantly changed. Ethnic groups on the bottom of the social pyramid have managed to rise over the generations, moving up in a series of waves determined by time of arrival. The New Immigrants who came from southern and eastern Europe in the early twentieth century and the first Asian immigrants were very impoverished and poorly educated (Table 4.1). By the third quarter of the twentieth century, however, the descendants of the New Immigrants and Asians had largely escaped poverty and illiteracy. The descendants of the Jews, Japanese, Italians, West Indians, and Poles, some of the most ostracized immigrants of the

Table 4.1.   Ethnic Groups Ranked by Income (1910) and Poverty (1970)

Differences in low income separated native-born and immigrant groups in 1910, but by 1970 these differences had closed.

NATIONALITY	PERCENTAGE OF FAMILIES IN BOTTOM TENTH IN INCOME (1910)	PERCENTAGE OF FAMILIES BELOW POVERTY LINE (1970)
Native white	10	10
Foreign white	26	10
Swedish	5	10
French Canadian	8	—
English	9	9
Irish	9	9
German	11	13
Bohemian	17	—
French	20	11
Portuguese	20	9
Lithuanian	25	—
Hebrew	26	—
Italian (North)	28	6
Slovenian	28	5
Croatian	29	a
Magyar	32	6
Polish	34	6
Slovak	34	8
Syrian	38	6
Italian (South)	40	6
Black	40	35
American Indian		40
Japanese		8
Chinese	40+	12
Filipino		14
Hawaiian		14
Korean		30

[a]Combined with Slovenian.

Source: Stanley Lebergott, *The American Economy: Income, Wealth, and Want* (Princeton: Princeton University Press, 1976), Table 2, p. 47.

century's early decades, had gained average incomes even higher than those of Americans of British descent.[14]

The European immigrants of the twentieth century ascended through small, cumulative steps of occupational mobility in the industrial economy. In

Boston, for example, only a quarter of low-skilled workers moved up to white-collar occupations in their lifetime. Greater progress occurred over generations. Of the native-born sons of working-class immigrant families in Boston, 40 percent rose to white-collar jobs. Similar patterns of two-generation occupational mobility were found in New York, Cleveland, Pittsburgh, and Somerville, Massachusetts. The rates of occupational mobility persisted well into the twentieth century. The immigrants saved earnings derived from jobs in the industrial labor market and invested in property and schooling for their children. Accumulation of these forms of real and human capital furthered social and geographic mobility. External conditions such as the local economy and patterns of discrimination produced variations in the rates and levels of social mobility, as did internal qualities such as family structure and cultural organization. The pathways of mobility also varied from group to group; for example, the Italians, Irish, and Poles aimed at homeownership more than secondary or college education for their children, while the Jews and Japanese used schooling as the chief vehicle for economic progress.[15]

The effects of cumulative social mobility winnowed away the subgroup identities of the Old Immigrants, who arrived from the early nineteenth century, and the New Immigrants of the early twentieth century. By the second generation in the twentieth century, social class became as important as ethnicity in shaping the group life of European immigrants and their children. For third or fourth generation descendants of the Italian, Jewish, or Slavic immigrants, ethnic differences had so diminished that mutual assimilation between them and the descendants of Old Immigrants occurred to a significant degree. They increasingly formed social relations on the basis of class and geography, a process embodied in the movement of multigenerational immigrant descendants into the suburban lower middle class. Intermarriage rose between Protestant, Catholic, and Jewish immigrant subgroups.[16]

The succession of social mobility cycles did not obliterate inequalities among groups, however. Groups advanced at different rates and to different levels on the social pyramid. Class barriers were never insurmountable for immigrants as some social pessimists believed, but still ethnic origins remained an important influence on progress. Native-born workers with native parents moved upward faster than did the sons of immigrants. The Germans, Jews, and Japanese achieved faster economic progress on the average than other groups such as the Irish, Slovaks, and Puerto Ricans. Nevertheless, virtually all immigrant peoples steadily improved their economic position with their length of residence in the United States. Furthermore, particular ethnic hierarchies in social mobility existed in different areas of the country. In Boston, the Jews, Germans, Scandinavians, Italians, and Irish formed an order of high to low mobility; in Cleveland, Romanians moved ahead of

Italians, who moved ahead of Slovaks; in New York City, the Jews rose more quickly than the Irish and Italians; in Pittsburgh, Italians made more economic gains than Poles; in Honolulu, the Chinese, Japanese, Portuguese, and Filipinos attained economic ranking in that order.[17]

The varieties of ethnic group life shaped adjustment to economic opportunities. Immigrants were drawn from dissimilar cultural backgrounds and thus had different orientations toward savings, entrepreneurship, and occupational preferences. Families from different groups were disposed to particular patterns of consumption, discipline, schooling, and investment in the future welfare of their children. These internal factors produced the tactics, expectations, and motivations that affected efforts to capitalize on opportunities. Some groups were able to benefit from strategic connections and status within their communities while others found that discrimination blocked paths to progress.[18]

Asian Patterns of Mobility

Among Asian Americans, two historically distinct generational cycles shaped the patterns of social mobility. These cycles, in turn, were rooted in two separate eras of immigration—the late nineteenth and early twentieth centuries, marked by male laborer migration, and the post-1965 period, in which middle-class families were well represented. Anti-Asian restrictionist admission policies ensured that relatively little immigration occurred between the two eras (see Chapter 1).[19]

The Chinese, Japanese, and Koreans of the early labor immigration took two to three generations to penetrate the middle class. By the 1950s, they expanded their base in white-collar employment and began to rise into its higher strata. Like the Jews and Armenians, their rapid ascent sprang from heavy investment in education to qualify for professional and white-collar occupations. Japanese Americans in particular closely paralleled in socioeconomic advances the most upwardly mobile European immigrant groups. They made sufficient cumulative gains after three generations to become well established in the suburban middle class by the 1960s and 1970s. The capacity of the Japanese to rebound after the heavy loss of property caused by their internment in relocation camps during World War II made their ascent especially noteworthy.[20]

A substantial group of post-1965 Asian immigrants moved more quickly and directly into middle-class employment. Many Chinese, Koreans, Filipinos, and Asian Indians came from the middle class in their homelands with resources, education, and skills that the earlier Asian immigrants had lacked. Their starting point was substantially higher on the economic pyramid than it was for the industrial and agricultural workers in the first cycle of Asian migration. Because of declining racial prejudice and growing tolerance, they were blocked by fewer discriminatory barriers than Asians of the first wave.[21]

From the founding of their earliest communities to the most recent, Asian immigrants engaged in entrepreneurship to a far greater degree than most other immigrant groups. In 1920, Japanese and Chinese immigrants ran a disproportionate share of the commercial enterprises in the urban centers of Hawaii, California, and Washington State. In Honolulu, they virtually dominated the metropolitan small-business economy. The post-1965 immigrants also found small enterprises to be profitable. Professionals and managers who could not immediately find jobs in their fields of expertise because of language and certification barriers were able to set up retail and grocery stores. The federal census of 1980 reported that Asian ethnic groups had the highest rate of firm ownership of all immigrant minorities.[22]

The most comprehensive studies of Asian American income levels have shown that although they varied enormously among different groups, they have tended to converge on the income level of whites over time, far more so than for blacks or Hispanics. The movement of income toward convergence was more evident when the depressing effects of recent immigration was factored out. Among Japanese and Asian Indians in California and New York in 1980, annual incomes of males were higher on the average than the incomes of white males. Nevertheless, on a national level, whites tended to have higher individual incomes than Asians in the same occupations. Among Asian groups, labor intensity in the form of employment of spouses and children played a vital role in lifting family incomes closer to or above those of whites.[23]

Hispanic Patterns of Mobility

Mexicans and Puerto Ricans, the two largest early Hispanic immigrant groups, faced unique conditions that affected their social mobility. The concentration of Mexican laborers in rural outposts limited opportunity in the initial stages of settlement. Puerto Ricans flocked to central cities in the Northeast, where, like many blacks, they found diminishing opportunities in the fading manual job market of the postindustrial economy. The Mexican and Puerto Rican populations were relatively young on average: many were poor workers in the early stages of their earning cycle. The close contact they enjoyed with their homelands encouraged persisting Spanish usage that complicated their efforts to take advantage of opportunities calling for contact with English speakers. The cumulative process of intergenerational investment in the host country was limited by their transfer of earnings home and disrupted by the frequency of return. The combined effects of these structural conditions probably reduced the pace of socioeconomic mobility.[24]

Nevertheless, Mexican and Puerto Rican employees increased their income at a slightly faster pace than that of non-Hispanic whites in the 1960s; Mexicans stayed above the rate of white income growth but Puerto Ricans fell behind in the 1970s.[25]

Mexicans and Puerto Ricans, however, defined two diverging and separate paths in the economic sphere. Mexican Americans, despite the depressing economic effect of massive labor migration, displayed much higher rates of economic progress than Puerto Ricans. The proportion of Mexicans living in poverty in 1980 was one-third less than the proportion of Puerto Ricans. Puerto Ricans in fact fell below blacks in per capita income. In other words, the earnings gap between Mexicans and Puerto Ricans grew steadily.[26]

The material differences separating Mexicans and Puerto Ricans were indicative of the range of economic status among Hispanic nationality groups after 1965. Cubans and Colombians, for example, had faster and higher mobility trajectories than did Puerto Ricans. Recent immigrants from Central America also ranked behind in income and jobs. Newcomers from Cuba, Colombia, Ecuador, and Argentina were the most active in small business during the 1970s. These entrepreneurs opened restaurants and *bodegas* (grocery stores). In the 1980s, Dominicans became dominant in the Hispanic small-business economy in New York City. Mexicans lagged behind somewhat in entrepreneurship, but in neighborhoods such as Pacoima and North Hollywood in Los Angeles, Mexican stores, stands, and restaurants sprouted. Puerto Ricans were the slowest to establish enterprises. The timing, route, and level of economic ascent among Hispanic groups were very heterogeneous, indicating that cultural and resource factors, especially those formed before migration, produced significant variations in economic adjustment.[27]

West Indian and Haitian Patterns of Mobility

Over the course of the twentieth century, black immigrants from the British West Indies made socioeconomic gains surpassing those of other African Americans and comparable to those of various European and Asian immigrant groups. A high percentage of the enterprises owned by blacks in New York City historically were West Indian businesses. West Indians operated in banking, real estate, insurance, advertising, publishing, taxis, and retail clothing. West Indians and Haitians arriving in the 1970s and 1980s established stores and restaurants, often next to those of Koreans. Many blocks in Brooklyn were lined with West Indian and Caribbean storefronts. The cycle of economic progress begun in the early West Indian communities of the 1920s continued in the 1970s and 1980s. In 1972, only 13 percent of West Indian immigrant families earned annual incomes of at least $15,000, while 30 percent of second-generation families earned that much. The rate of high school graduation increased from 48 percent for first-generation West Indians to 73 percent for the second generation. By the 1960s and 1970s, West Indians held nearly the same representation in white-collar and skilled occupations as whites and exceeded the proportions of native American blacks in the same jobs. West Indian median annual family income was $8,880 in 1967, lower than the average annual income of $10,672 for white families, yet higher than the average of $6,440 for native African Americans. In 1980, West Indians continued to hold on to this position relative to native blacks and whites. The 1980 federal census disclosed that West Indian-headed families had a median yearly income of $15,645, compared with a median of $17,361 for native families. Anthropologist Philip Kasinitz reported that median family income for Jamaican immigrants in 1980 was "higher and their poverty rate [was] far lower than that of native blacks (close to that of Koreans)."[28]

After 1965, West Indians and Haitians were particularly effective in penetrating the expanding service job market. They worked as cabdrivers and in the maintenance of offices, hotels, and hospitals. Female immigrants had unusually high rates of employment. In 1979, about 32 percent of West Indian women in New York City were nurses or nurses' aides. The unusual labor force participation of West Indian women probably was crucial in keeping poverty rates low among West Indians. Haitians too moved into the service sector of the labor market. Many Haitian women also worked as nurses and as domestics.[29]

The Changing Face of Mobility and Inequality

In the long run and on the whole, immigrants to the United States achieved a better economic life for themselves because they helped to build a dynamic economy that improved overall material welfare. Different immigrant groups found different and complementary economic niches for themselves. Immigrants elevated their standing consistent with their length of residence. Over time, the social and economic dynamics of the United States repositioned ethnic communities to cut across class boundaries, but at rates that varied according to time of arrival, context of settlement, and the material and behavioral resources intrinsic to families and communities.

In the short run, however, waves of immigration created transitional economic changes that reduced the rate of earnings and increased inequality. This impact was particularly salient in the peak periods of immigration at the beginning and at the end of the twentieth century. Immigration tended to depress wages and income by bringing a large addition of cheap labor with lower levels of skill and education. This phenomenon probably accounted for the downward trend in median income among Mexicans, Cubans, Puerto Ricans, and Central and South Americans in the mid-1970s when the rate of Hispanic influx accelerated sharply.[30]

Large waves of immigrants with lower levels of skill, education, and income contributed to the short-term widening of social class distances in American society. In the early twentieth century, as a result of the absorption of immigrant labor from southern and eastern Europe, income inequality in American society reached a high point. The decline of mass immigration in the mid-twentieth century combined with intergenerational social mobility in the New Immigrant communities to move income distribution closer toward equality. The burst of immigration from poor third world regions in the late twentieth century produced a return of trends toward greater inequality.

The growth of economic inequality expressed itself in two basic ways. First, new material disparities appeared within individual ethnic groups. In the Jewish community at the turn of the century, for example, the arrival of impoverished Russian Jews introduced new social class tensions, while in the Chinese community of the 1970s and 1980s, the arrival of low-skilled laborers spawned internal economic divisions. The growth of a large low-income subcommunity was particularly evident in New York City's Chinatown. Chinese males in New York State earned only 58 percent of the median annual income of their white counterparts in 1980. Although poverty has been historically low in the Asian communities, the waves of poor immigrants raised the proportion of welfare recipients. Mexican American communities that had developed a growing middle class were also divided by the waves of undocumented workers and poor immigrants that crowded the barrios.[31]

Second, economic distances between groups widened in response to economic resources and conditions, time of arrival, and internal capacity to organize for economic gain. In the early twentieth century, a substantial number of poor laborers from Europe became part of a "floating proletariat" of transient labor migrants. They drifted around the country, a large pool of reserve labor that could be tapped for low-skilled work. They were an underclass sharply divided from the Anglo-Protestant middle class. The arrival of many poor and undereducated illegal immigrants after 1965 caused an analogous phenomenon as they formed an invisible and profoundly separate lower class. Nevertheless, the degrees of persistence within the underclass and escape from it are still not understood with any precision. By the 1980s, the ethnic groups with the cumulative gains of multigenerational social mobility stood far ahead of many newly arrived groups. For example, Japanese Americans gained over three generations great occupational, educational, and wealth advantages over first-generation Vietnamese, Cambodians, and Lao-tians. However, some newly settled groups also surged past static multigen-erational groups. Recent arrivals such as Cubans and Colombians penetrated the middle class, while Puerto Ricans improved their income and education relatively little between World War II and the 1990s. Moreover, among the first generation, economic differentials were very high. On the average, Asian Indians, Iranians, and Koreans possessed more savings, job skills, and educa-tion than Southeast Asians, Dominicans, Greeks, and Salvadorans.[32]

Economically homogeneous blocs labeled "Asian," "Hispanic," "Euro-pean," and "African" never existed. To see changes on the socioeconomic pyramid, we must consider these blocs in terms of their constituent subgroups. Subgroups from different blocs often had more in common in their rate and form of mobility than did subgroups from within an ethnic bloc. Thus Japanese had more in common with Jews than they had with Laotians in education and acculturation, Cubans had more in common with West Indians than with Puerto Ricans in occupational progress. The same was true for low-mobility groups from different blocs: Puerto Ricans had more in common with native American blacks than with Mexicans in the persistence of low earnings; Cambodians had more in common with the Irish than with Koreans in welfare status. The social process of upward mobility cut across ethnic and racial lines; so did the drag of poverty. A multiethnic array of groups formed the vanguard of economic progress; another heterogeneous set constituted a group whose poverty and lack of skills made them the immigrant component of an American underclass.[33]

Educational Gains

Virtually all the immigrant groups arriving since the early twentieth century displayed rising levels of schooling over the course of two or three generations. Many immigrants from Europe, especially those from the southern and eastern areas, were either illiterate or had very basic functional ability in reading, writing, and speaking English. During the twentieth century, how-ever, the children of European immigrants achieved higher levels of schooling. Moreover, the more recent the second generation, the higher was its average level of schooling. The children of immigrants who were born after 1915 had, on the average, a high school education comparable to that of whites of native parentage.[34]

Among Hispanics and Asians, schooling levels also rose intergeneration-ally. Hispanic groups from 1960 to 1980 showed steady rises in school years completed and achieved about the same average of completed school years as the white population. There was also evidence of rising college attendance: among various Hispanic groups, the percentage of the college-educated in the first and second generation doubled and tripled from 1960 to 1980. By 1970, before the return of large waves of Asian immigrants, the Chinese, Japanese, Koreans, and Filipinos—historic and multigenerational populations—ranked higher in average years of schooling than the white population.[35]

Despite a common ability to increase schooling from the first to the second generation, ethnic groups varied immensely in the rate at which their levels of schooling rose. Groups such as the Jews, Japanese, Chinese, West Indians, and Armenians placed a higher premium on schooling, and their children realized quicker educational gains than groups such as the French Canadians, Irish, Italians, and Poles. The former possessed specific material and cultural resources and achieved the modicum of economic mobility that provided the surplus income to prolong the schooling of children who might otherwise enter the labor market to help their families. In 1910 in Hawaii, the Chinese and Japanese sent a disproportionate share of children to high school. They possessed traditions of disciplined family saving and role cooperation in which siblings would take turns working to maximize resources for schooling. Since professional and high-level white-collar jobs required secondary and college education, the groups who successfully invested in education usually achieved the highest degree of economic mobility.[36]

The post-1965 immigrants were often better established to sponsor the schooling of their children than the New Immigrants of the early twentieth century. Large numbers of college-educated professionals and managers came from India, the Philippines, Korea, and China (Figures 3.5 and 3.6, pp. 64 and 66). Their children thus benefited from parents who themselves knew the value of education and would make extraordinary efforts to keep their children in school.

At the same time, however, many low-skilled and poorly educated immigrants were not well positioned to boost their children's schooling. They lacked the resources for sponsoring extended schooling and were not as committed to it as a form of economic utility. These immigrants included many laborers who possessed only elementary levels of schooling. Their children constituted a growing pool of school-age youngsters disadvantaged by the poverty and undereducation of their parents.[37]

Although evidence is sketchy, many immigrants since 1965 appeared to be replicating the cycle of intergenerational educational mobility achieved by earlier European immigrants and the variable levels of achievement associated with ethnic background. A large-scale population survey of immigrants in 1960, 1970, and 1980 showed that, on average, they sponsored schooling for their children at higher rates than did native parents. A study of the nation's eighth largest school district in San Diego, California, showed that many children of post-1970 immigrants surpassed in educational achievement children of American birth, both black and white. In tendency to complete secondary school and in scholastic averages, children of Asian and European parents excelled over the children of native-born Americans. The results of the study in San Diego also demonstrated significant inequalities in school achievement among ethnic groups. Children of parents from Latin America and the Pacific Islands achieved lower grades and rates of promotion than students of Asian and European parentage. If historical precedents serve as a guide, however, these children and their progeny will probably climb to higher levels of schooling over time.[38]

Linguistic Assimilation

The peak periods of linguistic diversity in American history probably occurred in the early twentieth century and the late twentieth century when the largest and most culturally variegated waves of immigrants arrived. In 1910, the federal census reported that more than fifty foreign languages were in use across the country. After 1990, the number of foreign languages in use probably rose even higher and certainly included many more non-European tongues.

As a key to the resources and opportunities of the surrounding culture, linguistic assimilation to English improved immigrants' chances of moving into better occupations and increasing their education. The first generation of immigrants was usually hampered by unfamiliarity with English, which often endured through adulthood and was symbolized by an ineradicable foreign accent. The level of linguistic assimilation in the first generation probably acted as an important limiting factor on occupational mobility. Many immigrants from non-English-speaking backgrounds found it hard to progress from blue-collar to white-collar jobs. Conversely, linguistic assimilation boosted chances for social and economic advancement. The higher rates of movement into white-collar and skilled jobs among immigrants' American-born children, who gained much more effective command of English than their parents, indicated the crucial advantage of linguistic assimilation in occupational mobility.[39]

At the same time that command of English served as a key to enhancing opportunity, American communities insisted that only English could be the language of instruction in public schools. This monolinguistic policy sprang from the ideology of the common school movement, which sought to provide a core of shared knowledge and culture. Because American government historically refrained from supporting the customs and traditions of ethnic groups, no other official languages ever gained a foothold in public schools. However, government never went so far as to establish English as an official state language.[40]

The combination of practical incentives to learn English and the monolinguistic basis of public school instruction made the number of foreign language speakers dwindle rapidly. By 1980, in the native-born population, which included the children of immigrants and their descendants, only 6.8 percent spoke a language other than English at home (Table 4.2). Usage of a foreign language had decreased steadily with each succeeding generation after the first. Even within the lifetime of the foreign-born, adoption of English and the loss of the mother tongue occurred. While only 16 percent of immigrants who arrived in the 1970s used English at home, more than 38 percent of those immigrants who had been in the United States longer—those arriving before 1970—became English speakers at home. In the last several decades, first-generation Asian Americans improved in English ability and the second generation became proficient. A study of Spanish-language immigrants in 1980 showed that their children achieved English proficiency at the same rate as the children of German-speaking immigrants earlier in the century.[41]

The second generation by and large achieved basic literacy and oral competency in English, but the quality of English mastery varied significantly within and among ethnic groups. Usually it depended on the degree of educational mobility. Not surprisingly, persons from families who stressed

Table 4.2. Linguistic Assimilation, 1980

Although most immigrants came to the United States speaking a language other than English, societal pressures and incentives led them and their children to use English increasingly in and out of the home. In 1980, the vast majority of the American population was English-speaking, and English usage among immigrants increased with their length of residence.

	LANGUAGE SPOKEN AT HOME		
	ENGLISH ONLY (%)	OTHER THAN ENGLISH (%)	TOTAL NUMBER
All Persons over Age 4 in 1980			
Immigrants arrived from 1970 to 1980	16.3	83.7	5,340,000
Immigrants arrived before 1970	38.2	61.7	8,520,000
Native-born	93.2	6.8	196,400,000

Source: Computed from U.S. Bureau of the Census, *1980 Census: Detailed Population Characteristics*, PC80-1-D1-A (Washington, D.C.: U.S. Government Printing Office, 1984), Table 255.

and prolonged their children's schooling tended to achieve high levels of English proficiency. Historically, these individuals were found more often among the Japanese, Jews, and Armenians and less frequently among the Italians, Mexicans, and French Canadians. Among recent immigrant groups, East Asians acquired high-level English proficiency faster than Hispanics and Pacific Islanders.[42]

Adult female immigrants often gained English literacy and proficiency at a slower rate than men, partly because they generally had lower levels of education in their homelands as well as lower literacy rates. Also, the insulation of domestic life and their limited choices for employment made it less likely that women speaking a foreign language would be exposed to environments where using English was encouraged. In the second generation, however, gender differences in linguistic assimilation were leveled out as females learned English in the public schools. Indeed, the daughters of immigrants often surpassed the sons of immigrants in scholastic achievement in English.[43]

Even among recent Hispanic immigrants whose leaders have supported official bilingualism, the acquisition of English language skills proceeded at a rapid pace. In the twentieth century, the large majority of American-born Hispanic adults spoke English chiefly or exclusively. A 1976 study showed that 72 percent of Mexicans, 84 percent of Puerto Ricans, 80 percent of Cubans, and 96 percent of Central and South Americans used English as their main or sole language.[44]

Bilingualism in the home was not necessarily an impediment to scholastic performance. The Japanese and Jewish students of the 1920s and 1930s came from homes where foreign languages were used, but they still excelled in academics. The study of the San Diego public school system in the mid-1980s demonstrated that students from bilingual households frequently achieved the highest scholastic averages in high school. Moreover, familiarity with more than one language perhaps enhanced school and job performance in an era of growing internationalism, when knowledge of different cultures and the linguistic keys to them became more useful in enterprise and professional achievement.

FAMILY AND POPULATION

Fertility and Immigration

Because the twentieth century experienced the largest waves of immigration in history, its citizens also suffered from periodic anxieties about the submergence of the native population under a tide of aliens. The fear that immigrants would outbreed natives reached a crescendo during the rise of restrictionism in the first decades of the twentieth century. Alarmists worried about "race suicide," the inability of Anglo-Saxons to reproduce at the same rate as immigrants. This anxiety was vividly expressed in Lothrop Stoddard's shocking forecast in 1923 that in two hundred years one thousand Harvard graduates would have only fifty living descendants while one thousand Romanians would have a hundred thousand. The 1920 federal census reported that the foreign-born had one more child on the average than the native-born; furthermore, the primary nationality groups from Europe all tended to have more children on the average than did native whites. But the impact of these fertility differentials in favor of immigrants was vastly overrated. The host population continued to grow through natural increase, and the Anglo-Saxon stock reproduced at a healthy rate.[45]

In the 1990s, journalists and advocacy groups declared that the mass migrations from Asia, Latin America, and the Caribbean would soon make whites a demographic minority. They reached this conclusion by extrapolating current rates of immigration into the next century, neglecting the possibility that current policies could change so as to reduce admissions in the future. Moreover, these predictions suggested an unprecedented scale of foreignization, an exaggerated sense that America was being engulfed by an alien tide as never before. A historical perspective shows that recent fears of post-1965 immigration as an overwhelming flood were probably as dubious as the old notion of "race suicide."[46]

The annual levels of immigration since 1965 had not been so high since the peak years early in the century, but their demographic impact did not lead to radical displacements or imbalances between natives and immigrants. The host society had grown much larger, making its absorptive capacity greater. Thus, since the 1960s the rate of yearly immigration relative to the size of the host population was low in comparison with its magnitude before 1930 (Figure I.5, p. 11). Even the rate of immigration in the immigration-heavy 1980s was decidedly smaller than in the decades of the industrial revolution from 1830 to 1930. Also, the representation of the foreign-born in the American population was comparatively lower. While the foreign-born made up 13 to 14 percent of the population from 1860 to 1920, they composed 6 percent and 9 percent in 1980 and 1990, respectively (Figure 4.1). The decades of the New Immigration in the early twentieth century were actually the peak historical era of foreignization. The size of yearly immigration relative to the size of the receiving population in the first decade of the century was twice as high as in 1980.[47]

It is true that post-1965 immigration brought new ethnic groups who had the potential for higher fertility rates—the number of children born to females of childbearing age—than found among natives. The age structure of the

Figure 4.1.   Foreign-Born in the United States, 1900–1990

Annual immigration totals since 1965 have been the highest since the early twentieth century, but the total population of the United States has grown so much larger that the percentage of foreign-born, although rising, has been lower than earlier.

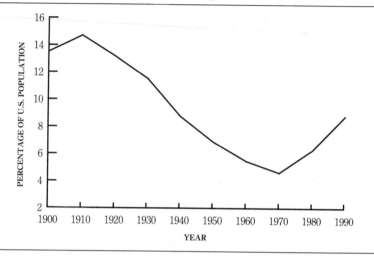

Source: Computed from the total of foreign-born reported by the decennial census of the United States.

immigrants yearly arriving since the 1980s was widest between twenty and thirty-nine and narrowest among the elderly and those in early childhood (Figure 4.2). In comparison, the age structure of the American population was narrower in the young adult range but fuller in the elderly and early childhood brackets. To put it graphically, the age structure of immigrants resembled a triangle while that of the host population resembled a rectangle. According to demographers, the triangular age structure has a much greater potential to produce population growth than the rectangular form. The former had a disproportionate mass in the prime childbearing and family-forming years, while the latter included many old people who would not affect natural increase and many children who would not raise fertility rates until they matured into the next adult generation.

During the peak historic intervals of mass immigration, some groups stood out as pacesetters for high fertility. Polish, German, and Irish groups displayed fertility rates twice as high as native white Americans in 1880. Recently, Mexicans and Puerto Ricans exhibited the highest fertility rates in the population. In 1980, the fertility rate of Mexican women was almost 40 percent higher than for native white women, and for Puerto Rican women it was more than a third higher.[48]

Figure 4.2. Age and Sex Distribution of U.S. Population and Immigrants Admitted, 1989

The immigrant population since the 1980s tended to have the potential for a higher growth rate than the general U.S. population, as proportionately more recent immigrants were between the ages of twenty and thirty-nine.

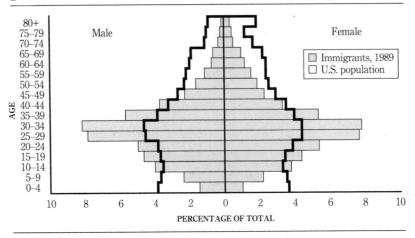

Source: 1989 Statistical Yearbook of the Immigration and Naturalization Service (Washington, D.C.: U.S. Government Printing Office, 1990), p. xxii.

Nevertheless, immigrants of the late twentieth century were so varied that the demographic effects of groups that were pacesetters in fertility were counterbalanced by the effects of others with low fertility. Even among Hispanics, often perceived to have high rates of fertility, a number of groups had low fertility rates. In 1980, the fertility rate of Cuban immigrants was lower than for whites; the fertility rate for immigrants from Central and South America was only slightly higher. Asian immigrants on the average had fertility rates lower than whites. The concurrence of high fertility rates among certain ethnic groups and lower rates among others leveled the natural increase of the entire foreign population. Indeed, demographers thus found that the average fertility rate of immigrant women whose childbearing ended in 1960, 1970, and 1980 was lower than that for native-born women; and, as a consequence, immigrant families were smaller on the average. In the 1980s and 1990s, however, young immigrant women had a higher rate of fertility than young native women, indicating that they would ultimately have more children than native women at completion of their childbearing period and thus could raise the foreign-born fertility above that of the native.[49]

Most important, historical patterns showed that fertility rates tended to decrease among all immigrant groups in the second and third generations. This trend occurred in the Hispanic population from 1960 to 1980. Mexicans,

Puerto Ricans, and Cubans displayed declining fertility rates as the American-born generation succeeded the foreign-born. The rates of natural increase among the two oldest Asian populations—the Chinese and Japanese—declined more rapidly than among whites. The Japanese exhibited the most linear and pronounced slowing of natural population growth.[50]

In spite of the immense wave of immigration in the 1970s and 1980s, the presence of many low-fertility groups and the tendency toward intergenerational decline in fertility made unlikely immense and abrupt shifts in the relative numbers of racial minorities and whites, or of foreigners and natives, as a result of the natural increase of immigrants.

Intermarriage

One of the most sensitive signs of the extent of intergroup or mutual assimilation in the twentieth century was the progressive rise of intermarriage rates. Whether one defined groups by religion, race, or ethnic identity, intermarriage clearly involved an expanding variety of groups. A well-known study of religious intermarriage in 1940 showed that only 16 percent of Roman Catholics and 6 percent of Jews married outside their religious group, thus inspiring the theory of the "triple melting pot"—that religion would act to limit intermarriage to one of the three religious supercategories of Protestant, Catholic, and Jew. In the 1970s, however, the rate of religious intermarriage climbed to 40 percent and upward for Catholics and Jews. Sociologist Richard D. Alba demonstrated in 1990 that "the rising tide of intermarriage is also sweeping across religious lines," thus showing that the triple melting pot theory "does not seem to be holding up." The Japanese and the Jews constituted important examples of groups who went from nearly universal endogamy to frequent exogamy after three or more generations. Changes in intermarriage among the Japanese also demonstrated the decline of race as a boundary. Half the Japanese Americans marrying in the 1970s and 1980s married into another ethnic group. Although the census did not supply results for respondents by Jewish ancestry, separate studies showed that intermarriage likewise involved half of all Jewish spouses by the 1980s. A historical pattern of generational increase in intermarriage also existed among Mexicans. One out of three third-generation Mexican Americans intermarried by the 1960s.[51]

The dramatic story of the rise of intermarriage was recorded in the multiple ancestry table of the 1979 *Current Population Reports* (Table 4.3 and Table A.12, p. 167). About two of every five Americans claimed more than one specific ethnic ancestry. In nearly all European ancestry groups, the majority of respondents reported multiple ancestry. The rates of multiple ancestry conformed to the sequence of arrival of immigrant waves. The Old Immigrant

Table 4.3. Selected Data on Multiple Ancestry, 1979

Data on multiple ancestry indicate the prevalence of intermarriage and mutual assimilation among ethnic groups.

TYPE OF ANCESTORY	NUMBER (thousands)	PERCENTAGE
Total persons responding	216,613	100.0
At least one specific ancestry	179,078	82.7
Single ancestry	96,496	44.5
Multiple ancestry	82,582	38.1
Did not report specific ancestry	37,535	17.3
American or United States	13,592	6.3
Other	195	0.1
Not reported	23,748	11.0

TEN LARGEST ANCESTRY GROUPS	NUMBER	PERCENTAGE OF TOTAL RESPONDENTS	PERCENTAGE WITH MULTIPLE ANCESTRY
German	51,649	28.8	66.8
Irish	43,752	24.4	77.7
English	40,004	22.3	71.3
African	16,193	9.0	7.0
Scottish	14,205	7.9	88.6
French	14,047	7.8	78.3
Spanish	12,493	7.0	21.9
Italian	11,751	6.6	48.0
American Indian	9,900	5.3	79.3
Polish	8,421	4.7	58.5

Source: Compiled from U.S. Bureau of the Census, Current Population Reports, Series P-23, No. 116, Ancestry and Language in the United States: November 1979 (Washington, D.C.: U.S. Government Printing Office, 1982), Table A and Table 1, pp. 1, 7.

stock, from northern and western Europe, displayed the highest level of multiple ancestry, the New Immigrant stock displayed a lower level of multiple ancestry, followed by the newest immigrants from the third world who reported the lowest levels of multiple ancestry. Among the Old Immigrant ancestry groups, 89 percent of the Scottish, 83 percent of the Dutch, 82 percent of the Welsh, 78 percent of the French, 78 percent of the Irish, and 75 percent of the Swedes reported multiple ancestry (Table A.12). Among the later-arriving New Immigrants of the twentieth century, lower but substantial percentages also reported multiple ancestry. Sixty-seven percent of Hungarians, 61 percent of Romanians, 58 percent of Poles, and 48 percent of Italians reported multiple ancestry. The newest Asian and Hispanic nationality groups also exhibited substantial and rising rates of intermarriage. Thirty-one percent of Filipinos, 23 percent of Chinese, and 22 percent of Japanese reported multiple ancestry, while nearly 22 percent of the Spanish population claimed multiple ancestry.[52]

The rates of multiple ancestry were highest among the earliest immigrant groups to arrive and lowest among the most recent, but even the latter showed signs of rising exogamy. The strong association between time of arrival and degree of multiple ancestry shown by these data indicated that the rise of intermarriage was a by-product of generational succession. Sociologist Richard Alba argued that intermarriage produced "the most profound ethnic change among whites: the wide dispersion of ethnically mixed ancestry." The 1979 ancestry survey showed that more than 13.6 million respondents reported their ancestry as "American" or "United States," suggesting that many Americans, particularly whites, had become so mixed that they identified themselves as a new supra-ethnic "American" ethnic group. The multiple ancestry data comprised a broad array of compelling evidence for the historic existence of an assimilative potency that made American society "a melting pot in the making."[53]

TRANSITIONS IN IDENTITY
AND COMMUNITY

In a special population survey in 1972, about 40 percent of the sample group chose not to identify with a specific ethnic heritage. They represented a transnational group that continued to grow in size and importance. The 1979 ancestry survey encouraged respondents to choose ethnic ancestries, but still 13.6 million refused, giving "American" or "United States" as their ancestry, the seventh largest response category that year, trailing English, German, Irish, black, Italian, and French. Examining these data, sociologists Stanley Lieberson and Mary Waters inferred the genesis of a "new American ethnic group," one whose members did not identify with premigration antecedents.[54]

Many Americans who were descended through generations from immigrant ancestors no longer identified with a particular ethnic group. They included the large and increasing number of people of mixed ethnic and racial parentage who took their identity primarily from their occupation, consumer habits, generation, residential location, and cultural lifestyle as social mobility and intergroup acculturation reduced ethnic ties.

The open conditions that promoted loss of specific ancestral identity also supported the preservation of cultural heritages. The American polity left groups alone to conserve their tradition as much as it left them alone to change it. The American government allowed the Irish, Jews, Poles, Greeks, Armenians, and Koreans to pursue their religion, build their own neighborhood institutions, and start their own schools, while in their homelands they suffered from the persecution of hostile neighbors, imperial powers, oppressive overlords, and church establishments. They found in America a place of refuge that ensured greater tolerance for their way of life.

The American city provided the organized and expansive conditions that supported intergroup tolerance and coexistence. The industrial city created new regimented patterns of work, transportation, and consumerism that provided an orderly set of mutual relations for people from radically different backgrounds. The spread of police-enforced public order and the legalization of social and economic relations provided new sources of control over behavior. The dynamic forces of economic change injected such sufficient and differential possibilities for occupational and property mobility that competition between immigrant groups did not reach hostile or destructive levels. Each group could find its economic niche. Residential space expanded to the extent that different groups could find geographic slots that permitted the security of insulation from outsiders.[55]

The urban neighborhoods were the key to the coexistence of groups. The geographic separation of immigrant nationalities into enclaves limited the amount of contact between groups who were alien or antagonistic toward each other. It allowed each group to manage the degree and character of interaction with outsiders whether for political, economic, or benevolent purposes. Immigrant newcomers were voluntarily able to preserve aspects of their transplanted culture as well as to control the absorption of different elements from surrounding neighbors on their own terms. The Poles and the Jews, the Koreans and the Japanese, and Pakistanis and the Indians—who had antagonistic relations in their homelands—were able to coexist in the United States by having their own autonomous communities.[56]

The ethnic neighborhoods generated a working-class public culture that satisfied special and exclusive group needs while providing for organized social and cultural exchanges between groups. Ethnic communal institutions such as fraternal welfare societies, churches, saloons, and theaters satisfied these needs, but as they brought together provincial and village subgroups they broke down local variations into the broader forms of a new ethnicity defined as Italian American, Polish American, Japanese American, and so on. Civic institutions such as schools, parks, and local government agencies supplied the cross-group ties that underpinned citizenship. These neighborhood institutions transmitted common sets of public values and conduct within groups and between groups. Under their influence, citizenship and ethnicity became defined in terms of residential and communal identity rather than occupational identity.[57]

The mass culture of the cities penetrated powerfully into the ethnic neighborhoods to affect traditions supplied by religion, family, and folk culture. Indulgence in the market of mass culture—spectator sports, amusement parks and districts, movie and radio entertainment, shopping, and fashion styles— was often seen by foreign-born parents and group leaders as a wasteful and escapist excess of the American-born. Encouraging the individualist pursuit of pleasure and novel sensation, consumerist mass culture was at odds with certain aspects of their tradition that emphasized moralistic and ascetic values, the stoical acceptance of self-denial and abstention for the sake of family propriety. The standards of taste, conduct, and values from mass culture gained adherents steadily in immigrant neighborhoods, especially among the young, but not without resistance from older forms and adaptations to conservative immigrant tastes. Immigrants and their children absorbed mass culture into their new ethnic identities. Mass culture became a part of their developing sense of self as "ethnic" Americans.[58]

In the second half of the twentieth century, the cities lost their industrial base, and the enclaves built by immigrants of the early twentieth century dwindled in size and social vitality as the forces of urban renewal and suburbanization depleted their populations. Nevertheless, the post-1965 wave of immigrants became an unexpected new force for recolonizing the neighborhoods abandoned by the Irish, the Italians, the Jews, and the Poles. Asian, Latin American, and Caribbean immigrants were the new players of the old roles held by the previous immigrant waves, who themselves had once taken over the neighborhoods that the Protestants and Anglo-Saxons left behind. In Brooklyn neighborhoods like Prospect Park and Sunset Park, in the Elmhurst section of Queens, in the Boston community of Allston, in the Chicago enclave of Rogers Park, and in Los Angeles districts such as Koreatown and Silver Lake, the newest immigrants built homes and businesses. They resuscitated and expanded residential buildings. They started new internal ethnic economies that linked themselves with external buyers and sellers. Koreans, Chinese, Vietnamese, Thai, Indians, Pakistanis, Colombians, Dominicans, Brazilians, Ecuadorans, Haitians, and Lebanese opened thriving stores, newsstands, restaurants, and food stands. These networks of production and trade produced new jobs. A new fusion of international popular cultures formed on streets where stores sold Latino music CDs, videos from India, and magazines from China. Cuban-Chinese and Japanese-Korean restaurants catered to syncretic new-wave food styles. New ethnic markets supplied the commodities that defined the lifestyles mingling in the Asian, Hispanic, and Caribbean neighborhoods. The newest immigrants kindled a rebirth of the public culture of the neighborhood by installing new forms of entrepreneurship, consumerism, art, and entertainment. Their enclaves became the visible human face of the new world melting pot.[59]

The newest immigrants injected a positive public spirit into neighborhoods demoralized by urban decay. A New York urban journalist reported in 1993, "To the American neighborhoods, the immigrants bring a refreshing enthusiasm to excel at school and in business, and enviable ethics concerning family and community." Their children stimulated scholarship and learning in the public schools. The newcomers learned how to register their demands for better facilities and public order in their playgrounds, schools, and sidewalks, starting neighborhood and civic organizations to lobby for vital services in their enclaves. In Flushing, New York, a coalition of Chinese, Korean, and other ethnic associations launched cooperative street-cleaning efforts and pressured the city government to upgrade sanitation codes and improve conditions for small business and consumerism. Although many immigrants maintained an interest in homeland politics, they eagerly learned how to gain access to the opportunities of municipal government and manipulate its institutional mechanisms. The "new people in old neighborhoods" were gradually organizing into a new constituency for American civic reform.[60]

THE SOCIETAL IMPACT
OF CHANGING IMMIGRATION

Throughout the twentieth century, mass immigration deeply affected the transitions between stages of social and economic organization. The New Immigrants in the early twentieth century provided massive labor input to the industrial economy and expanded the social infrastructure of cities. The next wave of immigration in the restrictionist era from 1924 to 1965 reduced the flow of international labor and enabled the geographic and social stabilization of the ethnic working-class populations brought by the first wave. The post-1965 wave tied into the reorganization of urban life and the postindustrial economy. The newest immigrants revitalized blighted residential and commercial districts. They worked in low-skilled service and light manufacturing jobs created by a consumer-oriented economy.[61]

By the early cold war era, the descendants of the New Immigrants and the early Asian, Hispanic, and Caribbean immigrants achieved a significant level of inclusion and positive coexistence with surrounding groups. The Italians, Slavs, and Jews reshaped the culture of the industrial North; the Mexicans in the Southwest and the Chinese and Japanese in California and Hawaii put their cultural imprint on these regions. Widespread multigenerational social mobility and assimilation made subgroup differences among those of southern and eastern European ancestry a declining factor in residential, occupational, and intermarital patterns by the late twentieth century. The achievement of absorbing the New Immigrants should not be underestimated. Europeans who were often in conflict in their homelands were able to live and work together in the United States.

In public opinion, it is usually assumed that post-1965 immigrants were more "diverse" than relatively "homogeneous" Italians, Jews, Irish, Greeks, and Slavs of the early twentieth century and so different from these European predecessors that assimilation patterns that once worked are irrelevant today. It is easy, however, to overstate this comparative difference. The New Immigrants had been in fact enormously diverse and profoundly divided at first from the communities of native-born Americans. The New Immigrants consisted of myriad ethnic subgroups in a time when nationalistic, regional, and religious differentiation, and even mutual antagonism, were very high. They were generally poor and undereducated and came from homeland societies quite removed from the influences of the United States. They also were classified racially as separate and inferior to Americans from northern Europe.

The success of assimilating the New Immigrant was a precondition for opening admissions to all regions of the world. In hindsight, the fissures created by immigration in the early twentieth century prepared the way for a more pluralistic society. The national fabric grew more complex in its forms of cohesion, developing a capacity to accept greater diversity.

The wave of immigrants in the late twentieth century produced social, economic, and cultural effects analogous to those created by the New Immigrants. Like the New Immigrants, the most recent group contributed to short-term increases in economic inequality that reinforced ethnic differences. Impoverished workers and refugees from Latin America and Asia who were handicapped by linguistic and cultural barriers had few immediate economic options besides low-income jobs. The newest immigrants also widened the cultural distances that had been closing with the assimilation of southern and eastern European ethnic groups. They increased the variety and living presence of non-European cultures and languages in American society. The multiplication of unprecedented groups raised the imperative to enlarge American national identity and the national culture to make them more inclusive of diversity. The pursuit of a better life by new multitudes challenged the economy to produce fair opportunities and the governing institutions to assist the immigrants in obtaining decent living conditions.

Nevertheless, the degree of social division and strain from post-1965 immigration may indeed have been smaller than in the early twentieth century. The key indicators of demographic impact were lower in magnitude.

The rate of immigration was 60 percent smaller and fertility rates of immigrants were probably no greater. The immigrants in the postrestrictionist era possessed skills and qualities that helped them integrate with the host society, in part because of the effects of selective policies toward family reunification and occupation. Many post-1965 newcomers arrived in families or joined them and thus reinforced social, communal, and institutional stability. A large contingent consisted of skilled and educated workers who contributed to a technological economy. An even higher number, drawn mostly from the West Indies, Haiti, Mexico, and other Latin American nations, dominated occupations in the fast-expanding service sector of the economy. Post-1965 immigrants arrived with a greater previous knowledge of American institutions and culture; many had advanced premigration training and schooling allowing them to learn English, job skills, and the requirements for naturalization faster. Indeed, many empirical studies of the social mobility and acculturation of immigrants arriving after 1965 showed that they were moving gradually toward convergence with the position of the native white population.[62]

After 1965, government expanded public services and welfare assistance that helped impoverished newcomers and even undocumented aliens adjust. Congress established a mechanism for normalizing the status of the latter. The growth of ethnic tolerance and antidiscrimination kept arenas for assimilation such as education, the mass media, and intermarriage more open to post-1965 immigrants than they were to their counterparts earlier in the century. Throngs of poor and uneducated newcomers came as they had earlier in the century, but unlike their predecessors they entered a welfare state that smoothed the difficult transition process. American government expanded the nation's instruments for the absorption of immigrants in the decades after the 1960s.

American society in the twentieth century never lost its cohesion despite the unparalleled size and diversity of immigration. The dynamics of economic and social integration produced a flexible and stable social structure. Because mass culture encouraged consumer choice and individual pursuit of lifestyle, persons of dissimilar origins joined together in an inclusive, open, and shared cultural fabric. These common bases of experience supplied order and unity to the American immigrant nation.

NOTES

[1] Marvin Gottlieb, "Bubble and Trouble in New York's Venerable Melting Pot," *New York Times,* 29 August 1991, p. B1.

[2] Dino Cinel, *From Italy to San Francisco: The Immigrant Experience* (Stanford: Stanford

University Press, 1982), pp. 10–13; Diane Ravitch, *The Schools We Deserve: Reflections on the Educational Crises of Our Times* (New York: Basic Books, 1985), pp. 128–29; Peter Skerry, *Mexican Americans: The Ambivalent Minority* (New York: The Free Press, 1993), pp. 28–29, 355–58.

[3] Richard Brown and Herbert Bass, *One Flag, One Land* (Morristown, N.J.: Silver Burdett, 1985), p. 449; John Horton, "The Politics of Diversity in Monterey Park, California," in Louise Lamphere, ed., *Structuring Diversity: Ethnographic Perspectives on the New Immigration* (Chicago: University of Chicago Press, 1992), p. 240.

[4] Oscar and Mary Handlin, *The Dimensions of Liberty* (Cambridge: Harvard University Press, 1961), pp. 130–31.

[5] Arthur Mann, *La Guardia: A Fighter against His Times, 1882–1933* (Chicago: University of Chicago Press, 1959), p. 21.

[6] Aiji Tashiro in *New Outlook,* September 1934, quoted in Carey McWilliams, *Prejudice* (Boston: Little, Brown, 1944), p. 99, as cited by Roger Daniels, *The Politics of Prejudice: The Anti-Japanese Movement in California and the Struggle for Japanese Exclusion* (Berkeley: University of California Press, 1962), p. 14.

[7] Stephen S. Fugita and David J. O'Brien, *Japanese American Ethnicity: The Persistence of Community* (Seattle: University of Washington Press, 1991), pp. 47–62, chs. 6–9; Richard D. Alba, *Ethnic Identity: The Transformation of White America* (New Haven: Yale University Press, 1990), pp. 4–21.

[8] Andrew Dawson, "The Paradox of Dynamic Technological Change and the Labor Aristocracy in the United States, 1880–1914," *Labor History* 20 (1979): pp. 334–35; Reed Ueda, "The High School and Social Mobility in a Streetcar Suburb," *Journal of Interdisciplinary History* 14 (1984): 751–71.

[9] Kenneth T. Jackson, *Crabgrass Frontier: The Suburbanization of the United States* (New York: Oxford University Press, 1985); Matthew Edel, Elliott D. Sclar, and Daniel Luria, *Shaky Palaces: Homeownership and Social Mobility in Boston's Suburbanization* (New York: Columbia University Press, 1984); Sam B. Warner, Jr., *Streetcar Suburbs: The Process of Growth in Boston, 1870–1900* (Cambridge: Harvard University Press, 1962); Handlin, *The Dimensions of Liberty,* pp. 145–54.

[10] Handlin, *The Dimensions of Liberty,* pp. 142–44; Reed Ueda, *Avenues to Adulthood: The Origins of the High School and Social Mobility in an American Suburb* (Cambridge: Cambridge University Press, 1987).

[11] Ivan H. Light, *Ethnic Enterprise in America: Business and Welfare among Chinese, Japanese, and Blacks* (Berkeley: University of California Press, 1972), chs. 1–5; Stephan Thernstrom, *The Other Bostonians: Poverty and Progress in the American Metropolis, 1880–1970* (Cambridge: Harvard University Press, 1973), pp. 136–37; Ivan Light and Edna Bonacich, *Immigrant Entrepreneurs: Koreans in Los Angeles, 1965–1982* (Berkeley: University of California Press, 1988), ch. 6; Philip Kasinitz, *Caribbean New York: Black Immigrants and the Politics of Race* (Ithaca: Cornell University Press, 1992), pp. 68–70; Thomas Muller, *Immigrants and the American City* (New York: New York University Press, 1992), pp. 126–36; Roger Daniels, *Asian America: Chinese and Japanese in the United States since 1850* (Seattle: University of Washington Press, 1988), pp. 74–81, 157–61.

[12] Vernon M. Briggs, Jr., "Employment Trends and Contemporary Immigration Policy," in Nathan Glazer, ed., *Clamor at the Gates: The New American Immigration* (San Francisco: Institute for Contemporary Studies, 1985), p. 157; Muller, *Immigrants and the American City,* ch. 5.

[13] Briggs, "Employment Trends," p. 156; Jack Miles, "Blacks versus Browns: The Struggle for the Bottom Rung," *The Atlantic,* October 1992, pp. 41–68. On historic conflict between immigrant minorities and blacks, see Lawrence H. Fuchs, "The Reactions of Black Americans to Immigration," in Virginia Yans-McLaughlin, *Immigration Reconsidered: History, Sociology, and Politics* (New York: Oxford University Press, 1990); Lawrence H. Fuchs, *The American Kaleidoscope: Race, Ethnicity, and the Civic Culture* (Hanover, N.H.: University Press of New England, 1990), pp. 145–48.

[14] Thomas Sowell, *Ethnic America: A History* (New York: Basic Books, 1981), p. 5.

[15] Thernstrom, *The Other Bostonians,* pp. 67–68, 129–30; William Petersen, *Japanese Ameri-*

cans: Oppression and Success (New York: Random House, 1971), pp. 113–25; Thomas Kessner, *The Golden Door: Italian and Jewish Mobility in New York City, 1880–1915* (New York: Oxford University Press, 1977), pp. 120–26; Josef J. Barton, *Peasants and Strangers: Italians, Rumanians, and Slovaks in an American City, 1890–1950* (Cambridge: Harvard University Press, 1975), pp. 113–16; Ueda, *Avenues to Adulthood*, ch. 7; John Bodnar, Roger Simon, and Michael Weber, *Lives of Their Own: Blacks, Italians, and Poles in Pittsburgh* (Urbana: University of Illinois Press, 1982), chs. 6, 8; Nathan Glazer and Daniel P. Moynihan, *Beyond the Melting Pot: The Negroes, Puerto Ricans, Jews, Italians, and Irish of New York City*, 2nd ed. (Cambridge: MIT Press, 1970).

[16] Olivier Zunz, *The Changing Face of Inequality: Urbanization, Industrial Development, and Immigrants in Detroit* (Chicago: University of Chicago Press, 1982), ch. 13; Stanley Lieberson and Mary C. Waters, *From Many Strands: Ethnic and Racial Groups in Contemporary America* (New York: Russell Sage Foundation, 1988), ch. 5; Alba, *Ethnic Identity*, ch. 1; Will Herberg, *Protestant-Catholic-Jew* (Garden City, N.Y.: Doubleday, 1965), ch. 3.

[17] Thernstrom, *The Other Bostonians;* Barton, *Peasants and Strangers;* Kessner, *The Golden Door;* Bodnar, Simon, and Weber, *Lives of Their Own;* Glazer and Moynihan, *Beyond the Melting Pot;* Lawrence H. Fuchs, *Hawaii Pono: A Social History* (New York: Harcourt Brace, 1961).

[18] Handlin, *The Dimensions of Liberty*, pp. 147–48; Kessner, *The Golden Door*, pp. 95–99; Judith E. Smith, *Family Connections: A History of Italian and Jewish Immigrant Lives in Providence, Rhode Island, 1900–1940* (Albany: State University of New York Press, 1985), ch. 2; Joel Perlmann, *Ethnic Differences: Schooling and Social Structure among the Irish, Italians, Jews, and Blacks in an American City, 1880–1935* (Cambridge: Cambridge University Press, 1988), chs. 3–4.

[19] Peter I. Rose, "Asian Americans: From Pariahs to Paragons," in Glazer, *Clamor at the Gates*, pp. 186–210; Richard T. Gill, Nathan Glazer, and Stephan Thernstrom, *Our Changing Population* (Englewood Cliffs: Prentice-Hall, 1992), ch. 19.

[20] Sowell, *Ethnic America*, chs. 6–7; Fuchs, *Hawaii Pono*, pp. 436–41; Fugita and O'Brien, *Japanese American Ethnicity*, chs. 7–8; Edna Bonacich and John Modell, *The Economic Basis of Ethnic Solidarity: Small Business in the Japanese American Community* (Berkeley: University of California Press, 1980), ch. 15; Roger Daniels, *Coming to America: A History of Immigration and Ethnicity in American Life* (New York: HarperPerennial, 1991), p. 353.

[21] David M. Reimers, *Still the Golden Door: The Third World Comes to America* (New York: Columbia University Press, 1985), pp. 107–16.

[22] Roger Daniels, *Asian America*, pp. 75–79, 105–08, 157–58; S. Frank Miyamoto, *The Social Solidarity among the Japanese in Seattle* (1939; Seattle: University of Washington Press, 1984), pp. 16–23; John Modell, *The Economics and Politics of Racial Accommodation* (Urbana: University of Illinois Press, 1977), ch. 5; Light, *Ethnic Enterprise in America;* Ivan H. Light, "Immigrant Entrepreneurs in America," in Glazer, *Clamor at the Gates;* Clarence E. Glick, *Sojourners and Settlers: Chinese Migrants in Hawaii* (Honolulu: University Press of Hawaii, 1980), pp. 88–92; Fuchs, *Hawaii Pono*, pp. 100–01, 122–23; Illsoo Kim, *New Urban Immigrants: The Korean Community in New York* (Princeton: Princeton University Press, 1981), ch. 4; Bonacich and Modell, *Economic Basis*, ch. 3; Ivan Light and Edna Bonacich, *Immigrant Entrepreneurs*, ch. 11; Alejandro Portes and Ruben Rumbaut, *Immigrant America: A Portrait* (Berkeley: University of California Press, 1990), Table 10, p. 76.

[23] Herbert R. Barringer, Robert W. Gardner, and Michael J. Levin, *Asians and Pacific Islanders in the United States* (New York: Russell Sage Foundation, 1993), p. 9; U.S. Civil Rights Commission, *The Economic Status of Americans of Asian Descent: An Explanatory Investigation* (Washington, D.C.: U.S. Commission on Civil Rights, 1988); Gill, Glazer, and Thernstrom, *Our Changing Population*, Table 19-8, p. 341.

[24] Michael J. Piore, *Birds of Passage: Migrant Labor and Industrial Societies* (Cambridge: Cambridge University Press, 1979), ch. 3.

[25] Frank D. Bean and Marta Tienda, *The Hispanic Population of the United States* (New York: Russell Sage Foundation, 1987), Table 6.13, p. 198.

[26] Ibid., Table 3.6, p. 92.

[27] Portes and Rumbaut, *Immigrant America*, Table 9, p. 74; Frank Bonilla and Ricardo Campos, "A Wealth of Poor: Puerto Ricans in the New Economic Order," *Daedalus* 110 (1981); pp. 133–76;

A. J. Jaffe, Ruth M. Cullen, and Thomas D. Boswell, *Spanish Americans in the United States: Changing Demographic Characteristics* (New York, 1976), pp. 60, 66, 421; Bean and Tienda, *The Hispanic Population,* Table 6.13, p. 198; Paul Cowan and Rachel Cowan, "For Hispanos It's Still the Promised Land," *New York Times,* 22 June 1975; Linda Chavez, *Out of the Barrio: Toward a New Politics of Hispanic Assimilation* (New York: Basic Books, 1991), pp. 122–25, 139–51.

[28] Margaret Katzin, "'Partners': An Informal Savings Institution in Jama...," *Social and Economic Studies* 8 (1959): pp. 436–40; Reed Ueda, "West Indians," in Stephan Thernstrom, ed., *Harvard Encyclopedia of American Ethnic Groups* (Cambridge: Harvard University Press, 1980), Table 1; Virginia Dominguez, *From Neighbor to Stranger: The Dilemmas of Caribbean Peoples in the United States* (New Haven: Yale University Press, 1975); Kasinitz, *Caribbean New York,* pp. 68–70, 93–95, 101–02; Sowell, *Ethnic America,* pp. 219–20.

[29] Kasinitz, *Caribbean New York,* pp. 103–05; Reimers, *Still the Golden Door,* p. 149; Nancy Foner, "The Jamaicans: Race and Ethnicity among Migrants in New York City," in Nancy Foner, ed., *New Immigrants in New York* (New York: Columbia University Press, 1987), p. 200.

[30] Bean and Tienda, *The Hispanic Population,* Table 3.1, Figure 10.1, pp. 59, 342; Thomas Muller and Thomas J. Espenshade, *The Fourth Wave: California's Newest Immigrants* (Washington, D.C.: Urban Institute Press, 1985), ch. 4.

[31] Peter Kwong, *The New Chinatown* (New York: Hill and Wang, 1987), pp. 25–33, 62–70; Gill, Glazer, and Thernstrom, *Our Changing Population,* Table 19–8, p. 341.

[32] Thernstrom, *The Other Bostonians,* p. 231; Alexander Keyssar, *Out of Work: The First Century of Unemployment in Massachusetts* (Cambridge: Cambridge University Press, 1986), chs. 3–5; Robert M. Jiobu, *Ethnicity and Assimilation: Blacks, Chinese, Filipinos, Japanese, Koreans, Mexicans, Vietnamese, and Whites* (Albany: State University of New York Press, 1988), pp. 84–97, 104–05.

[33] Donald Horowitz and Gerard Noiriel, eds., *Immigrants in Two Democracies: French and American Experience* (New York: New York University Press, 1992), Introduction, p. 26;

[34] Lieberson and Waters, *From Many Strands,* pp. 110–16; Stanley Lieberson, *A Piece of the Pie: Blacks and White Immigrants since 1880* (Berkeley: University of California Press, 1980), Tables 7.1 and 7.2, pp. 163–64.

[35] Bean and Tienda, *The Hispanic Population,* Tables 8.1, 8.2, pp. 234, 238; Gill, Glazer, and Thernstrom, *Our Changing Population,* Table 19-7, p. 340.

[36] Barringer, Gardner, and Levin, *Asians and Pacific Islanders,* pp. 165–66; Tamara Hareven, *Family Time and Industrial Time: The Relationship between the Family and Work in a New England Industrial Community* (Cambridge: Cambridge University Press, 1982), pp. 105–8, 189–94; Ueda, *Avenues to Adulthood,* pp. 101–18; Perlmann, *Ethnic Differences,* pp. 203–4; U.S. Bureau of the Census, *Chinese and Japanese in the United States,* Bulletin 127 (Washington, D.C.: U.S. Government Printing Office, 1914), Table 40, p. 17.

[37] George J. Borjas, *Friends or Strangers: The Impact of Immigrants on the U. S. Economy* (New York: Basic Books, 1990), pp. 45–46.

[38] Guillermina Jasso and Mark R. Rosenzweig, *The New Chosen People: Immigrants in the United States* (New York: Russell Sage Foundation, 1990), ch. 10; Portes and Rumbaut, *Immigrant America,* Tables 25 and 26, pp. 192, 194.

[39] Jasso and Rosenzweig, *The New Chosen People,* ch. 8.

[40] Oscar Handlin, "Education and the European Immigrant, 1820–1920," in Bernard J. Weiss, ed., *American Education and the European Immigrant, 1840–1940* (Urbana: University of Illinois Press, 1982), p. 14.

[41] Nancy Faires Conklin and Margaret A. Lourie, *A Host of Tongues: Language Communities in the United States* (New York: Free Press, 1983), Table 4, p. 54; Jasso and Rosenzweig, *The New Chosen People,* p. 336; Barringer, Gardner, and Levin, *Asians and Pacific Islanders,* Table 6.8, p. 186.

[42] Barringer, Gardner, and Levin, *Asians and Pacific Islanders,* pp. 182–87; Portes and Rumbaut, *Immigrant America,* Tables 26, 27, pp. 192–97.

[43] Fuchs, *Hawaii Pono,* pp. 278, 282–83.

[44] Portes and Rumbaut, *Immigrant America,* Table 31, p. 208.

[45] Lothrop Stoddard, *The Revolt against Civilization: The Menace of the Under Man* (New York: Scribner's, 1923), pp. 112–13; Niles Carpenter, *Immigrants and Their Children, 1920* (Washington, D.C.: U.S. Government Printing Office, 1927), Table 83, p. 184.

[46] Stephan Thernstrom, "American Ethnic Statistics," in Donald Horowitz and Gerard Noiriel, eds., *Immigrants in Two Democracies: French and American Experiences* (New York: New York University Press, 1992), pp. 88, 103, 105.

[47] Thernstrom, "American Ethnic Statistics," pp. 87–88, 95.

[48] Zunz, *The Changing Face of Inequality*, Table 3.6, p. 74; Bean and Tienda, *The Hispanic Population*, Table 7.1, p. 207.

[49] Bean and Tienda, *The Hispanic Population*, Table 7.4, p. 218; Barringer, Gardner, and Levin, *Asians and Pacific Islanders*, Table 3.1, p. 55; Gill, Glazer, and Thernstrom, *Our Changing Population*, Table 19-4, p. 332; Jasso and Rosenzweig, *The New Chosen People*, pp. 382–96, 410.

[50] Lieberson and Waters, *From Many Strands*, pp. 99–100; Bean and Tienda, *The Hispanic Population*, Table 7.4, p. 218; Gill, Glazer and Thernstrom, *Our Changing Population*, Table 19-4, p. 332.

[51] Ruby Jo Reeves Kennedy, "Single or Triple Melting Pot? Intermarriage Trends in New Haven, 1870–1940," *American Journal of Sociology* 49 (1944): pp. 331–39; Herberg, *Protestant-Catholic-Jew*, pp. 32–34; Alba, *Ethnic Identity*, p. 14; Leo Grebler, Joan W. Moore, and Ralph C. Guzman, *The Mexican-American People: The Nation's Second Largest Minority* (New York: Free Press, 1970), pp. 408–10.

[52] Lieberson and Waters, *From Many Strands*, pp. 6–8.

[53] Alba, *Ethnic Identity*, pp. 15, 310–13; Paul R. Spickard, *Mixed Blood: Intermarriage and Ethnic Identity in Twentieth-Century America* (Madison: University of Wisconsin Press, 1989), pp. 343–72.

[54] U.S. Bureau of the Census, "Characteristics of the Population by Ethnic Origin: March 1972 and 1971," *Current Population Reports*, P-20, No. 249 (Washington, D.C.: U.S. Government Printing Office, 1973); John Higham, *Send These to Me: Immigrants in Urban America*, (Baltimore: Johns Hopkins University Press, 1984), pp. 9–11; Lieberson and Waters, *From Many Strands*, pp. 264–68.

[55] Oscar Handlin, "The Modern City as a Field of Historical Study," in Oscar Handlin and John Burchard, eds., *The Historian and the City* (Cambridge: MIT Press, 1963); Roger Lane, "Urbanization and Criminal Violence," *Journal of Social History* 2 (1968); 156–63; Zunz, *The Changing Face of Inequality*, chs. 9–10; Warner, *Streetcar Suburbs*, chs. 4, 5; Thernstrom, *The Other Bostonians*, chs. 6–7; Bodnar, Simon, and Weber, *Lives of Their Own*, chs. 3, 6, 8; Kessner, *The Golden Door*, ch. 5.

[56] Oscar Handlin, *Boston's Immigrants: A Study in Acculturation, 1790–1880*, rev. ed. (Cambridge: Harvard University Press, 1969), ch. 4–6; Zunz, *The Changing Face of Inequality*, chs. 4, 7; Pontes and Rumbaut, *Immigrant America*, pp. 53–54.

[57] Nathan Glazer, "Ethnic Groups in America," in Morroe Berger, Theodore Abel, and Charles H. Page, eds., *Freedom and Control in Modern Society* (New York: Van Nostrand, 1954); Kathy Peiss, *Cheap Amusements: Working Women and Leisure in Turn-of-the-Century New York* (Philadelphia: Temple University Press, 1986), pp. 17–21; Oscar Handlin, *The Uprooted*, 2d ed. (Boston: Little, Brown, 1973), pp. 152–65; Roy Rosenzweig, *Eight Hours for What We Will: Workers and Leisure in an Industrial City, 1870–1920* (Cambridge: Cambridge University Press, 1983), chs. 2, 5; Couvares, *The Remaking of Pittsburgh*, pp. 111–26; Lizabeth Cohen, *Making a New Deal: Industrial Workers in Chicago, 1919–1939* (Cambridge: Cambridge University Press, 1990), ch. 2; Ira Katznelson, *City Trenches: Urban Politics and the Patterning of Class in the United States* (New York: Pantheon, 1981), chs. 2, 3.

[58] Peiss, *Cheap Amusements*, ch. 3; John F. Kasson, *Amusing the Million: Coney Island at the Turn of the Century* (New York: Hill and Wang, 1978), pp. 39–40, 50; Cohen, *Making a New Deal*, pp. 97, 157–58; Jane Addams, *Twenty Years at Hull House* (1910; New York: New American Library, 1961), chs. 15–16; Handlin, *The Uprooted*, pp. 214–28; Oscar Handlin, "Comments on Popular and Mass Culture," *Daedalus* (Spring 1960): 3–12.

[59] Kasinitz, *Caribbean New York*, pp. 57–73, chs. 4–5; Fuchs, *The American Kaleidoscope*, ch. 16; Louis Winnick, *New People in Old Neighborhoods: The Role of New Immigrants in Rejuvenating*

New York's Communities (New York: Russell Sage Foundation, 1990), chs. 3, 5, 7; Paul Cowan and Rachel Cowan, "For Hispanos It's Still the Promised Land," *New York Times Magazine,* 22 June 1975; Karen De Witt, "Washington's Hispanic Community Grows Rapidly," *New York Times Magazine,* 13 February 1978; Muller, *Immigrants and the American City,* ch. 4; Peter Kwong, *The New Chinatown* (New York: Hill and Wang, 1987), pp. 37–39.

[60] Keith Elliot Greenberg, "Letter from Flushing," *City Journal Journal* 3 (Spring 1993): 102–06; John Horton, "The Politics of Diversity in Monterey Park, California," in Lamphere, *Structuring Diversity;* Winnick, *New People in Old Neighborhoods,* pp. 164–71; Linda Basch, "The Vincentians and Grenadians: The Role of Voluntary Associations in Immigrant Adaptation to New York City," in Foner, *New Immigrants in New York City,* pp. 169–85.

[61] Walter Nugent, *Structures of American Social History* (Bloomington: Indiana University Press, 1981), pp. 112, 126.

[62] Barry R. Chiswick, *An Economic Analysis of the Economic Progress and Impact of Immigrants,* Report to U.S. Department of Labor, June 1980; David S. North, *Seven Years Later: The Experiences of the 1970 Cohort of Immigrants in the United States* (Washington, D.C.: U.S. Department of Labor, 1974); A. J. Jaffee, Ruth M. Cullen, Thomas D. Boswell, *The Changing Demography of Spanish Americans* (New York: Academic Press, 1980); Fuchs, *The American Kaleidoscope,* chs. 14–19; Portes and Rumbaut, *Immigrant America,* pp. 9–14.

5

The Immigrant
and American Democracy

THE PATH TO AMERICAN CITIZENSHIP

American government historically developed a flexible political and legal framework to accommodate the ethnic pluralism produced by mass immigration. Like the American economy and cultural institutions, it worked effectively to produce a cohesive nation for most of the twentieth century. As government expanded its role in combating discrimination, it brought increasingly fair opportunities for newcomers to rebuild their lives, thus furthering the social aspects of democracy. Beginning in the 1960s, however, the governmental framework for ethnic pluralism began diverging sharply from historic patterns, portending an uncertain future for American nationhood and democracy.

In the United States, weak and fluid boundaries between immigrant groups have been the historical key to national cohesion. Support for the principle of inclusive citizenship and nationality was the strongest guarantor of these boundary conditions. The American civic culture with its emphasis on individual rights provided a key support for the principle of inclusiveness. Another vital support came from the central historical role of immigration. The experiences of immigration, settlement, and the rebuilding of lives and communities shared by ethnic groups provided a common social foundation for a national identity that transcended group boundaries.[1]

The strength of American civic identity over group boundaries derived, in addition, from the mechanisms of the American political system that limited the ability of groups to turn government into an instrument for advancing their interests as a group. The American system rested on a federal principle that had important consequences for the struggle for power among ethnic groups. The lack of political centralization meant that ethnic politics usually resided within local networks and operated through the historic regional constellations of groups: the Japanese vied for power with the Chinese in Honolulu, the Irish and Italians clashed in Boston, Mexicans and blacks jostled for control in Los Angeles. Because group politics was compartmentalized locally, it was difficult for interethnic struggles to penetrate the arena of national government.[2]

Ethnic identities that could not be salient in the framing of national policy could achieve enormous political resonance in local government. The phenomenon of the big-city political machine sprang from the local power of ethnic solidarity and leadership. The machine took care of its loyal partisans by providing jobs, welfare, and a voice for their aspirations. The leadership style of the "pol"—the nickname for machine politician—was a curious blend of feudal lordship and democratic pandering. Boston's James Michael Curley, "Hiz Honor, the Mayor," and George Washington Plunkitt of New York's Tammany Hall nakedly affected the air of royalty, but the masses were willing to defer to the pol who served their needs as a kind of paternalistic sovereign. For the immigrant, American democracy was not inconsistent with a quasi-aristocratic cult of political personality.[3]

From the first Irish voters in antebellum Boston to the Mexican voters in San Antonio of the 1990s, the urban machine would become the most useful and direct embodiment of American democracy for the immigrant masses. The Irish pol of the nineteenth century paved the way for subsequent immigrant power brokers to be elected to city hall; early in the twentieth century, they would be Italian, Polish, Jewish, and Greek; in the late twentieth century, in the multicultural immigrant cities of Los Angeles, Miami, and New York, they were Mexican, Chinese, Puerto Rican, and West Indian. As the succession of immigrant waves swept over the country, federalism functioned as a safety valve that let out group impulses to power locally where ethnic organization keyed political integration.

The historical relation of religious organizations to government indirectly affected the relation of ethnic groups to government. As a consequence of the separation of church and state, the political system tolerated the development of ethnic subcultures and institutions based on a variety of religions. Government policy toward ethnicity basically followed the principle of disestablishment—nonsupport and nonrecognition of political status for cultural institutions.

As a result, the voluntary principle shaped ethnic institutions and communities far more than government did. State officials did not sponsor the operation of religious institutions, ethnic newspapers, language schools, and ethnic mutual aid societies. Ethnic groups had to take the initiative to establish their own language schools, churches, hospitals, cemeteries, and social welfare agencies. The ability of the group to maintain adherence to tradition depended on the vigor of voluntarism. Since no ethnic group could get government to pass laws ordering that its members abide by ethnic traditions, ethnic groups had to compete for the loyalty of the youngest generations and new members who entered the group through marriage and religious conversion. Despite the lack of government involvement in ethnic maintenance, groups were generally able to sustain and cultivate their ethnic institutions for at least two generations. The success of longer-term group identification varied according to race, cultural organization, and group size.[4]

The historic distance of government from ethnic life produced weak legal boundaries between groups. One boundary that all immigrants faced, however, was the line between the status of alien and that of citizen.

The Changing Distance
between Aliens and Citizens

Changes in the treatment of aliens have been a sensitive indicator of civic and political life for the American immigrant. Throughout the nineteenth-century era of open and unrestricted admissions, government treated aliens with tolerance, casualness, and even generosity. The need for settlers and industrial workers induced government to accept newcomers without strict qualifications for residency. States permitted aliens virtually the same rights as citizens with respect to property, occupation, education, and residency. To attract settlers, various states and territories in the South and West even granted voting rights to aliens who had filed a declaration of intention to become American citizens. The difference between alien and citizen was small and almost indistinguishable.

In the early twentieth century, however, lawmakers began to worry that immigrant aliens constituted a source of danger. The alien franchise was the first issue to awaken new concerns. In 1906, John S. Wise, a legal scholar, warned that the federal government itself was threatened by alien voting. "In many of the States," he explained, "the qualifications for electors of the most numerous branch of the State legislature are bestowed upon aliens who have made their preliminary declarations; consequently, it happens that in many instances the persons who vote for members of the Congress of the United States are not even citizens of the United States." Under these conditions, he feared that "the votes of aliens ... might ... control the action of the Congress of the United States." In 1912, Hattie Plum Williams published in the *Political Science Quarterly* a study of alien voting in Lancaster County, Nebraska. She reported that "the great majority of declarations made in Lancaster County have been the direct result of inducements from political campaigners." She noted, "Some one had an ax to grind ... [and] got the foreigner to turn the grindstone awhile." Although "the lax enforcement of a lax law" was a serious problem, Williams warned that it could produce the even greater threat of encouraging aliens not to acquire citizenship. She stressed,

If a marriage license gave to the contracting parties the chief privileges of the married state, how many would visit the minister or judge, secure witnesses and pay the marriage fee? . . . And so with the foreigner. The mere declaration of intention is vested with the sanctity of citizenship by the state. What more should the alien desire?[5]

Scholars and policymakers agreed that alien status had to be compartmentalized as separate and inferior to preserve citizenship and the proper distribution of its rights and obligations. Alien suffrage could no longer be tolerated in a nation state facing modern security dangers. During World War I, for instance, some states feared that alien suffrage would permit enemy aliens to influence government. Thus, in the war years and afterward, the remaining states with alien suffrage amended their constitutions to abolish it. In fact, the historic tradition of overlapping rights for both aliens and citizens appeared incongruous in a time when the new immigrants appeared to be less qualified for membership in American civil society and for participation in the arenas of opportunity. The separation of the status of aliens and citizens had to be made categorical and functional.[6]

The derogation of alien rights also occurred in the area of the male alien's opportunity for marriage to a native. A congressional act of 1907 ordered "that any American woman who marries a foreigner shall take the nationality of her husband." By making it impossible for a male alien to marry without penalizing a spouse with denaturalization, this law indirectly reduced his opportunity to marriage. This law was a corollary of a legal precedent affirmed in 1855 that an alien wife acquired the citizenship of her American husband. Moreover, federal courts found in *In re Rionda* (1908) and *United States v. Cohen* (1910) that an American woman who lost her citizenship by marriage to an alien was not eligible for naturalization because of the general principle that the nationality of the wife was determined by that of her husband. Thus, if a former female citizen who married an alien wished to regain her citizenship, her husband had to naturalize first. Penalizing marriages between male aliens and female citizens through denaturalization of female spouses was finally abolished in 1922 by the Cable Act, which granted "independent citizenship for married women." Henceforward, no female citizen could lose her citizenship by marriage to an alien and no alien woman could acquire citizenship by marriage to an American citizen or by the naturalization of her husband. All alien women had to apply for naturalization independently to obtain citizenship.[7]

The movement toward compartmentalizing alienage was expressed in municipal actions to limit aliens' right to work. The fear of alien competition and social influence lay behind these measures. According to the federal Supreme Court decision in *Barbier v. Connolly* (1885), a state could enact laws that discriminated against all aliens as a class or against certain classes of aliens, such as those who were ineligible for citizenship, without violating the equal protection clause of the Fourteenth Amendment. The legitimacy of anti-alien restrictions on employment also derived from the police powers of state governments to regulate morals and resources. In the early twentieth century, some states used their police power to deny aliens licenses for use of natural resources, fish, and game. Municipalities took steps to exclude aliens from public works employment. The city of Fall River, Massachusetts, refused in 1923 to hire aliens in the street department. In the 1930s, eighteen states imposed some type of restriction on the acquisition of property by aliens; fifteen states placed limits on the amount of property they could hold and the duration of ownership. Various forms of commercial licensing came to reflect the derogation of alien rights. In 1924, the New York State judiciary upheld a law preventing the issuance of licenses to aliens to sell soft drinks. A Cincinnati municipal ordinance denied aliens licenses to operate poolrooms. An alien plaintiff challenged this law before the U.S. Supreme Court in 1927, claiming that his Fourteenth Amendment rights had been violated. The Court, however, upheld the ordinance, reasoning that because of their unfamiliarity with the laws and customs of this country, alien proprietors of pool halls were more likely than natives to allow their establishment to cause public nuisances. Almost all states banned aliens from the legal profession. Many excluded aliens from architecture, engineering, surveying, medicine, dentistry, optometry, and other health professions. The states with the most anti-alien statutes tended to be those with the largest concentrations of aliens, but even far western states with few aliens passed such laws to bar them from use of natural resources. Government allowed private enterprises to refuse to hire aliens. Some department stores in eastern cities excluded aliens from qualification for most of their positions. Industrial labor organizations also excluded aliens from their ranks and consequently from entry positions in various blue-collar fields.[8]

States used the status of "aliens ineligible for citizenship" to restrict rights to opportunity for Asian immigrants. In the late nineteenth century, even before the restructionist era, state and local government in California experimented with a variety of laws limiting the economic activity of Chinese aliens. Discriminatory laws against "aliens incapable of becoming electors" were considered legally valid since the interests of those aliens were so marginal as to warrant treatment different from that accorded to aliens eligible for naturalization. A California law of 1913 barred aliens ineligible for citizenship from purchasing or transmitting land for commercial agricultural purposes. The effect of the law was to exclude Asians, especially Japanese aliens, from the market for agricultural land. By the 1930s, nine states, mostly in the West, where the Asian populations were largest, prohibited ineligible aliens from purchasing real property.[9]

The boundary between alien and citizen was sharpest for Asian immigrants. The ban on their naturalization placed them completely and permanently outside the civic tradition of individual and voluntary allegiance. Denial of American citizenship to Asian immigrants set them apart from all other immigrants by cutting them off entirely from American nationality. The original immigrant generation of Chinese and Japanese had to establish the basis for group life in a separate compartment as state and local governments restricted the employment, welfare, residency, and property rights of Asian aliens. The status of "aliens ineligible for citizenship" reinforced the boundaries of race, generation, and class.[10]

The permanent alienage of Asian immigrants had important consequences. Asian immigrants could neither gain access to industrial jobs controlled by nativist labor organizations such as the American Federation of Labor nor achieve a role in the politics of democracy. In the Chinese and Japanese community, mobilization into mass party politics was slowed by the absence of a first-generation electorate. In addition, Asian aliens were deprived of an important safety valve because they could not remove the stigma of alien identity by gaining naturalized citizenship. Because the Issei, the foreign-born first generation of Japanese Americans, could not remove the formal ties of loyalty to and association with Japanese sovereignty, they were more vulnerable to suspicions of disloyalty. At the same time, they could not formally affirm their Americanism and American loyalties. This was highly problematic at the time of international crisis during World War II, when the plight of Japanese Americans was exacerbated by xenophobic reactions to their alienage. During the war the Issei and their children, the Nisei, who were citizens but were regarded as children of an "enemy" race, were evicted without due process from their homes on the West Coast and interned in relocation camps.[11]

The effort of government to separate aliens and citizens also affected the status of Mexican Americans. The Mexican American population included an exceptionally high number of aliens. Two conditions affected the extent of alienage. First, Mexican immigrants naturalized at a slow rate, probably because many were transient migrants and had difficulty becoming proficient in English. Second, the guest worker program that brought *braceros* to work as migrant farm laborers produced a large pool of aliens who were not part of American civil society. Some authorities tended to deal with Mexicans as a special class of aliens. During the Great Depression, officials pressured Mexicans to return to Mexico to remove them from welfare support; in the process, they sent back legally resident aliens fully entitled to stay. *Braceros* who stayed after their contracts expired and those who chose illegal entry to avoid the formalities of quota admissions added another large contingent of aliens to the Mexican American population. Mexican American citizens and legal aliens feared they might suffer from discrimination in employment and other areas of opportunity because of uncertainty about their legal status.[12]

After World War II, the abolition of racial restrictions on naturalization ushered in a new era when the status of aliens drew closer to that of citizens. Indeed, the civil rights movement and the drive to rescind discriminatory admissions policies in the 1960s indirectly expanded the civil rights of aliens. Aliens received more powerful and versatile rights in gaining admissions for immediate and extended relatives. By the 1980s, aliens qualified for unprecedented levels of support and adjustment services through state welfare programs. In the areas of employment and schooling pursued by aliens, differences between their opportunities and those of native citizens shrank and were often nearly equalized. Scholars who analyzed the conditions for immigrant assimilation began to point out that with the expansion and protection of alien rights, the only important status difference remaining between aliens and citizens was the vote. But even there, efforts were under way in the 1980s to equalize the rights of aliens and citizens. The Mexican American Legal Defense and Education Fund advocated suffrage rights for aliens. Whereas nineteenth-century traditions of alien suffrage rested on the need to attract settlers to territories, the new call for the alien franchise was aimed at heightening the power of Hispanic minorities.

Government showed rising interest in increasing opportunities to bridge the gap between alien and citizen through naturalization. The Senate Subcommittee on Immigration and Naturalization Policy studied the feasibility of reducing the minimum residential requirement for naturalized citizenship. In the late twentieth century, the historical pendulum had swung back toward a contraction of the distance between aliens and citizens.[13]

Naturalization of Aliens

For all aliens, naturalization became an increasingly important right in the early twentieth century. Its utility increased as the rights of aliens were gradually withdrawn and restricted. More immigrants realized that naturalization was becoming necessary to claim rights to opportunity and gain full membership in American society. Naturalization offered the opportunity to declare and affirm symbolically American national identity, an important advantage during times of war and international conflict when nativism and xenophobia spread. William S. Bernard, a student of American immigration, noted in 1950 that naturalization was "a significant index of the integration of the foreign born into American life."[14]

Yearly naturalization totals followed a cycle that differed in subtle and significant ways from the course of annual immigration. It rose with the onset of the New Immigration in the early twentieth century and peaked at times when external events made aliens anxious about their status, during World War I and the 1920s when the government established restrictive quotas (Figure 5.1). Naturalizations reached a historic high point during World War II. Annual naturalizations plummeted to the lowest level of the century after the war, jumped in the years after the first refugee acts (1948, 1950, 1953), and then gradually returned in the 1970s to the levels of 1910–1930.

In his inimitable style, President Theodore Roosevelt described his vision of voluntary and homogeneous American identity. He announced that immigrants could become American citizens, equal to all others, by an act of will and individual decision. Furthermore, he repudiated any distinction implying that natives were better Americans than naturalized immigrants.

There is no room in this country for hyphenated Americanism. When I refer to hyphenated Americans, I do not refer to naturalized Americans. Some of the very best Americans I have ever known were naturalized Americans, Americans born abroad. But a hyphenated American is not an American at all. This is just as true of the man who puts "native" before the hyphen as of the man who puts German or Irish or English or French before the hyphen. Americanism is a matter of spirit and of the soul. Our allegiance must be purely to the United States. We must unsparingly condemn any man who holds any other allegiance. But if he is heartily and singly loyal to this republic, then no matter where he was born, he is just as good an American as anyone else.

　　　　　　　　—Theodore Roosevelt, "Americanism," address to the
　　　　　　　　Knights of Columbus, New York City, 1915

Source: Arthur Mann, *Immigrants in American Life,* rev. ed. (Boston: Houghton Mifflin, 1974), p. 180.

Figure 5.1.   Persons Naturalized by Provision of Law, 1908–1990

Naturalization rates tended to peak in troubling political times when aliens were most anxious about their status. Otherwise, they have tended to be high when immigration itself was high.

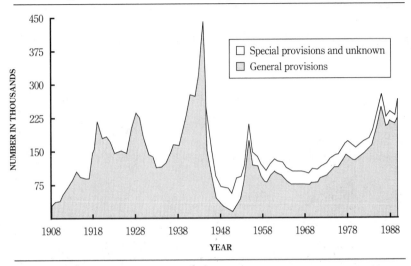

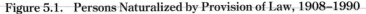

Source: 1990 Statistical Yearbook of the Immigration and Naturalization Service (Washington, D.C.: U.S. Government Printing Office, 1991), p. 188.

The character of the population being naturalized changed dramatically over the course of the century. Immigrants from northern and western Europe constituted the overwhelming majority of those gaining citizenship before the 1920s. From the 1920s to the 1940s, the naturalization of immigrants from southern and eastern Europe accelerated. After the 1970s, immigrants from the third world constituted the large majority of the naturalized.[15]

Among recent immigrant groups, Asians—Vietnamese, Filipinos, Koreans, and Chinese—gained naturalization at the fastest rate, by a sizable percentage over other groups (Figure 5.2). Moreover, Asians consistently took seven years or less, on the average, to gain citizenship, the shortest duration found among all nationality groups. Asians totaled more than 33 percent of naturalizations in the 1970s and nearly 50 percent in the 1980s (Figure 5.3).

Another significant trend since World War II has been the rising naturalization rate of immigrant women. Only since 1922, when Congress passed the Cable Act, did alien wives begin to file for naturalization separately from their husbands. Women were slow to participate in the naturalization process: prior to World War II, many more men naturalized than women each year (Figure 5.4). The pool of male aliens shrank faster and actually became smaller than

Figure 5.2.   Immigrants Admitted, 1970–1979, and Naturalizations of Those Immigrants, 1970–1990

While Asians have tended to become naturalized citizens within seven years of their arrival in the United States, immigrants from the Western Hemisphere and Europe have been more likely to retain longer their citizenship in their native countries.

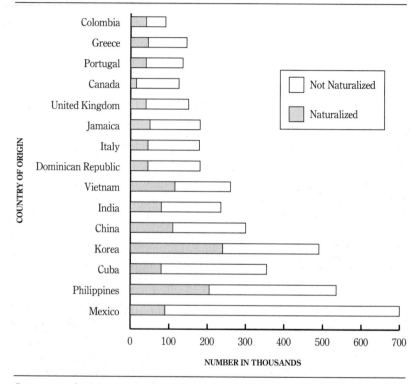

Source: 1990 Statistical Yearbook of the Immigration and Naturalization Service (Washington, D.C.: U.S. Government Printing Office, 1991), p. 141.

the pool of female aliens by 1940. But with the coming of the war, many immigrant women who had held back from naturalization decided that they would be safer during the crisis if they too became citizens. Thus during World War II, the number of women naturalizing surpassed men for the first time in history; indeed, annual naturalization totals for women rose far above the highest annual naturalization totals ever registered for men. The international crisis of war ended the time lag in female naturalizations. Alien women would henceforth be as committed as alien men to the goal of becoming citizens. From the postwar years to the 1990s, the annual number of naturalizations for men and women remained close, with the number of women slightly higher in most

Figure 5.3.   Persons Naturalized, by Decade and Selected Region of Birth, 1951–1990

From 1951 to 1970, most naturalized citizens had immigrated from Europe. From 1971 to 1990, immigrants from Asia and the Western Hemisphere were a growing majority of naturalizations, while the number of naturalizations by Europeans was much smaller than it had been.

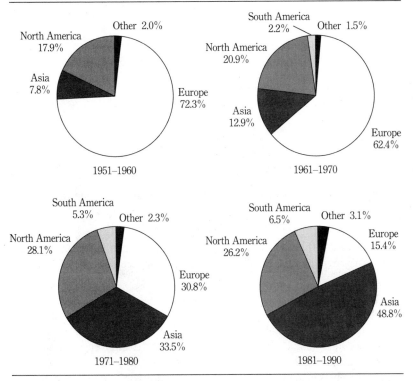

Source: 1990 Statistical Yearbook of the Immigration and Naturalization Service (Washington, D.C.: U.S. Government Printing Office, 1991), p. 139.

years. The small edge in female naturalizations was sustained by the postwar admissions pattern, in which more female immigrants arrived annually than males, thus producing a larger pool of alien women applying for naturalization.

Because naturalization was the result of voluntary achievement, immigrants used it to serve their self-interest. They saw the protections of American citizenship as a way to consolidate their personal and family security. They also wished to gain the vote. Throughout the century, most new citizens at the time of naturalization were in the early middle stage of adulthood when

Figure 5.4.   Aliens Naturalized, by Sex, 1923–1980

Because women did not naturalize independently from their husbands before 1922, there was a "catch-up" period in the 1920s and 1930s when women gradually achieved parity with men in annual naturalizations. In the years since the Second World War, more women than men have become U.S. citizens each year.

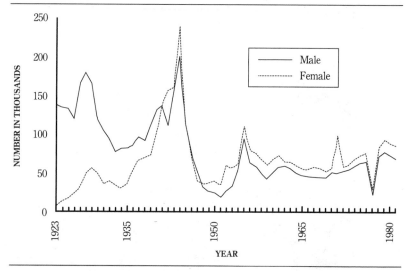

Source: Computed from tabulations of naturalizations in annual reports of the U.S. Immigration and Naturalization Service.

they were negotiating important life transitions. The individual matter of deciding when naturalization was most useful to an immigrant usually determined its timing. By being able to choose when to naturalize, immigrants could use naturalization to augment the stages of family development and to avail themselves of social and economic opportunity in a timely fashion.

These patterns of motivation and self-interest became evident in the rise of naturalization early in the century among immigrants from southern and eastern Europe. Beginning with the First Quota Act of 1921, naturalized citizens had the right to bring their nonresident spouses and children above any quota limitations. For immigrants from the restricted area of southern and eastern Europe, the right to family reunification irrespective of the immigration quota law made naturalization highly desirable. Naturalization was an important adjunct to the establishment of the family in the United States.

The political motives for naturalization, like the personal motives, changed enormously over the century. In the years surrounding World War I, nativist anxiety over the capacity of New Immigrants to fit into American society made naturalization an important political question. Advocates of Americanization felt it was the responsibility of immigrants to prove their commitment to the United States by speedily achieving citizenship. In the post-1965 era of global immigration, nativists were more concerned with the presence of illegally resident aliens rather than the naturalization of immigrants. Indeed, the forces seeking to naturalize immigrants were mainly concentrated in minority advocacy groups who saw naturalization as a necessary step toward political power. Hispanic Americans, especially Mexicans, moved to the forefront of efforts to promote the naturalization process.

Mexicans long found it difficult to mobilize their growing numbers into electoral power. Although large Mexican enclaves existed for decades, Mexican aliens were among the slowest to naturalize and thus disproportionately lacked voting rights. Many deferred naturalization because of the possibility of a return to Mexico. Others did not learn sufficient English to pass the test or feared contact with naturalization officers. Even as recently as the 1960s, only 2.4 to 5.0 percent of Mexicans eligible for citizenship each year were naturalized, compared with 23 to 33 percent of eligible aliens from other groups.

The low rate of naturalization among Mexicans was not unusual among immigrants with high rates of return or circular migration. Immigrants from Canada and eastern Europe, who had often migrated home, also historically exhibited low rates of naturalization. Transient immigrants felt it was not in their best interest to give up their nationality because it would be useful if they returned home.

Learning American National Identity

For children of immigrants, schooling was the chief formal means of absorbing official American national identity. For most of the twentieth century, educators expected students to leave behind their ethnic identities when they entered the public schools, where they would gradually assume American national identity from their studies in history, literature, and social studies. Through readings and lessons students encountered an iconology of great figures in American history who personified the distinctive values of the country. They learned about the character of American institutions by learning about the history of building a democratic nation.[16]

The schools constructed national history, ideals, and heroes as universal symbols available for adoption by all and sought to make learning about them inspirational. The children of immigrants learned about individual rights, self-government, and equality. The schools taught students to develop a self-image as individual citizens that served as the mold of national identity.[17]

By cultivating ideological identification with the nation and its institutions, the public schools introduced subjective attachments to an official culture transcending ethnic identification. In this way schooling served as a force for creating a sense of nationality, assimilating immigrant groups by substituting civic inclusion for ethnic differentiation.[18]

For most of the twentieth century, schools did not make it part of their mission to develop sensitivity to ethnic identity. In fact, educators sought to counteract the private culture of immigrant families and the public culture of ethnic neighborhoods. Indeed, these teachers were aided by textbooks and curricula that eschewed or discouraged ethnic identification. In their effort to promote an "American" style of classroom behavior and performance, some teachers were not above using intimidation. Sociologist Nathan Glazer recalled that one of his teachers derided him for speaking "like a Jewish tailor." Historian Oscar Handlin observed that the teacher "could twist the knife of ridicule" into her students since "there was so much in their accent, appearance, and manners that was open to mockery." Even classmates marginalized newcomers for their strange language and manners.[19]

Education in national identity was highly variable in style and results. Many teachers failed to inspire their students, who were often passive and indifferent. The school's role in propagating the civic culture was probably most effective among groups that sponsored prolonged schooling and exceptional learning rates such as Japanese Americans and Russian Jews. These groups also shared a distance from official middle-class social and cultural values, making the effects of schooling significantly different from the influences learned at home.[20]

Nevertheless, the classroom that focused on American national identity did help to democratize political consciousness and identity. It empowered the children of immigrants by including them in what political scientist Lawrence H. Fuchs called the "civic culture," a democratic culture of equal individual rights, popular consent, and voluntary pluralism. Ethnic students gained from schooling a new conception of their rights as American citizens that had the residual power to encourage their struggle for equality through adult life.[21]

The educational history of the children of Japanese immigrants, the Nisei, supplies an insight into how schooling served not just as a means of supervised acculturation but as an outlet for projecting and claiming national identity. The second-generation Japanese in early twentieth-century Los Angeles were regarded as outstanding scholar-citizens in the public schools, receiving high marks in academic and citizenship grades and engaging actively in the institutional programs of the public school. Many Nisei probably felt that scholastic success demonstrated their American national identity and represented initial acceptance as citizens.[22]

The extracurriculum was a set of institutional programs organizing the representation of second-generation public identity. Its effects can be glimpsed in a secondary school heavily attended by the children of Japanese immigrants, Honolulu's McKinley High School (nicknamed "Tokyo High School"), in the 1920s. Student body elections and officeholding acquainted students with the mechanisms of democratic government, while student service and activities groups created vehicles for civic activism. The Japanese American editors of *The Pinion,* the student weekly of McKinley High School, wove the rhetoric of official Americanism into their editorials and stories, expounding from time to time on American ideals and symbolic role models such as Abraham Lincoln and George Washington. Student writers clarified the civic meaning of school elections, activity programs, and athletics for their student readers.[23]

The persistent residual effects of civic socialization in the schools was illustrated by the movement of the Nisei electorate into mass party politics in Hawaii, which was galvanized by a living democratic vocabulary learned in the schools. Sympathetic teachers had urged their Nisei students to work toward assuming leadership in a more democratic future. Masayuki "Spark" Matsunaga, who became a U.S. senator, recalled how his high school civics teacher had encouraged him to aspire toward representing Hawaii in Congress.[24]

National identity learned in school was used to assert the rights of the second generation in a climate of ethnic prejudice. The ethnic defense organization formed in 1930 as the Japanese American Citizens' League (JACL) used the learned vocabulary of democracy in its public relations. Its creed, written by the pioneer JACL organizer, Mike Masaoka, read before the U.S. Senate on May 9, 1941, and printed in the *Congressional Record,* announced:

> I am proud that I am an American Citizen of Japanese ancestry, for my very background makes me appreciate more fully the wonderful advantages of this Nation. I believe in her institutions, ideals and traditions; I glory in her heritage; I boast of her history; I trust in her future. She has granted me liberties and opportunities such as no individual enjoys in this world today. She has given me an education befitting kings.[25]

This type of second-generation nationalist rhetoric can be seen as a call for ethnic inclusion and equality. "I am firm in my belief," Masaoka stated, "that American sportsmanship and attitude of fair play will judge citizenship and patriotism on the basis of action and achievement, and not on the basis of physical characteristics." The JACL creed was predicated on a democratic faith in universal and egalitarian standards and defined empowerment in terms of the expansion of the national identity of the individual.

The function of national identity in the public self-representation of the Nisei raises broader possibilities for understanding the experiences of different groups. For example, the JACL creed possessed parallels to the concluding tributes to American democracy in *The Promised Land* (1912), the autobiography of the Russian Jewish immigrant Mary Antin. Both Masaoka and Antin (who celebrated the public school scholar as citizen) projected their national identity by accepting and appreciating the gift of an American civic culture of opportunity. From a vantage point in a Boston tenement far away from the Little Tokyos of the Pacific coast, Antin declared how her life

> traced the way an immigrant child may take from the ship through the public schools, passed on from hand to hand by the ready teachers; through free libraries and lecture halls, inspired by every occasion of civic consciousness; dragging through the slums the weight of private disadvantage, but heartened for the effort by public opportunity . . . seeking in American minds, the American way, and finding it in the thoughts of the noble—striving against the odds of foreign birth and poverty, and winning, through the use of abundant opportunity, a place as enviable as that of any native child.[26]

Though heartfelt, Antin's and Masaoka's expressions were also calculated because both wished to make clear their adoption of American citizenship and seal their claim on its opportunities. The second generation in groups whose capacity for citizenship was severely doubted, such as the Japanese and the Jews, relied heavily on the projection of national identity as a device for securing their public acceptance in American society. Moreover, to the new Americans, national identity implied an advantageous contract: if they, the second generation, ideologically embraced American citizenship and official institutional values, the nation was bound to accept them as equals.[27]

The ideological values underpinning national identity as learned in school also influenced the history of the family, for schooling taught democratic and individualist values contesting the traditional authoritarianism of families. When the Nisei learned in public school about individual equality and rights, it became hard to submit unquestioningly to the dictates of parents, grandparents, and age- and gender-privileged siblings in a traditionalist family. The ideological power of second-generation democratic rhetoric also probably drew significantly from the psychological urge of children to separate their identity from that of their parents by transferring their allegiance to the ideals of national identity.[28]

Second-generation immigrant Americans from a variety of backgrounds found the symbols of official Americanism inspiring and politically powerful. The embrace of official Americanism and national identity was consistent with the empowerment of immigrant groups throughout national history. In the nineteenth century, Irish Americans learned that public displays of patriotism defused nativist suspicions of the Irish as subversive minions of "international popery"; in the early twentieth century, Italian, Jewish, and Slavic community leaders went to great lengths to engage other members of their ethnic groups in American patriotic rituals and celebrations to counteract charges that they were not good citizens. The assimilation of American national identity by second-generation Japanese Americans was indicative of the way in which immigrants appropriated official nationalist values and ideology in developing group strategies of self-defense and the pursuit of equality. Historian Gary Gerstle has pointed out that civic education often helped European immigrant youths gain political self-consciousness and directed them toward social justice:

> They took their American civics lessons truly to heart and sought to reinterpret them in light of their own social experience. Rather than accept the equation of Americanism with political conservatism, they began to point out that poverty and inequality violated the promise of American life, and they found in American political traditions the ideals and language to legitimate liberal and radical politics.[29]

The civic education of Vito Marcontonio, an Italian American congressional representative, and Walter Reuther, the German American labor leader, helped produce their political activism, according to Gerstle. Marcontonio discovered that studying the lives of the country's early leaders and heroes at New York's DeWitt Clinton High School provided the understanding of equality and liberty that helped him combat the neglect of poor working people. Marcontonio taught citizenship courses at an Italian American community center in East Harlem to equip the immigrants with a knowledge of their rights as citizens. When he was a member of Congress in 1947, a constituent asked him how to tell his new wife from Czechoslovakia about American life. Marcontonio advised reading "the writings of Jefferson, Paine, Lincoln, and Franklin Delano Roosevelt," and especially recommended Carl Sandburg's biography of Lincoln to "give her a thorough idea of the traditions and lives of the American people."[30]

Walter Reuther's initial inspiration to lead labor unions in the automobile industry came when he attended high school in Dearborn in his early twenties. He joined a 4C club (standing for cooperation, confidence, comradeship, and citizenship), promoted by the local chamber of commerce, from which he learned that American civic values were a spur to the worker's quest for equality. Walter Reuther, like Vito Marcontonio, found the life of Lincoln especially appealing and relevant to poor working people. Reuther even refashioned the Gettysburg Address into a speech advocating reform of the economy and the elimination of poverty.

The Constitution and citizenship formed the guiding compass of group political agendas. The German philosopher of history Wilhelm Dilthey once argued that the great challenge of modern historiography was to determine how the many who constituted society were mobilized in concert by shared thoughts. Historian Oscar Handlin proposed a variation of Dilthey's assertion—that the United States early faced the key question of the modern world, how dissimilar people of different origins can act together under democratic conditions. The United States responded effectively to this problem because different peoples were unified by their adoption of the values of the Constitution. The shared pursuit of making the Constitution apply equally and fully to all people was a key aspect of the mutual endeavor of ethnic minorities intrinsic to American nation building.[31]

THE EXPANDING ROLE OF GOVERNMENT IN ETHNIC RELATIONS

Toward Equal Opportunity for New Americans

Facing ostracism as strange newcomers, immigrants organized themselves to combat discrimination and prejudice. As Catholics and Jews, as newcomers from southern and eastern Europe, the New Immigrants faced natives and Anglo-Protestants who wished to deny them fair treatment. It was perfectly legal until well after World War II to deny immigrant Americans equal access to jobs, homes, education, and, in the case of those who were not white, intermarriage. Italians, Jews, Mexicans, Chinese, and Japanese faced occasional violent assaults. Color barriers limited the rights of Asian, Hispanic, and African immigrants. In Texas, Mexicans were segregated in schools, neighborhoods, and public facilities, and, to a certain extent, Asians encountered segregation in California and Hawaii. As a result of these conditions, the political leaders of immigrant groups supported government efforts to delegitimize and reduce ethnic discrimination.[32]

Ethnic leaderships explicitly or implicitly agreed on the need for an informal mutual security alliance among all marginal groups that protected their common citizenship. Jewish and black self-defense organizations recognized a type of "domino theory" in which discrimination against one group opened up the potential for discrimination against others. According to this logic, the security of each ethnic group was dependent upon others'. Jews supported organized efforts to outlaw lynching and to provide legal justice to blacks. Blacks joined with immigrants and labor to make the pursuit of antidiscrimination an administrative function of government.[33]

From the New Deal, government gradually abandoned its traditional policy of nonintervention in group relations and institutionalized laws and programs to reduce prejudice and discrimination. The New Deal provided a leadership example for antidiscrimination by appointing Catholics, Jews, and blacks to administrative posts and by desegregating federal programs. To curb anti-alien employment discrimination, some states passed laws prohibiting certain businesses from using "nationality" as a restriction in hiring. Various states after World War II established commissions to monitor and combat acts of discrimination. Antidiscrimination had hitherto consisted of equal-access statutes and isolated judicial remedies for plaintiffs suffering from violations of protective laws. The operation of state antidiscrimination commissions superseded piecemeal and defensive legal tactics with offensive programs that were precedents for future federal antidiscrimination agencies. The commissions investigated complaints and ordered remediation for damages. Using statistical records, they monitored patterns of discrimination in employment and housing and experimented with the idea that government administration could change race relations through law and education.[34]

The assault on prejudice gained additional impetus and intellectual sophistication from the reaction against Nazism during and after World War II. Jewish self-defense organizations sponsored research and educational campaigns that treated prejudice as a psychological pathology. To the extent that scholars demonstrated that prejudice was a learned and socially constructed behavior, they uncovered the pathways by which prejudice could be unlearned and neutralized by active measures. The antidiscrimination movement expressed the liberal impulse to free the potential of individuals from irrational and unproductive restrictions.[35]

A positive vision of American ethnic history developed in the postwar decades. It sprang from the search by American intellectuals, reacting to international fascism and communism, for the roots of democratic traditions in the United States. They found that immigration had been a key to liberal and democratic pluralism. The leading social historian of the era, Oscar Handlin, envisioned a pan-immigrant nationhood in which all Americans shared a social identity as immigrants that served as the basis for American national identity. He contended that blacks and Puerto Ricans were joined with European immigrants by the shared process of migrating from a traditional world to a modernizing society. Nathan Glazer, perhaps the most influential sociologist of ethnic relations, anticipated that racial minorities would travel the path toward becoming ethnic groups taken by European immigrants and their descendants.[36]

Scholars such as Handlin and Glazer supported a form of cultural pluralism that can be called the "democratic pluralism model." They sought to chart the conditions under which a liberal government would promote ethnic pluralism, leaving individuals free to cultivate ethnic identity or to change it. While the melting pot described by Anglo supremacists in the early twentieth century

With the exception of the Indian, all Americans or their forefathers came here from other countries. This map shows where they live, what they do, and what their religion is.

stressed linear acculturation toward Anglo conformity, the democratic pluralism model eschewed Anglo conformity and tolerated all degrees of voluntary ethnic identification. The democratic pluralism model seemed more consistent with the tenets of liberal democracy because it permitted groups to determine their way of life. It worked best where the extinguishing of prejudice and discrimination against blacks, Catholics, Jews, Asians, and Hispanics created an arena nurturing tolerant and pluralistic ethnic relations. Government would guarantee equal opportunity for all people and would desist from supporting the privileges, the power, and the identities of particular groups. To the extent that these conditions could be fulfilled, ethnic pluralism in the United States guided the nation's destiny toward the realization of democracy.[37]

The Rise of Official Group Identity

In the 1960s, the Vietnam War and the evolution of the civil rights movement into the black power movement inaugurated a profound shift in attitudes toward American nationhood. Antiwar leaders and black power advocates portrayed American democracy as enduringly flawed by racism and capitalist imperialism. Minority leaderships concluded that historically rooted racism made impractical a reliance on the mechanisms of equal opportunity for individuals. They espoused an anti-assimilationist ideology based on a historical critique of American social development and institutions.

As the institutional symbol of assimilationist ideology, the melting pot

Left: Just after World War II began in Europe, public and government organizations concerned with the rights of minorities began to publicize a new formula of American nationalism. All Americans, no matter how different, had a common heritage in the immigrant experience that served as the social foundation for national identity. This pan-immigrant vision of American nationhood was pictured in a map (part of which is reprinted here) published with a handbook for refugees and aliens.

Source: The New American: The Handbook of Necessary Information for Aliens, Refugees, and New Citizens, compiled and edited by Francis Kalnay (New York: Greenburg Publishers, Inc., 1941).

became the target for wide-ranging and intense criticism. Minority activists in the late 1960s rejected assimilationist ideology as well as the democratic pluralism model. Black, Hispanic, Asian, and American Indian militants conceded that the assimilation model—the melting pot—may have worked for European immigrants, but it was irrelevant to their history of racial subjugation and marginalization. Some even asserted that the melting pot was a historical fraud designed to deceive minorities into acquiescing to the white power structure. Concurrently, spokespersons for the descendants of European immigrants began to equate the melting pot with the coerced dissolution of ethnic groups. At hearings for the federal Ethnic Heritage Studies Act in 1970, they attested to the harmful ways in which the dominant melting pot policy had stripped away their ethnic identities.[38]

As a result of these developments, a momentous change occurred in antidiscrimination policy just as the "race-blind" integrationism of Martin Luther King, Jr., was consolidating into national policy during the Great Society of President Lyndon Johnson. Minority leaders sought to expand the federal Civil Rights Acts with preferential policies called "affirmative action"—compensation for historic discrimination against the racial minority group, not individuals. Minority advocates argued that the individual rights of citizenship had to make way for group minority rights determined by racial criteria because of the inescapable power of racism. They began the process of reorganizing the political system into ethnic and racial categories with the intention of converting government from a device for maintaining individual opportunity into an arena for balancing group forces.[39]

The post-1965 black, Hispanic, and Asian immigrants arrived after the federal government established unprecedented social welfare programs to end poverty and after state governments increased their aid programs. Welfare politics connected the issue of rights for immigrant minorities with socioeconomic status. The affirmative action goal to empower minorities overlapped with the goal of welfare policies to ensure that the newest immigrants would have the support to stay above the poverty line. Aliens qualified for benefits, and even undocumented immigrants received aid to help support their American-born children. The welfare provided by the liberal state reached out beyond those who were citizens to include those without American nationality—to Hispanic, Asian, and Caribbean aliens—causing friction with taxpayers and citizens seeking welfare benefits.[40]

Engaging government actively in ethnic management unavoidably fostered the politicization of group relations. As ethnicity became officially recognized and accommodated, ethnic groups allowed themselves to be classified and managed to further the benefits to them of antidiscrimination policies. The adoption of the view that groups had discrete, separate identities contradicted the liberal tradition of inclusive civic identity in which ethnicity was incidental or voluntary. As government offered services on the basis of group identity, individual, voluntary, and heterogeneous identity became less useful.

Victimhood became the qualification for remedial awards through judicial or administrative action. Increasingly, "disparate representation" —that is, inequities in social or economic patterns—was taken as proof of historical discrimination as well as ongoing discrimination against the group. Statistically, discrimination became measurable by deviation from proportional membership in the population. By 1970, government officials decided that four major ethnic categories qualified for remediation because of their historical exclusion: Afro-Americans, Asian and Pacific Island Americans, Hispanic Americans, and Native American Indians.

Lawmakers established the rights of groups to affirmative action quotas, bilingualism in schools and society, busing of schoolchildren to ensure equity in education, minority electoral representation, and institutional representation. They constructed or restructured federal agencies to program group rights and expanded the administrative power of state antidiscrimination commissions. The net result of legal remediation through ad hoc interventions by a variety of agencies at all levels of government was the creation of official groups. The division of the nation into political blocs of preferentially empowered minorities eclipsed the integrationist approach of uniting all ethnic groups in a single legal relation to government through a common citizenship. Unlike the political climate that absorbed immigrants of the early twentieth century according to individual identities, the reorganization of the political system based on ethnic identity led to the absorption of immigrants not as individuals but as members of official groups.[41]

The radicalization of minority leadership accompanied these developments. A "third world liberation front"—a loose alliance of Afro-American, Hispanic American, Asian American, and Native American movements— emerged as the organizational vehicle of empowerment in the 1960s, particularly in California. This front was united by a racial liberation ideology predicated on shared victimization and heroic resistance to white supremacist oppression. It repudiated the liberal assumption that racial minorities shared with European immigrants a path of assimilation leading toward equality and social inclusion. Third world front adherents contended that the true position of "people of color" was properly described as a state of "internal colonialism." As a result, they studied how elements of Cuban, Maoist, and third world models of racial liberation could be substituted for ethnic assimilation through the melting pot or free pluralism.[42]

By the 1970s, minority advocates retreated from third world liberation and began a reformist program to expand society's commitment to the empowerment of official groups. They claimed that racial discrimination was not only historical but an ongoing, living reality that was structural and covert, just not as overt as in the restrictionist 1920s. Prejudice and discrimination permeated institutions, the social fabric, and popular culture. Basically, minority leadership contended that pervasive discrimination gave "people of color" a deeply rooted, "fixed" group interest separate from whites that must be protected.

But minority leaders also enunciated a positive rationale for empowering official groups. As functional political groups, minorities would police the political system to ensure that discrimination and prejudice as general social ills would be systematically counteracted for the sake of the larger good. Because of their historical and ongoing experience with discrimination, minorities were in a unique position to perform this task.[43]

Chicano activists took the lead in efforts to empower both the legal and illegal alien community. They lobbied for more government activity to provide rights, welfare, and protections to all Mexican immigrants. Some requested a return to nineteenth-century traditions of alien enfranchisement, aiming at increasing the political power of the official Hispanic category. The achievement of American citizenship was no longer paramount.[44]

The minority empowerment movement paved the way for fundamental changes in the operation of public schools. The education profession had many members who were eager to cooperate and who worked with minority leaders to transform schools into vehicles for cultivating group identities and cultures. This process began in the early 1970s when a leading educationalist announced that "America's culture is unalterably pluralistic" and another called for schools to encourage "the qualitative expansion of existing ethnic cultures" through multicultural education. Educators looked to multiculturalism as the preferred replacement to the rejected melting pot or assimilationist paradigm.[45]

From the 1970s to the 1990s, multiculturalism grew into the dominant reform movement in American schools. Although multicultural schooling was not uniform in content and often stressed ethnic differences as part of individual identity, by the 1990s many school systems supported the teaching of whole cultures and group identities. "No One Model American," a manifesto of the movement, declared that multicultural education did not stop at "awareness and understanding of cultural differences" but aimed ultimately at "cultural equality." The setting of this educational goal marked a complete revolution in the role of schools in the socialization of the children of immigrants. Whereas schools for most of the twentieth century endeavored to build a supra-ethnic identity, in the late twentieth century schools gave priority to the preservation and inculcation of group identities and cultures. The schools still taught about the shared values that underlay American national identity, but they also cultivated alternative identities and cultures. The children of immigrants as well as the multigenerational descendants of immigrants would learn that they were Germans, Koreans, Italians, Haitians, Mexicans, and Jews.[46]

The most ambitious multiculturalists urged that schools be transformed totally into a multicultural milieu. James A. Banks, a University of Washington education professor, published several books and articles describing how to reform "the total school environment in order to implement multicultural education successfully." By the 1990s Banks's views were widely accepted. The American history course syllabus for New York City schools announced, "In the final analysis, all education should be multicultural education."[47]

The institutionalization of multicultural education resonated with the emergence of official groups in the political system. The schools aimed to cultivate the identities and cultures that would serve as the building blocks for identification with official groups. In this way, multicultural education reinforced the new pluralism of functional minority groups.

The growth of multicultural ideology enabled supporters of preferential policies to move in the 1980s beyond the justification of remedial antidiscrimination policies. Advocates of preferential rights de-emphasized their former rationalization of group preferences as a temporary emergency measure of reparations. They stressed a new rationale based on the special capacity of minorities to serve as mechanisms for ensuring pluralism. By the 1980s the social good of pluralism was popularly known as "diversity." Minority advocates coupled affirmative action with multiculturalism, and the result was a practical model for managed diversity: affirmative action would ensure the social good of diversity in institutions and competitive outcomes.

Affirmative action thus complemented multiculturalism and formed a new combined ideology resting on specific axioms: First, that diversity was inescapable and predetermined. Second, that the preservation and empowerment of ethnic identities and cultures were socially beneficial. (A tacit corollary of this view was that assimilation represented a loss rather than a gain.) Third, that an entitlement system had to replace the historic opportunity system to facilitate multicultural conditions. Fourth, that racial classification and enumeration were technically required to produce appropriate (usually proportional) group representation.[48]

Despite these confident justifications for preferential policies, they became the subject of much popular disagreement and political debate. The debate intensified over the appropriateness of preferential policies for new immigrants, for women, and for historic minorities. Many ordinary citizens charged "reverse discrimination" and objected to the "my turn" rationale for preferential rights. Supporters of preferential policies often dismissed this protest as a retrograde "white backlash." However, revisionists felt that preferential policies could be reserved for blacks only, but not for Asians and Hispanics.

Among intellectuals, old liberals and new conservatives worried that preferential policies engendered self-defeating divisions in a nation with the inherent potential to unite whites and minorities through expanding equal opportunity. They pointed out that such policies heightened division, mistrust, and resentment in group relations because qualification criteria for preferential rights raised difficult questions of fairness and application. By what criteria, they asked, should a group be given entitlements, and were these criteria politically or ethically defensible? Should whites who had a Hispanic ancestor be given preferences? Should groups without a history of victimization in America such as Pakistanis and Cambodians be given entitlements? What were the grounds for urging that middle-class minorities needed or deserved preferential rights? They also worried that preferential policies would produce undemocratic tendencies, fostering the decline of citizenship and expanding the power of the judiciary, administrative bureaucracy, and racial leadership power brokers—whom anthropologist Philip Kasinitz called "ethnicity entrepreneurs"—to allocate opportunities. Scholars using a comparative method demonstrated that while producing less than satisfactory remedial results in other countries, preferential policies heightened group conflict. For these reasons, the critics of preferential policies preferred broader-based and more fundamental efforts to integrate minorities in traditional opportunity structures of education and occupational mobility.[49]

Intellectual critics were troubled that minority advocates and their allies appeared to be uncritically committed to diversity. For example, under the leadership of multiculturalists, the New York City public schools adopted an American history syllabus declaring that diversity was "natural" and "inevitable." Critics worried that as multicultural diversity became the goal of schooling, a new kind of ethnic filiopietism would replace old-fashioned Americanism, creating a new potential for anti-intellectualism, chauvinism, and identity orthodoxy as great as that which had been used in the 1920s to glorify patriotism. Scholars with an international perspective on ethnicity warned that heightening ethnic pride and consciousness could have frictional and divisive effects as they had elsewhere. Stephan Thernstrom, a historian and the editor of *The Harvard Encyclopedia of American Ethnic Groups,* expressed this concern: "As the example of Lebanon reveals so clearly, ethnic awareness is not necessarily benign and colorful. It can be enormously destructive if cultivated to the point at which a sense of the ties that bind a nation together is lost." In the wake of the Los Angeles riot of 1992 and widespread racial clashes in public schools, even the strongest advocates of multiculturalism in California began to rethink their agenda along Thernstrom's cautionary line and began to discuss the need for revisions in the established multicultural curriculum that would build more integrated and inclusive identities.[50]

Throughout history, ethnic categorization was a by-product of political, administrative, and bureaucratic projects. As a result, it was never logically consistent and produced an artificial sense of the fixed nature of ethnicity. It ascribed more importance to the characteristics of the group and less to the characteristics of the individual, thus homogenizing all individuals. During the rise of restrictionist immigration policies early in this century, the U.S. Bureau of Immigration classified European immigrants by highly abstracted categories of race to justify discriminatory quotas for immigrants from southern and eastern Europe. While the government has abandoned such racial categories for European ethnic groups, it has preserved them on the federal census for Koreans, Vietnamese, Japanese, and Chinese. Since the 1960s, preferential policies required the invention of "supranational" identities such as Hispanic and Asian, a reductionist and arbitrary formalism incongruent with the fluidity and heterogeneity of historical group life. Hispanics who were treated as a unitary racial minority included whites, blacks, mulattoes, and *mestizos*; they consisted of highly variegated ethnic and national subgroups. Asians were combined with Pacific Islanders into a conglomerate Asian Pacific group that oddly homogenized groups as different as Samoans and Koreans.[51]

These new forms of ethnic classification helped to solidify racial boundaries in oversimplified ways. Noting that ethnicity "has always been a socially constructed project," sociologists Alejandro Portes and Ruben Rumbaut cautioned about "the gap between ethnic labeling and actual reality" established as heterogeneous nationality groups from Latin America and Asia were labeled "Hispanic-American" and "Asian-American." They described the artificial character of umbrella identities produced as different groups were "defined as single entities in numerous official publications, lumped together in affirmative action programs, counted together by the census, and addressed jointly in official rhetoric." Sociologist Nathan Glazer warned about the way such artificial superclassification could harden and divide groups. Ruminating on the "hypostatization" of identities and cultures under multiculturalism, Glazer commented, "We fall into the danger, by presenting a conception of separate and different groups fixed through time as distinct elements, in our society, of making our future one which conforms to our teaching, of arresting the processes of change and adaptation that have created a common society."[52]

In contrast to the ethnic typology of preferential policies, however, immigration and naturalization policies moved away after World War II from invidious racial and ethnic classification. To be sure, episodes of exclusionary xenophobia punctuated the development of immigration and naturalization policy, but the direction over the past half-century was toward a global and cosmopolitan definition of American nationality. The United States gradually abandoned discriminatory ethnic categorization in immigration and naturalization policy after World War II. Asians who were once the most excluded from admissions and naturalized citizenship became a large immigrant element and acquired citizenship faster and more frequently than other groups. Selective principles unrelated to ethnicity determined opportunities for admission, and citizenship was opened to all races. Government protected and enlarged the rights of aliens so that, apart from voting, in many respects they converged closely on the rights of citizens.

By the end of the twentieth century, ethnic social policy and immigration policy rested on contradictory premises. The former pivoted on the principle that opportunities and rights should be distributed differentially according to fixed ethnic categories. Ethnic social policy—epitomized by preferential policies—articulated a language of difference and separateness. Immigration and naturalization policy, in contrast, sprang from the idea of the irrelevance of ethnic differences to policy. It preserved the language of unity and inclusion that historically expressed the values of democratic universalism. The divergence between these two major areas of American policymaking toward immigrant groups revealed the inner disagreement and confusion besetting the nation over the best means to achieve ethnic democracy in an era of global immigration.

NOTES

[1] The key argument for the predominance of the civic culture is made by Lawrence H. Fuchs, *The American Kaleidoscope: Race, Ethnicity, and the Civic Culture* (Hanover, N.H.: University Press of New England, 1990). For the various ways the immigration experience provided a social basis for nationhood, see Oscar and Mary Handlin, *The Dimensions of Liberty* (Cambridge: Harvard University Press, 1961), pp. 3, 27, 28, 97, 108, 134, 157.

[2] Nathan Glazer, *Ethnic Dilemmas, 1964–1982* (Cambridge: Harvard University Press, 1983), pp. 274–92; Donald L. Horowitz, "Immigrants in Two Democracies: French and American Experience," in Donald L. Horowitz and Gerard Noiriel, eds. *Immigrants in Two Democracies: French and American Experience* (New York: New York University Press, 1992); Donald L. Horowitz, "Conflict and Accommodation: Mexican-Americans in the Cosmopolis," in Walker Connor, *Mexican Americans in Comparative Perspective* (Washington, D.C.: Urban Institute Press, 1985), pp. 59–65.

[3] William L. Riordon, *Plunkitt of Tammany Hall* (1905; New York: E. P. Dutton, 1963); John Bodnar, *The Transplanted: A History of Immigrants in Urban America* (Bloomington: Indiana University Press), pp. 202–05.

[4] Handlin, *The Dimensions of Liberty*, pp. 127–32; Nathan Glazer, *Affirmative Discrimination: Ethnic Inequality and Public Policy* (New York: Basic Books, 1975), pp. 25–30; Glazer, *Ethnic Dilemmas*, pp. 126–30.

[5] John S. Wise, *A Treatise on Citizenship* (Northport, N.Y.: E. Thompson, 1906), p. 7; Hattie Plum Williams, "The Road to Citizenship: A Study of Naturalization in a Nebraska County," *Political Science Quarterly* 27 (1912): 399–427.

[6] John Higham, *Strangers in the Land: Patterns of American Nativism, 1860–1925* (New Brunswick: Rutgers University Press, 1955), p. 214.

[7] Luella Gettys, *The Law of Citizenship in the United States* (Chicago: University of Chicago Press, 1934), ch. 5; Catherine A. Bradshaw, *Americanization Questionnaire* (New York: Noble and Noble, 1944), p. 24.

[8] *Barbier v. Connolly*, U.S. Reports, vol. 113, pp. 27–32; Milton R. Konvitz, *The Alien and the Asiatic in American Law* (Ithaca: Cornell University Press, 1946), chs. 5–7; Massachusetts, Division of Immigration and Americanization, *Annual Report, 1924;* Higham, *Strangers in the Land*, pp. 300–01; Harold Fields, *The Refugee in the United States* (New York: Oxford University Press, 1938), pp. 68–72.

[9] Konvitz, *The Alien and the Asiatic*, pp. 5–6, 10–12, 157–61, 162–69, 172–74; Stanford Lyman, *Chinese Americans* (New York: Random House, 1974), pp. 70–85.

[10] Yuji Ichioka, *The Issei: The World of the First Generation Japanese Immigrants, 1885–1924* (New York: Free Press, 1988), pp. 210–54; Lyman, *Chinese Americans*, pp. 125–26; Sucheng Chan, ed., *Entry Denied: Exclusion and the Chinese Community in America, 1882–1943* (Philadelphia: Temple University Press, 1991).

[11] Roger Daniels, *Concentration Camps: North America* (Malabar, Fla.: Robert E. Krieger, 1981).

[12] Fuchs, *The American Kaleidoscope*, pp. 250–52.

[13] U.S. Senate, Committee on the Judiciary, Subcommittee on Immigration and Refugee Affairs, *Hearing on Proposed Legislation to Modify Immigration and Naturalization Requirements,* 15 June 1989 (Washington, D.C.: U.S. Government Printing Office, 1990).

[14] William S. Bernard, ed., *American Immigration Policy* (New York: Harper and Brothers, 1950), p. 100.

[15] Reed Ueda, "Naturalization and Citizenship," in Stephan Thernstrom, ed., *Harvard Encyclopedia of American Ethnic Groups* (Cambridge: Harvard University Press, 1980), Table 4, p. 747; U.S. Immigration and Naturalization Service, *Annual Report, 1945* (Washington, D.C.: U.S. Government Printing Office, 1945), Table 45, pp. 104–05.

[16] Charles E. Merriam, *Civic Education in the United States* (New York: Charles Scribner's Sons, 1934), pp. 110–11; Charles E. Merriam, *The Making of Citizens* (Chicago: University of Chicago Press), p. 211; Ruth Miller Elson, *Guardians of Tradition: American Schoolbooks of the Nineteenth Century* (Lincoln: University of Nebraska Press, 1964), ch. 6; Frances FitzGerald, *America Revised: History Schoolbooks in the Twentieth Century* (Boston: Little, Brown, 1979), p. 153; Grace Hull Stewart and C. C. Hanna, *Adventures in Citizenship: Literature for Character* (Boston: Ginn, 1928).

[17] Merriam, *Civic Education*, pp. x–xi; Bessie Louise Pierce, *Civic Attitudes in American School Textbooks* (Chicago: University of Chicago Press, 1930), ch. 12; Michael R. Olneck, "Americanization and the Education of Immigrants, 1900–1925," *American Journal of Education* 97 (1989): pp. 398–423.

[18] Frank V. Thompson, *Schooling of the Immigrant* (New York: Harper and Brothers, 1920), pp. 15–17.

[19] David B. Tyack, *The One Best System: A History of American Urban Education* (Cambridge: Harvard University Press, 1974), pp. 229–41; Oscar Handlin, *The Uprooted*, 2d ed. (Boston: Little, Brown, 1973), pp. 220–21; Nathan Glazer, memorandum to author, August 1993.

[20] For a sociocultural analysis of intensive sponsorship of education among Japanese Americans, see Allison Davis, "The Public Schools in America's Most Successful Racial Democracy: Hawaii," unpublished manuscript (Chicago, 1947). M. Kent Jennings and Richard G. Niemi, *The Political Character of Adolescence: The Influence of Families and Schools* (Princeton: Princeton University Press, 1974), pp. 181–206.

[21] Fuchs, *The American Kaleidoscope,* pp. 1–6; Lawrence H. Fuchs, *Hawaii Pono: A Social History* (New York: Harcourt Brace, 1961), pp. 129–30, 282–91.

[22] John Mills Richardson, "A Comparative Study of Japanese and Native American White Children," unpublished M.A. thesis (University of Southern California, 1937), pp. 96–100; George Haywood Freeman, "A Comparative Investigation of the School Achievement and Socio-Economic Background of the Japanese-American Students and the White-American Students of Gardena High School," unpublished M.A. thesis (University of Southern California, 1938), pp. 49–56.

[23] "Lincoln's Birthday Anniversary," *The Pinion* (McKinley High School, Honolulu, Hawaii), 12 February 1926, p. 2; "Events," "Our Student Body Government Similar to That of U.S.; Every McKinleyite Votes," "George Washington," "Let's Stand by Yoshiko," "Girl Is Awarded Lincoln Medal," *The Pinion,* 19 February 1926, pp. 1–2; "American Legion Announces Flag Creed Contest," *The Pinion,* 26 February 1926; "Errors in Speech Will Be Criminal Offence Next Week," "Editorial," *The Pinion,* 19 March 1926, pp. 1–2; "His Soul Goes Marching On!" *The Pinion,* 8 February 1927, p. 1; "Pater Patriae Nostrae," *The Pinion,* 21 February 1927, p. 1; "Freshmen, Wake Up Now," "Student Body Election Discussed," *The Pinion,* 3 May 1927, p. 2.

[24] "Spark Matsunaga: The Path to Understanding," *Japanese American National Museum Newsletter* (Summer 1990), p. 5.

[25] Bill Hosokawa, *JACL: In Quest of Justice* (New York: William Morrow, 1982), pp. 133, 279–80.

[26] Mary Antin, *The Promised Land* (Boston: Little, Brown, 1912), pp. 357–58, 359.

[27] Werner Sollors, *Beyond Ethnicity: Consent and Descent in American Culture* (New York: Oxford University Press, 1986), pp. 45, 151, 215; Marcus Lee Hansen, "The Problem of the Third Generation Immigrant," in Dag Blank and Peter Kvisto, *American Immigrants and Their Generations* (Urbana: University of Illinois Press, 1989), pp. 192–93.

[28] Erik H. Erikson, *Young Man Luther: A Study in Psychoanalysis and History* (New York: W. W. Norton, 1958), pp. 40–43.

[29] Gary Gerstle, "The Politics of Patriotism: Americanization and the Formation of the CIO," *Dissent* 33 (1986): pp. 84–92; Gary Gerstle, *Working-Class Americanism: The Politics of Labor in a Textile City, 1914–1960* (Cambridge: Cambridge University Press, 1989), pp. 10, 177–87.

[30] Gerstle, "The Politics of Patriotism," pp. 84–92.

[31] Oscar and Mary Handlin, *The Dimensions of Liberty,* p. 4; Oscar Handlin, *Truth in History* (Cambridge: Harvard University Press, 1980), p. 95; Fuchs, *The American Kaleidoscope,* Preface.

[32] Oscar Handlin, *The American People in the Twentieth Century* (Cambridge: Harvard University Press, 1954), p. 47; Konvitz, *The Alien and the Asiatic,* pp. 228–30, 231–40; Ricardo Romo, *East Los Angeles: History of a Barrio* (Austin: University of Texas Press, 1983) pp. 94, 127; Higham, *Strangers in the Land,* pp. 169, 209, 264, 295; John Higham, *Send These to Me: Jews and Other Immigrants in Urban America* (New York: Atheneum, 1975), chs. 6–9; Leonard Dinnerstein, *The Leo Frank Case* (Athens: University of Georgia Press, 1966), pp. 66–72; Roger Daniels, *The Politics of Prejudice: The Anti-Japanese Movement in California and the Struggle for Japanese Exclusion* (Berkeley: University of California Press, 1962), pp. 33–34, 49; David Montejano, *Anglos and Mexicans in the Making of Texas, 1836–1986* (Austin: University of Texas Press, 1987), pp. 122, 204, 220–34; Rodolfo Acuna, *Occupied America: A History of Chicanos,* 2d ed. (New York: Harper and Row, 1981), pp. 326–27; Fuchs, *The American Kaleidoscope,* pp. 137–45.

[33] Oscar Handlin, *Firebell in the Night* (Boston: Little, Brown, 1964), pp. 28–29; Louis Ruchames, *Race, Jobs and Politics: FEPC* (New York: Columbia University Press, 1953).

[34] Morroe Berger, *Equality by Statute: Legal Controls over Group Discrimination* (New York: Columbia University Press, 1952); Leon H. Mayhew, *Law and Equal Opportunity* (Cambridge: Harvard University Press, 1968); Jack Greenberg, *Race Relations and American Law* (New York: Columbia University Press, 1959), ch. 1; Milton Konvitz, *A Century of Civil Rights* (New York: Columbia University Press, 1961), pp. 157–79, 197–250.

[35] T. W. Adorno et al., *The Authoritarian Personality* (New York: Harper, 1950); Bruno Bettelheim and Morris Janowitz, *Dynamics of Prejudice* (New York: Harper, 1950); N. W. Ackerman and Marie Jahoda, *Anti-Semitism and Emotional Disorder* (New York: Harper, 1950); Abram Kardiner and Lionel Ovesey, *The Mark of Oppression: A Psychosocial Study of the American Negro* (New York: Harper, 1951); Higham, *Send These to Me,* p. 219.

[36] Handlin, *The Uprooted;* Handlin, *The American People in the Twentieth Century;* Oscar Handlin, *The Newcomers: Negroes and Puerto Ricans in a Changing Metropolis* (Cambridge: Harvard University Press, 1959), pp. 77–104, 118–19; Oscar Handlin, *A Pictorial History of American Immigration* (New York: Crown Publishers, 1972); Handlin, *Firebell in the Night,* pp. 88–90; Nathan Glazer and Daniel P. Moynihan, *Beyond the Melting Pot: The Negroes, Puerto Ricans, Jews, Italians, and Irish of New York City* (Cambridge: MIT Press, 1963).

[37] Oscar Handlin, "Historical Perspectives on the American Ethnic Group," *Daedalus* (Spring 1961); 220–32; Oscar Handlin, *Out of Many: A Study Guide to Cultural Pluralism in the United States* (New York: Anti-Defamation League of B'Nai B'Rith, 1964), chs. 3, 4.

[38] Glazer, *Ethnic Dilemmas,* pp. 79–93; Morris Janowitz, *The Reconstruction of Patriotism: Education for Civic Consciousness* (Chicago: University of Chicago Press, 1983), pp. 106–12; Diane Ravitch, *The Schools We Deserve: Reflections on the Educational Crises of Our Times* (New York: Basic Books, 1985), pp. 219–20; Michael Novak, *The Rise of the Unmeltable Ethnics: Politics and Culture in the Seventies* (New York: Macmillan, 1971); Arthur Mann, *The One and the Many: Reflections on the American Identity* (Chicago: University of Chicago Press, 1979), pp. 37–38.

[39] Gordon S. Wood, *The Creation of the American Republic, 1776–1787* (Chapel Hill: University of North Carolina Press, 1969), p. 577; J. G. A. Pocock, *The Machiavellian Moment: Florentine Political Thought and the Atlantic Republican Tradition* (Princeton: Princeton University Press, 1975), p. 521; Samuel H. Beer, *British Politics in the Collectivist Age* (New York: Alfred A. Knopf, 1965), pp. 17, 71, 73; Reinhard Bendix, *Citizenship and Nation-Building* (Berkeley: University of California Press, 1977), p. 91. For civil rights legislation, see Glazer, *Affirmative Discrimination,* pp. 33–76.

[40] Peter H. Schuck and Rogers M. Smith, *Citizenship without Consent: Illegal Aliens in the American Polity* (New Haven: Yale University Press, 1985), pp. 107–15.

[41] Glazer, *Affirmative Discrimination,* ch. 6; Abigail Thernstrom, *Whose Votes Count?: Affirmative Action and Minority Voting Rights* (Cambridge: Harvard University Press, 1987), ch. 9; Terry Eastland and William J. Bennett, *Counting by Race: Equality and the Founding Fathers to Bakke and Weber* (New York: Basic Books, 1979), ch. 7; Linda Chavez, *Out of the Barrio: Toward a New Politics of Hispanic Assimilation* (New York: Basic Books, 1991), pp. 131–38, 161–71; Peter Skerry, *Mexican Americans: The Ambivalent Minority* (New York: Free Press, 1993), ch. 10.

[42] Stokely Carmichael and Charles V. Hamilton, *Black Power: The Politics of Liberation in America* (New York: Vintage, 1967), pp. 2–32; Robert Blauner, "Internal Colonialism and Ghetto Revolt," *Social Problems* 16 (1969): 393–408; Robert Blauner, *Racial Oppression in America* (New York: Harper and Row, 1972).

[43] The rationale of the specialized functionalism of political corporate groups is described in Beer, *British Politics,* p. 72.

[44] Peter H. Schuck, "Membership in the Liberal Polity: The Devaluation of American Citizenship," in William Rogers Brubaker, ed., *Immigration and the Politics of Citizenship in Europe and North America* (Lanham, Md.: University Press of America, 1989); Antonio Rios-Bustamente, *Mexican Immigrant Workers in the United States,* Anthology No. 2, Chicano Studies Research Center Publications, UCLA, 1981, Introduction, pp. 177–78; Chavez, *Out of the Barrio,* p. 133; Janowitz, *The Reconstruction of Patriotism,* p. 194.

[45] William A. Hunter, editorial, *Journal of Teacher Education* 24 (Winter 1973); William W. Joyce, "Minority Groups in American Society: Imperatives for Educators and Publishers," in Jonathan C. McLendon, William W. Joyce, and John R. Lee, *Readings in Elementary Social Studies: Emerging Changes,* 2nd ed. (Boston: Allyn and Bacon, 1970), pp. 289–90.

[46] AACTE Commission on Multicultural Education, "No One Model American: A Statement on Multicultural Education," *Journal of Teacher Education* 24 (Winter 1973): 264–65; John U. Michaelis, *Social Studies for Children: A Guide to Basic Instruction,* 7th ed. (Englewood Cliffs: Prentice-Hall, 1980), pp. 199–205; Diane Ravitch, "Multiculturalism: E Pluribus Plures," *American Scholar* 59 (1990): 337–54; Nathan Glazer, "In Defense of Multiculturalism," *New Republic,* 2 September 1991, pp. 18–22.

[47] James A. Banks, "Multicultural Education: Development, Paradigms, and Goals," in James A. Banks and James Lynch, eds., *Multicultural Education in Western Societies* (New York: Praeger,

1986). Also see James A. Banks, "Cultural Pluralism and the Schools," *Educational Leadership* 32 (December 1974): 163–66; James A. Banks, "Ethnic Studies as a Process of Curriculum Reform," *Social Education* 40 (February 1976); James A. Banks, *Multiethnic Education: Practices and Promises* (Bloomington, Ind.: Phi Delta Kappa Educational Foundation, 1977); James A. Banks, with Ambrose A. Clegg, Jr., *Teaching Strategies for the Social Studies: Inquiry, Valuing, and Decision-Making* (Reading, Mass.: Addison-Wesley, 1977); James A. Banks, *Teaching Strategies for Ethnic Studies,* 2nd ed. (Boston: Allyn and Bacon, 1979); James A. Banks, with Cherry McGee Banks, *Multicultural Education: Issues and Perspectives* (Boston: Allyn and Bacon, 1989).

[48] New York State Education Department, *Social Studies Program, Kindergarten,* updated ed. (Albany: Bureau of Curriculum Development, 1988), p. 9; Heather MacDonald, "Divided Self," *Commentary* 93 (1992): 60–62.

[49] Handlin, *Firebell in the Night,* pp. 56–63; Glazer, *Affirmative Discrimination,* ch. 6; Janowitz, *The Reconstruction of Patriotism,* pp. 121–22, 128–37; Thernstrom, *Whose Votes Count?* pp. 236–44; Philip Kasinitz, *Caribbean New York: Black Immigrants and the Politics of Race* (Ithaca: Cornell University Press, 1992), pp. 176–77; Thomas Sowell, *Preferential Policies: An International Perspective* (New York: William Morrow, 1990), Part II; Donald L. Horowitz, *Ethnic Groups in Conflict* (Berkeley: University of California Press, 1985), ch. 16.

[50] See, among American Federation of Teachers President Albert Shanker's regular editorials in 1991, "Where We Stand"; "The Danger in Multiple Perspectives"; "Sacrificing Accuracy for Diversity"; "Courting Ethnic Strife"; "Don't Stop Teaching the Common Heritage"; Ravitch, "Multiculturalism," p. 340; FitzGerald, *America Revised,* p. 104. Arthur M. Schlesinger, Jr., *The Disuniting of America: Reflections on a Multicultural Society* (Knoxville, Tenn.: Whittle Direct Books, 1991), ch. 4.; Nathan Glazer, "Additional Comments," in New York State Social Studies Review and Development Committee, *One Nation, Many Peoples: A Declaration of Cultural Interdependence* (Albany: New York State Education Department, 1991), pp. 35–36; Stephan Thernstrom, "The Humanities and Our Cultural Heritage," in Chester E. Finn, Jr., Diane Ravitch, and P. Holley Roberts, *Challenges to the Humanities* (New York: Holmes and Meier, 1985), p. 77; Sharon Bernstein, "Multiculturalism: Building Bridges or Burning Them?" *Los Angeles Times,* 30 November 1992, p. A1.

[51] Stanley Lieberson and Mary C. Waters, *From Many Strands: Ethnic and Racial Groups in Contemporary America* (New York: Russell Sage Foundation, 1988), p. 15; Stephan Thernstorm, "American Ethnic Statistics," in Horowitz and Noiriel, *Immigrants in Two Democracies.*

[52] Alejandro Portes and Ruben Rumbaut, *Immigrant America: A Portrait* (Berkeley: University of California Press, 1990) pp. 136–39; Glazer, "Additional Comments."

6

Immigration
and the National Future

To tell the story of an ethnic or racial group living within the confines of the U.S. without reference to the whole of America is to truncate its identity as well as the identity of all other Americans.

—Carl Degler, 1992[1]

The creation of a nation based on the coexistence and mutual life of a multiplicity of groups hinged historically on the maintenance of weak and fluid boundaries between groups. Inclusive citizenship and nationality formed the strongest support of these boundary conditions. Reinforcement of this support came from the role of public education in socializing the children of immigrants to a shared national identity and the function of naturalization as a voluntary movement ensuring the integration of aliens according to a common citizenship. The detachment of legal boundaries from ethnic boundaries enlarged the sphere of citizenship. Government treated ethnic identity as private rights by staying out of the maintenance of ethnic cultures and institutions.

The United States, however, did not escape periods of discrimination and restriction in citizenship and nationality. The necessary support for inclusive conditions fluctuated according to the changing pressures of immigration and material circumstances. Groups who wished to impose their agendas and protect their interests from newcomers manipulated government to manage ethnic relations to their own advantage.

These efforts introduced rigidities into the subtle dynamics of fusion and integration that operated within American society. During the arrival of the New Immigrants in the early twentieth century, a nativist backlash provoked a retreat from the civic universalism of long-standing admissions policies. Congress established restrictions on admissions and citizenship based on race and ethnicity. Employers discriminated against Italians, Jews, Poles, and Japanese. Local governments sharpened the boundary between the rights of citizens and those of aliens.

As in the early twentieth century, the rising tide of newcomers in the 1980s and 1990s engendered a new movement of immigration restriction. Experts cited the depressing effects of labor competition from low-skilled and illegal immigrants on the economic status of poor black and white natives. Some new restrictionists saw immigration from the third world as a force undermining the European or Christian basis of American culture. They invoked ideas cultivated by journalists and the mass media that whites would soon be a minority. As government increased spending on adjustment and welfare programs for immigrants, citizens worried about their economic and tax burdens. The expansion of the liberal welfare state produced a ground for conflict between native and foreigner that had not existed in the first decades of the century. In hard economic times, tensions between natives and immigrants rose over the costs of welfare. Where group rights and welfare rights intertwined, or were perceived to intertwine, these tensions spilled over into racial and ethnic antagonism. From Lowell, Massachusetts, to Philadelphia to Los Angeles, natives both black and white resented Asian and Hispanic newcomers who received government assistance.[2]

In the 1980s a growing nativism expressed itself in crude and menacing forms of bigotry. Government agencies recorded a rising number of assaults and intimidation against Asians and Latinos. The new nativism had multi-ethnic and multigenerational roots. Descendants of earlier immigrants and African Americans turned to defend their turf against the encroachment of Dominicans, Cambodians, and Koreans. Poor blacks boycotted Korean grocers in Los Angeles, New York City, and Philadelphia. Black students fought with newly arriving Chicano students in rioting at Los Angeles public schools. Poor whites in Massachusetts harassed new Cambodian and Vietnamese neighbors; in Wisconsin, white natives resented the resettlement of Laotian refugees.

To achieve protection, equity, and power in the climate of ethnic change and conflict, new immigrant minorities were drawn to the strategy of the most important historic minority—black Americans—by endeavoring to pressure the government to establish more mechanisms for managing ethnic relations. Official group identity and the advocacy of group rights became widespread through preferential and multicultural policies for "people of color" in jobs, education, and voting. As in the early twentieth century, prescribed racial lines defined ethnic hierarchies. The hierarchy of preferential empowerment rights formed an inverted image of the hierarchy of restrictive rights for minorities in the early twentieth century. The domain of ethnic relations was politicized as government managed intergroup relations in ways unimaginable in the era of Americanization. Although the trend was far from complete in the 1990s, the cumulative changes in ethnic policy since the 1960s moved the United

States much closer to a kind of state pluralism, the reorganization of the nation into official ethnic groups. Ironically, by adopting the strategic claims of blacks to group rights, Hispanics and Asians became a competing factor for empowerment programs. As such they cut into the welfare of blacks, and conflict and friction with blacks escalated.

The growing power of group identity underlay all these developments. This phenomenon constituted one of the most important changes in American politics and in ethnic relations. It derived from complex and subtle cultural forces. A type of sociological determinism holding that group identity ineluctably defined the characteristics and interests of individuals gained ascendancy. A popular sense of the natural and primordial magnetism of ethnicity always existed, but after the 1960s it was modified by journalism, racial advocacy leaders, and a host of policies in the areas of schooling, jobs, and voting. But at an even deeper and more paradoxical level, the rising strength of group identity was an indirect by-product of spreading social mobility and acculturation, of historically unprecedented group mixing and boundary crossing from the large scale of integrating institutions and communities to the small scale of intermarrying families. The unmooring and transition unsettled many who were accustomed to the security of the sheltered world of fellow ethnics. The newly liberated minorities and new immigrants, unsure of their new opportunities and capabilities, sought the solidarity of the group. Natives worried by coexistence and competition with unfamiliar newcomers fended off their challenges by withdrawing into their enclaves. Ethnic empowerment and xenophobia were two faces of the same phenomenon.[3]

The rise of official group identity will probably have a significant effect on the relation between national identity and ethnic identity. It is instructive to hypothesize about these possible changes using the historian Marcus Lee Hansen's well-known three-generation model of ethnic identity. Hansen postulated that the first generation of immigrants clung to their ethnic identity, the second tried to escape from it, while the third experienced an inevitable return of interest in ethnicity. Hansen suggested that the third generation was willing to reawaken its ethnic consciousness because assimilation at that stage freed its members from the repressive stigma and burdens of ethnicity. There is evidence that this prediction was realized in the third generation of Japanese, Chinese, and Mexican Americans. This generation of immigrant minorities moved beyond the station of their parents and grandparents in a postwar climate of middle-class expansion and intergroup tolerance. They laid claims to ethnic roots and racial justice. Their political consciousness was affected by the changing relationship of the political system to ethnicity wherein racial identity became a basis for remediation and the distribution of rights under the aegis of preferential and multicultural policies—a factor unforeseen by

Hansen. Under these conditions, has Hansen's law of third generation return become more predictive? Conversely, if official minority identity has become a powerful competitor with national identity, to what extent can Hansen's law capture descriptively the course of ethnicity in the future three-generation cycle? Perhaps the second-generation weakening of ethnicity in favor of tactical and personally liberating national identity will not occur normally as Hansen found and ethnicity will have a more or less constant intensity across generations produced by a politics of particularistic group identity. Perhaps Hansen's law is historically bound, a phenomenon of an earlier polity predicated on the assimilation of national identity rather than the empowerment of official groups. A survey of children of immigrants in 1993 revealed their growing tendency to eschew assimilation and the label "American" in favor of possessing a stronger ethnic identity.[4]

In the 1990s, a renewed commitment to the positive role of fluid and weak boundaries could facilitate intergroup linkages and a new stage of shared nation building. The cultivation of supra-ethnic identities or inclusive identities will be more necessary to counterbalance the trend toward official multicultural identities in the political system. Without the former, the nation will become a disunited collection of mutually exclusive groups.[5]

Supra-ethnic identities can grow from a common civic education in a shared national identity, as in the past; but perhaps the most fundamental ingredient for crossing boundaries will come from the private forces of social mobility and cultural fusion generating integrated and heterogeneous identities, also as in the past. Government can allow these forces to work effectively by limiting discrimination yet avoiding the overregulation of ethnic relations through the machinery of state pluralism.

The fluidity, complexity, and subtlety of mutual acculturation was never easy to encase in legal and formal identities. Only by risking oversimplification was it possible to partition Western from non-Western, to separate foreign and American, or to split the mainstream from subcultures. These dualisms were incomplete distortions of a more complex reality. The interaction between the core of American society and ethnic minorities on the margin included the positive as well as negative relations between the periphery and the center. These relations occurred at the subjective level of changing identities and the objective level of social mobility. There was a reality of native domination, but immigrants and minorities nevertheless took advantage of the chances for a better living, the freedoms of democratic society, the possibilities of inclusion in an American national identity, and representation in a national culture. They anticipated change and growth, which they made part of their lives.

The newest immigrants—the Pakistanis, the Haitians, and the Koreans—are changing the melting pot, as much as the melting pot is changing them. A world melting pot *is* forming in the United States in which the question "Whose identity and culture?" is increasingly irrelevant. Harvard sociologist Orlando Patterson observed that the ever-changing American culture is owned by no particular groups. According to Patterson, "Once an element of culture becomes generalized under the impact of a universal culture, it loses all specific symbolic value for the group which donated it. It is a foolish Anglo-Saxon who boasts about 'his' language today. English is a child that no longer knows its mother, and cares even less to know her. It has been adapted in a thousand ways to meet the special feelings, moods, and experiences of a thousand groups." Patterson concluded that the "ethnic WASP culture is no longer the culture of the group of Americans we now call WASP's." Journalist Jim Sleeper recalled how a stint teaching in a New York high school showed him that "the Chinese-American students in my class were [not] interested in adopting 'white' culture as much as they were interested in becoming part of the larger 'universal' culture of constitutional democracy and technological development." The mutual acculturation of immigrants, their vision of American democracy as the best haven for cultural pluralism, their need to establish interdependency with surrounding groups, and their common pursuit of equal citizenship under the Constitution can produce a nationalizing experience revolving on voluntary and fluid indentities.[6]

In a time of worldwide nationalism and xenophobia that stress the small picture with its internal definition of life, it is evermore necessary to see the large picture in which the local is dynamically connected to a greater exterior whole. The world society arising in twentieth-century America was not divisible into truncated, static, or homogeneous parts. As people from Africa, Asia, and the Western Hemisphere made society more culturally and racially pluralistic, the potential for assimilation increased because the host milieu developed a greater diversity of absorptive factors. As new groups added themselves to it over time and as the ingredients in its core grew more varied, the similarities increased between the host society and diverse newcomers. Those who argued that they could not assimilate in a Euro-centric core and those who tried to preserve it will have to face the absorptive power of the emergent multiracial and multicultural core of a world melting pot.

Global immigration can contribute to the nation, so long as conditions of social stability are maintained that permit immigrants and natives to adjust flexibly to each other. To maintain these conditions, government must effectively control illegal immigration and reregulate admissions to correspond with changing economic and social needs. Without proper management of the influx, conditions for mutual adjustment will be gridlocked from the resultant disorder, overcrowding, and anxiety. Many Asian and Hispanic Americans have reached this view as well. The further deterioration of control could fuel an extremist nativism that will seek to restrict immigration in a very severe and unnecessary fashion.[7]

Americans have long seen their country as the land of opportunity and individual freedom for immigrants. From Crèvecoeur's *Letters from an American Farmer* (1782) to Mary Antin's *The Promised Land* (1912) to Walt Disney's *The Girl Who Spelled Freedom* (1986), this theme has been eloquently chronicled. However, fears that the United States would disintegrate through the social changes wrought by immigration have surfaced time and again. In the early twentieth century, authorities such as anthropologist Madison Grant sounded the alarm that immigration was a force dividing the nation and corroding its institutions. Fearing the decline of Anglo-Saxon social dominance, they successfully advocated ending the tradition of open admissions and nationality and began the retreat into restriction.[8]

Ultimately, nativism fell before the ascendancy of the idea that immigration held a positive role in the development of the nation. The turning points in this intellectual and ideological change were marked by the work of historians Marcus Lee Hansen and Oscar Handlin. Because their studies of immigration reflected a subtle understanding of the historical condition in the United States of multicultural diversity without central government power, they perceived the dynamic and semiautonomous character of intergroup acculturation. They viewed immigration as a source of the national ethos of liberty and individualism. Handlin's historical writings in particular formed the intellectual and ethical apex of the vision of immigration as a liberating and nationalizing force. In his work, immigration rose to a historical saga about the creation of modern identity. The immigrant American became the archetype of the individual freed from the shackles of prescribed roles by a life of movement into an alien world to discover a changing, self-potentiating identity. Ultimately, immigration helped realize the national and global destiny of the United States as the prototypical modern nation unified by the joint effort of dissimilar groups to build a new shared identity under democratic conditions.[9]

The fulfillment of this destiny was possible only insofar as the relation between the ethnic group and the nation was freely and mutually adjusting. In such a situation, the ethnic part could derive its meaning from the national whole, and the qualities of the whole were imbedded in each part. Without this interdependency, it will be hard to sustain a vision of a greater nation that is more than a collection of groups and of a greater national destiny that is more than coexistence.[10]

NOTES

[1] Carl N. Degler, "In Search of the Un-hyphenated American," *Kettering Review* (Summer 1992): 43.

[2] Otis L. Graham, Jr., and Roy Beck, "Immigration's Impact on Inner City Blacks," and Raymond Rodriguez, "Closing Mexican Border Could Be a Blessing," *The Social Contract* (Summer 1992): 215–16; John Tanton and Wayne Lutton, "Welfare Costs for Immigrants," Lance T. Izumi, "The Costs of California's Porous Borders," and Wayne Lutton, "Costs of Illegal Aliens in San Diego County," *The Social Contract* 3 (Fall 1992): 6–15, 22–23, 27–28.

[3] John Higham, *Send These to Me: Jews and Other Immigrants in Urban America* (New York: Atheneum, 1975), pp. 228–46; Nathan Glazer, *Ethnic Dilemmas, 1964–1982* (Cambridge: Harvard University Press, 1983), pp. 254–73, 315–36.

[4] Reed Ueda, "American National Identity and Race in Immigrant Generations: Reconsidering Hansen's 'Law,'" *Journal of Interdisciplinary History* 22 (1992): 483–91; "A Fervent No to Assimilation in New America," *New York Times,* 29 June 1993, p. A10.

[5] Tim W. Ferguson, "The Sleeper Issue of the 1990s Awakens," *The Social Contract* 3 (Summer 1992): 237–38; Francis Fukuyama, "Immigrants and Family Values," *Commentary* 95 (1993): 26–32.

[6] Jim Sleeper, *The Closest of Strangers: Liberalism and the Politics of Race in New York* (New York: W. W. Norton, 1990), pp. 232–34.

[7] Vernon M. Briggs, Jr., "Employment Trends and Contemporary Immigration Policy," in Nathan Glazer, ed., *Clamor at the Gates: The New American Immigration* (San Francisco: Institute for Contemporary Studies, 1985), pp. 158–60; Lawrence W. Miller, Jerry L. Polinard, and Robert D. Wrinkle, "Attitudes toward Undocumented Workers: The Mexican American Perspective," in Rodolfo O. de la Garza, *The Mexican American Experience: An Interdisciplinary Anthology* (Austin: University of Texas Press, 1985), pp. 237–38.

[8] John Higham, *Strangers in the Land: Patterns of American Nativism, 1860–1925* (New Brunswick: Rutgers University Press, 1955); Barbara Miller Solomon, *Ancestors and Immigrants: A Changing New England Tradition* (Cambridge: Harvard University Press, 1956).

[9] Marcus Lee Hansen, *The Atlantic Migration, 1607–1860: A History of the Continuing Settlement of the United States* (Cambridge: Harvard University Press, 1940); Marcus Lee Hansen, *The Immigrant in American History* (Cambridge: Harvard University Press, 1940); Oscar Handlin, *The Uprooted* (Boston: Little, Brown, 1951); Oscar Handlin, *The American People in the Twentieth Century* (Cambridge: Harvard University Press, 1954); Oscar Handlin, *Boston's Immigrants: A Study in Acculturation, 1790–1880,* rev. ed. (Cambridge: Harvard University Press, 1959).

[10] Degler, "In Search of the Un-hyphenated American," p. 43; John Higham, "Multiculturalism and Universalism: A History and Critique," *American Quarterly* 45 (June 1993): 214.

APPENDIX A

Additional Tables

Table A.1. Alien Immigrants to the United States by Age, 1868–1989

YEARS	TOTAL NUMBER	PERCENTAGE OF TOTAL		
		UNDER 15	15–40	OVER 40
1868–1870	1,022,160	22.2	65.7	12.1
1871–1875	1,726,796	21.7	64.6	13.7
1876–1880	1,085,395	18.2	70.8	11.0
1881–1885	2,975,683	23.0	66.5	10.5
1886–1890	2,270,930	19.2	70.2	10.6
1891–1895	2,280,735	13.9	79.3	6.8
1896–1900[a]	1,563,685	14.6	76.9	8.5
		UNDER 14	14–44	OVER 44
1901–1905	3,833,076	12.1	82.5	5.4
1906–1910	4,962,310	12.0	83.4	4.6
1911–1915	4,459,831	13.2	80.9	5.9
1916–1920[b]	1,275,980	17.6	71.8	10.6
		UNDER 16	16–44	OVER 44
1921–1924	2,344,599	18.5	72.3	9.2
1925–1929	1,520,910	16.3	74.7	9.0
1930–1934	426,953	17.4	70.5	12.1
1935–1939	272,422	16.3	66.5	17.2
1936–1940	308,222	15.3	66.1	18.6
1941–1945	170,952	14.4	62.9	22.7
1946–1950	864,087	15.9	66.6	17.5
1951–1960	2,515,479	22.9	63.5	13.6
1961–1970	3,321,677	25.5	60.7	13.8
1971–1979	3,962,000	26.1	59.3	14.6
1980–1989	6,332,218	19.8	64.4	15.8

[a]For 1899 and 1900, age groups were under 14, 14–44, and over 44.
[b]For 1918–1920, age groups were under 16, 16–44, and over 44.
Sources: Imre Ferenzci and Walter F. Willcox, *International Migrations* (New York: National Bureau of Economic Research, 1929), vol. 1, p. 214; U.S. Bureau of the Census, *Statistical Abstract of the United States, 1942,* p. 123; *Statistical Abstract of the United States, 1954,* p. 106; *Statistical Abstract of the United States, 1962,* p. 99; *Statistical Abstract of the United States, 1984,* p. 93; *Statistical Yearbook of the Immigration and Naturalization Service, 1989,* p. 24.

Table A.2. Distribution of Immigrants by Sex, 1831–1989 (Percentage)

YEARS	MALES	FEMALES
1831–1835	65.6	34.4
1936–1840	63.3	36.7
1841–1845	58.3	41.7
1846–1850	59.8	40.2
1851–1855	57.8	42.2
1856–1860	58.1	41.9
1861–1865	59.5	40.5
1866–1870	61.0	39.0
1871–1875	60.4	39.6
1876–1880	62.8	37.2
1881–1885	60.5	39.5
1886–1890	61.6	38.4
1891–1895	61.2	38.8
1896–1900	61.6	38.4
1901–1905	69.8	30.2
1906–1910	69.7	30.3
1911–1915	65.0	35.0
1916–1920	58.3	41.7
1921–1924	56.5	43.5
1925–1929	60.0	40.0
1930–1934	45.2	54.8
1935–1939	44.0	56.0
1936–1940	45.2	54.8
1941–1945	41.0	59.0
1946–1950	40.3	59.7
1951–1960	45.9	54.1
1961–1970	44.8	55.2
1971–1979	46.9	53.1
1982–1985	50.4	49.6
1986–1989	50.2	48.8

Sources: Imre Ferenzci and Walter F. Willcox, *International Migrations* (New York: National Bureau of Economic Research, 1929), vol. 1, p. 211; U.S. Bureau of the Census, *Statistical Abstract of the United States, 1942,* p. 123; *Statistical Abstract of the United States, 1954,* p. 106; *Statistical Abstract of the United States, 1984,* p. 93; compiled from *Statistical Yearbook of the Immigration and Naturalization Service, 1985,* p. 46; *Statistical Yearbook, 1989,* p. 24.

Table A.3. Employed Immigrants, by Occupation, 1901–1985 (Percentage)

	1901–1910	1911–1920	1921–1930	1931–1940	1941–1945	1946–1950
Professional	1.4	2.7	4.5	17.3	24.2	16.2
Proprietors, managers	2.7	2.7	3.5	15.3	15.2	7.1
Clerical, sales	1.5	a	7.0	10.6	16.7	17.5
Skilled crafts, supervisors	17.8	22.4	23.7	19.3	21.9	30.7
Farmers, farm managers	1.6	2.2	4.9	4.2	2.3	9.1
Farm laborers	24.5	27.2	8.5	2.9	1.1	1.6
Laborers	35.1	25.7	24.7	8.6	5.2	5.3
Domestics	14.1	16.8	17.2	15.0	7.8	7.5
Service workers	1.3	0.4	6.0	6.7	5.6	4.9

	1951–1960	1961–1970	1971–1979[f]	1982–1985	1986–1989
Professional	15.6	23.0	25.0	19.4	13.9
Managers	4.5	4.5	7.3	9.5	7.4
Sales	b	b	2.1	4.3	4.4
Clerical	16.7	16.7	9.7	9.2	8.4
Skilled crafts	16.6	14.1	12.2	11.5	11.5
Operatives (nontransport)	14.3	11.1	13.8	22.7	26.0
Transport operatives	c	c	0.2	c	c
Laborers	11.3	8.8	9.0	c	c
Farmers, farm managers	4.2	1.8	1.0	5.0	5.3
Farm laborers	3.7	3.9	4.4	d	d
Service workers	5.9	7.4	9.4	18.3	23.0
Household workers	8.0	8.7	5.2	e	e

[a]Combined with proprietors and managers.
[b]Sales workers included with clerical.
[c]Transport operatives or laborers included with operatives.
[d]Farm laborers included with farmers and farm managers.
[e]Household workers included with service workers.
[f]No data available for 1980–1981.
Sources: Conrad Taeuber and Irene Taeuber, *Changing Population of the United States* (New York: John Wiley, 1958), p. 70; *Statistical Abstract of the United States, 1984*, p. 93; Commissioner-General of Immigration, *Annual Reports, 1927*, Tables 96, 97. Compiled from *Statistical Yearbook of the Immigration and Naturalization Service, 1985–1989.*

Table A.4. Preference System for Visa Admissions under Quota System (1924 and 1952) and Worldwide Limitation (1965 and 1990)

Preferences under 1924 Immigration Act

1. Persons aged twenty-one or over who are skilled in agriculture and their spouses and children.
2. Unmarried children under twenty-one, parents, and spouses of U.S. citizens aged twenty-one or over.

Preferences under 1952 Immigration Act

1. Highly skilled immigrants possessing urgently needed services or skills and their spouses and children.
2. Parents of U.S. citizens over age twenty-one and unmarried adult children of U.S. citizens.
3. Spouses and unmarried adult children of permanent resident aliens.
4. Brothers, sisters, and married children of U.S. citizens and accompanying spouses and children.
5. Applicants not entitled to preceding preferences.

Preferences under 1965 Immigration Act

1. Unmarried adult children of U.S. citizens.
2. Spouses and unmarried adult children of permanent resident aliens.
3. Members of the professions and scientists and artists of exceptional ability.
4. Married children of U.S. citizens.
5. Brothers and sisters of U.S. citizens over age twenty-one.
6. Skilled and unskilled workers in occupations for which there is insufficient labor supply.
7. Refugees given conditional entry or adjustment. Chiefly from Communist or Communist-dominated countries and the Middle East.
8. Applicants not entitled to preceding preferences.

Preferences under 1990 Immigration Act

FAMILY-SPONSORED PREFERENCES

1. Unmarried children of U.S. citizens and their children.
2. Spouses, children, and unmarried adult children of permanent resident aliens.
3. Married children of U.S. citizens and their spouses and children.
4. Brothers and sisters of U.S. citizens (at least twenty-one years old) and their spouses and children.

EMPLOYMENT-BASED PREFERENCES

1. Priority workers and their spouses and children. (Priority workers defined as persons of extraordinary ability, outstanding professors and researchers, and certain multinational executives and managers.)
2. Professionals with advanced degrees or aliens of exceptional ability and their spouses and children.
3. Skilled workers, professionals (without advanced degrees), needed unskilled workers, and their spouses and children.

Table A.4. *(continued)*

EMPLOYMENT-BASED PREFERENCES *(continued)*

4. Special immigrants and their spouses and children.
5. Employment creation ("investors") and their spouses and children.
6. Applicants not entitled to preceding preferences. Includes spouses and children of aliens legalized under 1986 Immigration Reform and Control Act and aliens from countries "adversely affected" by immigration laws since 1965.

Source: Combined and modified material from E. P. Hutchinson, *Legislative History of American Immigration Policy, 1798–1965* (Philadelphia: University of Pennsylvania Press, 1981), p. 194; Roger Daniels, *Coming to America: A History of Immigration and Ethnicity in American Life* (New York: HarperPerennial, 1991), Table 13.2, p. 342; Vernon M. Briggs, Jr., *Immigration Policy and the American Labor Force* (Baltimore: Johns Hopkins University Press, 1984), Table 11, p. 65; *1991 Statistical Yearbook of the Immigration and Naturalization Service* (Washington, D.C.: U.S. Government Printing Office, 1992), Table A, Appendix 2, pp. A.2–3.

Table A.5. Aspects of Transition to Quota System

	IMMIGRATION FROM NORTHERN AND WESTERN EUROPE		IMMIGRANTS FROM SOUTHERN AND EASTERN EUROPE	
	QUOTA (%)	NONQUOTA (%)	QUOTA (%)	NONQUOTA (%)
1925	80	20	30	70
1926	78	22	28	72
1927	53	47	23	77
1928	74	26	24	76
1929	70	30	23	77

Immigrants Who Were Spouses and Children of U.S. Citizens, as Percent of Annual Immigration

	FROM SOUTHERN AND EASTERN EUROPE	FROM NORTHERN AND WESTERN EUROPE
1925	27	1
1926	31	1
1927	29	2
1928	52	1
1929	56	2

Immigrants under Sixteen, as Percent of Annual Immigration

	HEBREW		SOUTHERN ITALIAN		POLISH	
	MALE	FEMALE	MALE	FEMALE	MALE	FEMALE
1925	26	21	24	20	24	20
1926	22	18	27	16	27	17
1927	28	23	56	26	14	16
1928	28	23	56	26	14	16
1929	36	24	53	27	20	17

	ENGLISH		GERMAN		SCANDINAVIAN	
	MALE	FEMALE	MALE	FEMALE	MALE	FEMALE
1925	19	20	16	19	11	18
1926	18	20	14	15	10	13
1927	16	17	12	13	8	14
1928	16	17	12	13	8	14
1929	17	17	12	12	10	13

Source: Computed from data in Commissioner-General of Immigration, *Annual Reports* and *Statistical Abstracts of the United States.*

Table A.6.   Aspects of Return Migration

Rate of Return Migration (Emigrants) in the Pre-Quota and Quota Decades

	NUMBER OF IMMIGRANTS	NUMBER OF EMIGRANTS	EMIGRANTS PER 100 IMMIGRANTS
1911–1920	5,735,811	2,146,994	37
1921–1930	4,107,209	1,045,076	25

Percentage of Return Migration, by Length of Residency in the United States

LENGTH OF RESIDENCY	1911–1917	1918–1920	1921–1924	1925–1930
Under 5 years	64	35	30	66
5–10 years	17	55	45	15
10–15 years	3	7	16	10
15–20 years	1	2	5	5
More than 20 years	1	2	4	5
Unknown	13	0	0	0

Number of Emigrants per 100 Immigrants, by Sex

	MALE	FEMALE	FEMALE/MALE RATIO
1911–1915	41	17	.42
1916–1920	75	26	.34
1921–1925	34	16	.46
1926–1930	30	16	.52

Number of Emigrants per 100 Immigrants, by Age

	UNDER 14	14–44	45 AND OVER
1910–1914	10	29	54
1915–1917	15	49	49

	UNDER 16	16–44	45 AND OVER
1918–1919	36	90	147
1920–1924	8	32	85
1925–1929	7	25	62

Number of Emigrants per 100 Immigrants, by Occupation

	1911–1915	1916–1920	1921–1925	1926–1930
Professional	22	30	17	116
Skilled	23	33	13	65
Semiskilled and unskilled	42	101	45	35

Source: Computed from data in Commissioner-General of Immigration, *Annual Reports.*

Table A.7. Immigrants from Asian and Latin American Countries, by Decade, 1961–1990 (Numbers in thousands)

	1961–1970	1971–1980	1981–1990
Asia			
Cambodia	1.2	8.4	116.6
China	96.7	202.5	388.8
Hong Kong	25.6	47.5	63
India	31.2	176.8	261.9
Japan	38.5	47.9	43.2
Korea	35.8	272	338.8
Laos	0.1	22.6	145.6
Pakistan	4.9	31.2	61.3
Philippines	101.5	360.2	495.3
Thailand	5	44.1	64.4
Vietnam	4.6	179.7	401.4
Latin America			
Mexico	443.3	637.2	1,653.3
Cuba	256.8	276.8	159.2
Dominican Republic	94.1	148	251.8
Costa Rica	17.4	12.1	15.5
El Salvador	15	34.4	214.6
Guatemala	15.4	25.6	87.9
Honduras	15.5	17.2	49.5
Nicaragua	10.1	13	44.1
Panama	18.4	22.7	29
Argentina	42.1	25.1	25.7
Brazil	20.5	13.7	23.7
Chile	11.5	17.6	23.4
Colombia	70.3	77.6	124.4
Ecuador	37	50.2	56
Peru	18.6	29.1	64.4
Venezuela	8.5	7.1	17.9

Source: Derived from *Statistical Abstract of the United States, 1992,* Table 8, p. 11.

Table A.8. Median Age of Immigrants by Country of Birth, 1986–1990

	1986	1987	1988	1989	1990
All Countries	27.4	27.9	27.9	30.0	30.1
North America					
Canada	27.1	27.5	27.7	28.4	29.5
Mexico	26.2	27.1	30.0	30.4	29.8
Central America					
El Salvador	26.4	26.6	27.5	32.2	31.2
Guatemala	26.3	26.7	27.6	33.0	31.8
Honduras	24.5	24.8	—	27.7	30.1
Nicaragua	—	—	—	30.8	30.4
South America					
Ecuador	—	27.1	—	29.7	31.2
Colombia	27.2	27.3	27.2	30.0	31.9
Peru	29.3	29.4	30.2	31.2	32.6
Guyana	24.9	25.4	25.2	26.7	28.4
Caribbean					
Cuba	36.7	38.3	37.6	38.3	39.1
Dominican Republic	23.4	22.3	23.2	22.6	26.2
Haiti	27.0	29.6	33.4	30.3	30.6
Jamaica	24.7	24.3	24.5	24.9	27.8
Asia					
Cambodia	23.6	24.7	26.0	—	—
China, People's Republic of China	38.5	36.5	37.1	39.3	40.4
Hong Kong	—	24.2	27.6	27.9	—
Korea	25.4	25.6	26.2	27.8	28.9
Laos	22.8	22.7	21.4	23.7	24.2
Philippines	28.8	29.3	29.9	31.4	31.9
Taiwan	28.4	28.9	30.1	30.1	31.2
Thailand	7.2	7.3	8.1	12.2	—
Vietnam	28.0	23.5	23.9	23.1	23.6
India	29.4	29.1	30.0	30.7	31.0
Pakistan	27.8	27.8	28.3	29.4	29.7
Middle East					
Iran	30.3	30.5	31.3	34.1	33.7
Lebanon	27.1	—	27.5	—	—
Europe					
Germany	24.8	24.8	25.3	—	—
Poland	31.0	30.9	30.7	36.2	35.4
Romania	30.8	—	—	—	—
United Kingdom	27.8	28.0	28.0	28.3	29.2
Ireland	—	—	26.1	—	27.2
Soviet Union	—	—	—	33.9	31.8

Source: Derived from *Statistical Yearbook of the Immigration and Naturalization Service,* 1986–1990.

Table A.9. Male Immigrants as Percentage of Total Immigration, by Country of Birth, 1986–1990

	1986	1987	1988	1989	1990
All Countries	50.0	49.9	50.5	50.4	53.3
North America					
Canada	48.1	48.0	48.3	48.8	50.0
Mexico	43.1	56.5	56.1	52.6	57.8
Central America					
El Salvador	47.0	47.0	47.1	49.7	50.8
Guatemala	47.7	48.3	47.7	49.0	51.3
Honduras	43.5	44.8	—	43.4	45.6
Nicaragua	—	—	—	45.5	46.7
South America					
Colombia	45.8	44.5	44.3	46.4	48.8
Ecuador	—	48.2	—	51.3	56.9
Peru	46.0	46.4	46.3	48.5	50.8
Guyana	47.5	47.4	47.7	48.3	47.5
Caribbean					
Cuba	55.8	56.8	56.0	56.2	55.2
Dominican Republic	48.6	47.7	48.8	48.0	50.5
Haiti	27.0	54.2	58.9	49.1	47.7
Jamaica	47.4	48.4	49.1	48.5	47.6
Asia					
Cambodia	48.6	47.6	48.3	—	—
China, People's Republic of China	47.0	47.8	47.2	50.8	48.9
Hong Kong	—	50.2	51.2	51.7	—
Korea	42.6	42.8	43.1	44.6	44.8
Laos	53.1	52.9	51.7	51.9	51.9
Philippines	40.9	41.6	41.6	41.8	40.5
Taiwan	46.8	46.4	46.8	46.7	46.6
Thailand	46.5	46.3	47.8	47.4	—
Vietnam	56.5	55.0	55.3	50.6	48.0
India	50.5	50.0	50.6	51.3	50.2
Pakistan	56.0	57.0	55.2	58.1	60.6
Middle East					
Iran	57.2	55.2	53.4	53.3	54.2
Lebanon	62.5	—	55.4	—	—
Europe					
Germany	26.7	26.8	27.9	—	—
Poland	51.3	50.7	51.1	48.9	49.3
Romania	51.3	—	—	—	—
United Kingdom	49.3	49.6	50.4	51.0	50.7
Ireland	—	—	56.4	—	55.7
Soviet Union	—	—	—	48.2	48.5

Source: Derived from *Statistical Yearbook of the Immigration and Naturalization Service,* 1986–1990.

Table A.10. Occupational Distribution of Employed Mexican Immigrants, 1971–1990

	1971–1979 (%)	1982–1990 (%)
Professional	3.0	1.8
Executive/Administration	2.3	2.2
Sales	1.0	2.5
Administrative support	3.5	4.1
Production/Craft	11.0	13.1
Operator/Laborer	48.7	41.2
Farming/Fishing	8.2	12.3
Service	19.1	22.9
Total Number of Immigrants	203,260	967,049

Source: Computed from Immigration and Naturalization Service, *Annual Reports,* 1971–1979, and annual *Statistical Yearbook of the Immigration and Naturalization Service,* 1982–1990.

Table A.11. Male Immigrants by Occupation for Selected Countries and Regions, 1983–1990

OCCUPATIONAL CLASS	MALES IN SELECTED COUNTRY AND REGION, AS PERCENT OF TOTAL MALES					
	CUBA	DOMINICAN REPUBLIC	WEST INDIES	CENTRAL AMERICA	SOUTH AMERICA	HAITI
Professional	6.1	8.4	12.9	4.5	12.6	5.3
Executive	3.1	5.1	5.3	3.8	7.3	2.0
Sales	5.3	5.0	4.3	3.9	5.3	2.0
Administration	9.0	7.1	15.1	7.9	11.5	5.2
Production/Crafts	18.0	17.0	16.4	13.6	13.7	13.6
Farm, Forestry	0.9	5.4	2.8	2.2	1.9	6.7
Operator/Laborer	36.1	25.9	11.2	27.4	22.8	23.2
Service	21.5	26.1	35.1	36.6	24.6	37.2

Source: Derived from *Statistical Yearbook of the Immigration and Naturalization Service,* 1983–1990.

Table A.12. Reported Single and Multiple Ancestries for Civilian Population, November 1979 (Numbers in thousands)

ANCESTRY	TOTAL	PERCENT OF TOTAL	PERSONS REPORTING SINGLE ANCESTRY		PERSONS REPORTING MULTIPLE ANCESTRY	PERCENT OF PERSONS BY KIND OF ANCESTRY RESPONSE	
			NUMBER	PERCENT		SINGLE ANCESTRY	MULTIPLE ANCESTRY
Reporting at least one specific ancestry	**179,078[1]**	**100.0[1]**	**96,496**	**100.0**	**82,582[1]**	**53.9**	**46.1**
Afro-American, African	16,193	9.0	15,057	15.6	1,136	93.0	7.0
American Indian	9,900	5.3	2,053	2.1	7,847	20.7	79.3
Asian Indian	182	0.1	156	0.2	26	85.7	14.3
Austrian	1,070	0.6	385	0.4	685	36.0	64.0
Belgian	448	0.3	113	0.1	335	25.2	74.8
Canadian	609	0.3	228	0.2	381	37.4	62.6
Chinese, Taiwanese	705	0.4	540	0.6	165	76.6	23.4
Czechoslovakian	1,695	0.9	794	0.8	901	46.8	53.2
Danish	1,672	0.9	438	0.5	1,234	26.2	73.8
Dutch	8,121	4.5	1,362	1.4	6,759	16.8	83.2
English	40,004	22.3	11,501	11.9	28,503	28.7	71.3
Filipino	764	0.4	525	0.5	239	68.7	31.3
Finnish	616	0.3	255	0.3	361	41.4	58.6
French	14,047	7.8	3,047	3.2	11,000	21.7	78.3
French Canadian	1,053	0.6	582	0.6	471	55.3	44.7
German	51,649	28.8	17,160	17.8	34,489	33.2	66.8
Greek	990	0.6	567	0.6	423	57.3	42.7
Hungarian	1,592	0.9	534	0.6	1,058	33.5	66.5
Iranian	118	0.1	103	0.1	15	87.3	12.7
Irish	43,752	24.4	9,760	10.1	33,992	22.3	77.7
Italian, Sicilian	11,751	6.6	6,110	6.3	5,641	52.0	48.0
Jamaican	184	0.1	158	0.2	26	85.9	14.1
Japanese	680	0.4	529	0.5	151	77.8	22.2
Korean	265	0.1	230	0.2	35	86.8	13.2

Table A.12. *(continued)*

ANCESTRY	TOTAL	PERCENT OF TOTAL	PERSONS REPORTING SINGLE ANCESTRY		PERSONS REPORTING MULTIPLE ANCESTRY	PERCENT OF PERSONS BY KIND OF ANCESTRY RESPONSE	
			NUMBER	PERCENT		SINGLE ANCESTRY	MULTIPLE ANCESTRY
Lebanese	322	0.2	179	0.2	143	55.6	44.4
Lithuanian	832	0.5	317	0.3	515	38.1	61.9
Norwegian	4,120	2.3	1,232	1.3	2,888	29.9	70.1
Polish	8,421	4.7	3,498	3.6	4,923	41.5	58.5
Portuguese	946	0.5	493	0.5	453	52.1	47.9
Romanian	335	0.2	132	0.1	203	39.4	60.6
Russian	3,466	1.9	1,496	1.6	1,970	43.2	56.8
Scandinavian	340	0.2	110	0.1	230	32.4	67.6
Scottish	14,205	7.9	1,615	1.7	12,590	11.4	88.6
Slavic	722	0.4	300	0.3	422	41.6	58.4
Spanish	12,493	7.0	9,762	10.1	2,731	78.1	21.9
Colombian	117	0.1	101	0.1	16	86.3	13.7
Cuban	675	0.4	558	0.6	117	82.7	17.3
Dominican	119	0.1	107	0.1	12	89.9	10.1
Mexican	6,682	3.7	5,889	6.1	793	88.1	11.9
Puerto Rican	1,333	0.7	1,107	1.1	226	83.0	17.0
Other Spanish	3,566	2.0	2,000	2.1	1,566	56.1	43.9
Swedish	4,886	2.7	1,216	1.3	3,670	24.9	75.1
Swiss	1,228	0.7	312	0.3	916	25.4	74.6
Ukrainian	525	0.3	231	0.2	294	44.0	56.0
Vietnamese	198	0.1	177	0.2	21	89.4	10.6
Welsh	2,568	1.4	455	0.5	2,113	17.7	82.3
West Indian	193	0.1	129	0.1	64	66.8	33.2
Yugoslavian	467	0.3	283	0.3	184	60.6	39.4
Other specified ancestry groups	4,942	2.8	2,372	2.5	2,571	48.0	52.0

[1] Number and percent by ancestry groups do not add to total, as persons may be counted in more than one ancestry group.
Source: U.S. Bureau of the Census, *Current Population Reports*, Series P-23, no. 116, *Ancestry and Language in the United States: November 1979* (Washington, D.C.: U.S. Government Printing Office, 1982), p. 7.

APPENDIX B

Chronology of Immigration and Naturalization Policy

1882: Chinese Exclusion Act bars the admission of Chinese laborers and declares Chinese immigrants to be aliens ineligible for naturalized citizenship. Act extended indefinitely by laws passed in 1892, 1902, and 1904.

1891: Congress establishes comprehensive federal control over immigration, establishes the Bureau of Immigration under the Treasury Department to administer immigration laws. Barred persons likely to go on public welfare are those having certain contagious diseases, felons, polygamists, and anyone guilty of "moral turpitude." Federal control extends to deportation of unlawful entries.

1898: In *United States v. Wong Kim Ark,* the U.S. Supreme Court finds that the children of Chinese immigrants are American citizens because they were born in the United States.

1903: U.S. Bureau of Immigration is placed under Department of Commerce and Labor. Congress passes act to recodify existing immigration laws, toughens deportation powers, and bars anarchists and subversives.

1906: Naturalization Act systematizes application for naturalized citizenship and makes knowledge of English a requirement.

1907–1908: Gentlemen's Agreement between the United States and Japanese government, which volunteers to stop emigration of laborers.

1911: The United States Immigration Commission publishes its forty-two-volume report asserting that immigration is damaging the nation and calling for restriction of immigrants from southern and eastern Europe.

1917: Immigration Act requires literacy test for admission and creates an Asiatic Barred Zone from which no immigration is permitted.

1921: First Quota Act limits annual admissions to 3 percent of foreign-born of a nationality in the United States in 1910. An annual ceiling of 355,000 quota admissions is imposed: 55 percent of all admissions to come from northern and western Europe, 45 percent from other countries, nearly all from southern and eastern Europe. Also, new selective measures are installed to permit nonquota or unlimited admissions of immediate relatives of American citizens and immigrants from the Western Hemisphere.

1922: The U.S. Supreme Court finds in *Takao Ozawa v. United States* that Japanese immigrants are aliens ineligible for citizenship.

1922: The Cable Act of 1922 overturns the position expressed by statute and judicial decision that the citizenship of a married woman follows that of her husband. Henceforward, citizenship for married women is established as independent.

1924: The Second Quota Act revises annual admissions quotas to 2 percent of the foreign-born of a nationality in the United States in 1890. This lowers the annual ceiling of total quota admissions to 165,000 while increasing the share of visas for immigrants from northern and western Europe to 86 percent (141,000) and decreasing the share for those from southern and eastern Europe to 12 percent (21,000). Declares immigrants from Asia inadmissible because they are aliens ineligible for citizenship.

1929: The discriminatory National Origins Quota system goes into full effect. Quotas are recalibrated to a complicated statistical breakdown of the American population in 1920 according to different national origin groups that gives 83 percent of annual quota admissions (127,000) to immigrants from northern and western Europe, 15 percent (23,000) to those from southern and eastern Europe, and 2 percent (4,000) to other areas. The annual ceiling of quota admissions drops to 154,000.

1934: Philippines Independence Act restricts immigration from Philippines to fifty admissions a year.

1940: The Smith Act requires registration and fingerprinting of aliens and widens the grounds for deportation. Congress passes a new Immigration and Nationality Act that recodifies existing immigration law and revises naturalization procedures and forms.

1942: Initiation of Mexican foreign laborer program known as the *bracero* program.

1943: Repeal of Chinese Exclusion Act of 1882 provides a small quota for Chinese admissions and makes Chinese immigrants eligible for naturalized citizenship.

1945: President Truman issues executive order permitting entry of 40,000 refugees and displaced persons.

1945: War Brides Act facilitates immigration of foreign-born spouses and children of armed services personnel.

1946: India receives an annual admissions quota and Indian immigrants are permitted to naturalize. Immigrants from the Philippines are also granted eligibility for naturalization.

1948: Congress passes the Displaced Persons Act, the first law expressing the need to admit people fleeing persecution. The law provides for entry of 202,000 refugees uprooted by the war in Europe over the next two years. Refugees are counted against annual quotas in each year and subsequent years (called quota mortgaging).

1950:   Internal Security Act expands the grounds for exclusion and deportation of subversives. Membership in the Communist party is made a ground for exclusion or deportation. The law requires aliens to report their address annually. Congress amends the 1948 Displaced Persons Act to increase the number of available visas from 202,000 to 341,000.

1952:   McCarran-Walter Act recodifies immigration and naturalization statutes. The discriminatory national origins quota system is retained. A system of occupational preferences is installed. Racial and gender discrimination in naturalization is prohibited.

1953:   Refugee Relief Act provides 205,000 nonquota visas and repeals quota mortgaging.

1954:   Operation Wetback removes one million Mexican aliens from the Southwest and causes numerous civil liberties violations. United States begins to admit Hungarian refugees.

1959:   United States begins to admit refugees from Cuba.

1965:   Hart-Celler Act abolishes the restrictive national origins quota system, and creates a worldwide system of equal per country visa limits (20,000 a year). For the first time, annual limits are placed on immigration from the Western Hemisphere. The annual ceiling of limited admissions is raised to 290,000: Eastern Hemisphere nations receive 170,000 admissions, Western Hemisphere nations 120,000. The law establishes an admissions class not subject to limitation that functionally replaces the old nonquota class. A revised occupational and family reunion preference system is to be applied to the Eastern Hemisphere only. The law requires that an admitted alien obtain labor preclearance from the secretary of labor stating that he or she will not displace or harm working conditions of an American worker.

1975:   The Indochinese Migration and Refugee Assistance Act establishes an administrative program for resettling refugees from Vietnam and Cambodia.

1976:   Congress passes a law to include Laotians in Indochinese resettlement program. Congress passes a law to apply Eastern Hemisphere visa preference system and annual 20,000 per country visa limit to the Western Hemisphere.

1980:   The Refugee Act reaffirms cooperation of the president and Congress in setting refugee admissions, and places refugees outside the quota system by removing "refugee" as a preference category. The law correspondingly reduces the worldwide ceiling on annual quota immigration to 270,000 and establishes an administrative program for domestic resettlement of refugees.

1986:   Immigration Reform and Control Act (IRCA) establishes amnesty for aliens unlawfully in the country and provides them an opportunity to legalize their status; produces sanctions prohibiting employers from knowingly hiring or recruiting illegal aliens; adjusts to permanent resident alien status Cubans and Haitians who had not been admitted officially and properly; and creates a small quota for aliens from countries underrepresented in annual immigration.

1990: Congress passes a law that revises the entire admissions system and creates an overall flexible cap of 700,000 admissions starting in 1992, to be replaced by a cap of 675,000 in 1995. Congress retreats from exclusion and deportation policies based on ideological and anti-Communist grounds; liberalizes naturalization qualifications and provides for administrative hearings in addition to traditional court hearings for naturalization; and expands the share of "diversity immigrants" from underrepresented countries.

Index